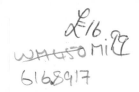

A SHORT INTRODUCTION TO
PSYCHOANALYSIS

Short Introductions to the Therapy Professions
Series Editor: Colin Feltham

Books in this series examine the different professions which provide help for people experiencing emotional or psychological problems. Written by leading proctitioners and trainers in each field, the books are a source of up-to-date information about

- the nature of the work
- training, continuing professional development and career pathways
- the structure and development of the profession
- client populations and consumer views
- research and debates surrounding the profession.

Short Introdutions to the Therapy Professions are ideal for anyone thinking about a career in one of the therapy professions or in the early stages of training. The books will also be of interest to mental health professionals needing to understand allied professions and also to patients, clients and relatives of service users.

Books in the series:

A Short Introduction to Clinical Psychology
Katherine Cheshire and David Pilgrim

A Short Introduction to Psychoanalysis
Jane Milton, Caroline Polmear and Julia Fabricius

A Short Introdution to Psychiatry
Linda Gask

A SHORT INTRODUCTION TO
PSYCHOANALYSIS

Jane Milton, Caroline Polmear
and Julia Fabricius

SAGE Publications
London • Thousand Oaks • New Delhi

First published 2004

Reprinted 2005

SAGE Publications Ltd
1 Oliver's Yard
55 City Road
London EC1Y 1SP

SAGE Publications Inc.
2455 Teller Road
Thousand Oaks, California 91320

SAGE Publications India Pvt Ltd
B-42, Panchsheel Enclave
Post Box 4109
New Delhi 110 017

British Library Cataloguing in Publication data

A catalogue record for this book is available
from the British Library

ISBN 0 7619 7186 6
ISBN 0 7619 7187 4 (pbk)

Library of Congress Control Number: 2003115328

Typeset by C&M Digitals (P) Ltd., Chennai, India
Printed in Great Britain by TJ International Ltd, Padstow, Cornwall

CONTENTS

PREFACE

What is psychoanalysis? There is no short or simple answer to this question, which concerns a complex and multi-faceted field of learning. In addition to provoking lively curiosity, psychoanalysis has become surrounded by much anxiety, misconception, prejudice and even myth. This book aims to give a succinct and accessible account of psychoanalysis, its theory, practice, history and applications, and to describe the psychoanalytic profession today.

Psychology, psychiatry, psychotherapy, psychoanalysis: how do they differ? The word root 'psych' comes from the Greek, meaning the soul or spirit as distinct from the body. In modern usage psyche usually refers to the mind. **Psychology**, then, is the study of all aspects of the mind and its functioning. It includes, for example, the study of perception, memory, thinking and of the working of complex psychophysical skills such as driving or operating machinery. Nearly everyone is interested in minds, their own and others', but more formally psychology is an academic discipline, a branch of science, that can be studied to degree level and beyond. Academic psychology in principle includes the study of psychoanalysis, although in practice it is only a small part of many academic courses. **Clinical psychology** is a branch of psychology concerned with helping people with psychological difficulties. Clinical psychologists have undertaken a degree in psychology followed by further training. They cannot prescribe drugs but assess patients and use various sorts of psychological treatment.

Psychiatry is a branch of medicine. All psychiatrists are doctors who have undertaken further specialist training and who treat people with disorders of the mind. Psychiatrists may use either drugs, psychological treatments that involve talking, or both. **Psychotherapy** is a generic term for talking treatments, which may be practised by psychiatrists, clinical psychologists and other specifically trained psychotherapists who do not come from either of these backgrounds. For example nurses, social workers and others may have received specialist training in psychotherapy. There are a number of types of psychotherapy, as we will describe in Chapter 8, each needing a specific type of training. **Psychoanalysis** is one of the original and most intensive forms of psychotherapy and has given rise to the less intensive practice of **psychoanalytic psychotherapy**

in its various forms. As we will describe in Chapter 2, psychoanalysis is not only a form of psychotherapy but also a body of theory about the mind and a method of observing and investigating mental processes.

The nine chapters are set out as follows. In Chapter 1 we start in the place where psychoanalysis happens, in the room with a patient and his or her analyst, in the middle of a psychoanalytic session. From there we move outwards to other patients and to a more general overview of what goes on in clinical psychoanalysis and who it is for. In Chapter 2 we give an overview of psychoanalytic theory. In Chapter 3 we outline the history of psychoanalysis and in Chapter 4 the way it has seeded and spread in different cultures. Chapter 5 turns to the serious issue of critiques of psychoanalysis and a discussion of these, and Chapter 6 to the complex field of research in psychoanalysis. Chapter 7 describes some ways in which psychoanalytic thinking has been used outside the consulting room. Chapter 8, on psychoanalysis and other psychotherapeutic approaches, tries to show where psychoanalysis fits into the range of psychological therapies. Finally in Chapter 9 we describe the psychoanalytic profession in the UK, the training, the professional bodies and the national and international structures involved.

We have found psychoanalysis a fascinating, intriguing, compelling, personally helpful, difficult and rewarding subject. Each of us is grateful to the teachers or mentors who introduced us to psychoanalysis and to the teachers and patients who have helped us along the lifelong path of learning. Here we hope to share our enthusiasm. We hope this book will be an engaging introduction which will answer some questions and raise curiosity for further reading. If we inform some of those without previous knowledge and capture the interest of a few then we will have succeeded in our aim.

ACKNOWLEDGEMENTS

The authors first of all gratefully acknowledge the generosity of patients who have given permission for vignettes from their analyses to be published here. We have taken care that they will be recognisable by no one but themselves.

We also thank the following colleagues who have contributed information and ideas at various stages: Anthony Bateman, David Bell, David Black, Catalina Bronstein, Donald Campbell, Anthony Cantle, Rachael Davenhill, Jenny Davids, Mary Donovan, Hella Ehlers, Steven Grosz, Wojtek Hanbowski, Rael Meyerowitz, Rosine Perelberg, Daniel Pick, Joscelyn Richards, Anne-Marie Sandler, Vic Sedlak, Emilia Steuerman, Sally Weintrobe.

Relatives, friends and colleagues who have kindly helped us by spending time reading through sections of the manuscript are: David Crease, Elizabeth Piercy, Richard Rusbridger, Lynne Ridler-Wall, Max Sasim, Katy Thomson and Sarah Thomson.

Our series editor Colin Feltham has been most helpful and supportive. We have also appreciated the friendly professionalism of the Sage team: Alison Poyner, Louise Wise, Rachel Burrows, Wendy Scott, Susie Home and Joyce Lynch.

1
WHAT IS PSYCHOANALYSIS?

At this moment you are a privileged fly on the wall. Alan, a 55-year-old man, is 15 minutes into his session with his analyst and is reporting a dream. In the way that flies do, you've noticed the atmosphere. It is still and calm. They both seem completely engrossed in something, though to you nothing appears to be happening. Alan seems to be talking to himself, yet his analyst is listening intently. He is searching for all the details of last night's dream, pulling them back from beneath the shroud which waking threw over them.

Alan says: 'I was on a landing; there were banisters'. He pauses before describing the exact shape and details of the banisters. 'There was a thin man there. I was toppling him over the banisters. He said to me: "When you have lost the 4 stone and the 14 stone, then you might topple over." That's all I can remember.' Alan is thoughtful a while then talks about the 'toppling over'. He thinks that the sense was that the man might get unbalanced and topple over. He considers whether he might be pushing him over in the dream. He thought there was a way in which the man was suggesting that when Alan had lost the 4 stone and the 14 stone then he might topple over too; might lose his balance.

As Alan thought about different parts of his dream he let his mind follow the thoughts, images and memories which came to him. He thought about his weight loss programme. He couldn't think why he was dreaming about 4 and 14 stone, but it didn't bother him that he couldn't understand that part, something would probably come up later. Perhaps it's because his next goal is 18 stone, he muses. He remembers being thin as a young man at school. In particular in athletics, competing against an arch-rival in running. He remembers something else which happened at that time too. He smiles with surprise, saying that he hasn't thought of it for 30 years until this moment. But now he notices that thinking about this memory makes him feel anxious.

Just as he's saying this, his analyst notices that as she begins to think of what she might say about the dream she finds herself feeling she'll have to be very careful not to say it insensitively and provoke a fight. Subtly and imperceptibly the atmosphere has become tense. He remembers fighting this rival; really fighting as if to the death. He thinks that he might have completely lost control and killed him if this strange thing hadn't happened at that point. He'd just gone like jelly; he got up and walked away.

After dwelling a little more on the fears he'd suffered as a young thin man about losing control and being violent, he remembers his father's sudden death from a heart attack when he was a boy. What his analyst knows is that this death, so traumatic for Alan, had precipitated his disturbance as a child. He had developed obsessional routines involving checking and re-checking that he had turned off the taps and secured the locks on the windows at night, as if he believed that in some way he was culpable for the death of his father.

Alan interrupts himself to say: 'I went to the doctor yesterday, by the way, to discuss coming off all the pills.' He reminds his analyst that he is currently taking four different pills. He reminds her what each is for: an antipsychotic, an antidepressant, a beta blocker and a blood pressure pill. They speak a bit about the visit to the GP and Alan stresses both his desire to give up all his medication now that he is improving with the help of his analysis and his need to do it very carefully. He knows someone who came off antidepressants suddenly, all at once, and nearly died because the doctors hadn't bothered to warn him that it was dangerous. He checked this out with the GP and is stopping at the rate of half a pill per fortnight. His analyst says: 'Perhaps this helps us understand the 4 and the 14 in the dream. While you very much want to be healthy and be doing well in your analysis, and to manage without taking the 4 pills by giving up more every 14 days, you are also afraid that without the pills and the fat jelly you've covered yourself with, you might get unbalanced and be compelled to fight and be violent. Perhaps you fear your violence towards me, your thin analyst, too. The banisters made me think of those outside the consulting room which you see as you come in.'

Alan says: 'Oh yes; I knew I'd seen them somewhere before! But how do I know I won't go mad and do something to you? I just thought of something, just then.' Alan is now very agitated. 'It makes my blood boil the way analysts never defend themselves when they are attacked in the press. You hear one slander after another about Freud and psychoanalysis, and what do your lot do? Nothing!'

We leave them at this point as they unravel the many layers of meaning held in each image of the dream and each communication of Alan's. Their activity resembles the task of going deeper and deeper into the meaning of a poem. Alan is rediscovering his unconscious wishes and fears, those that made him ill in the first place, and finds himself reliving them in the relationship with the analyst where they come alive again. Here he can be supported by her to know about them, however frightening or unpalatable they are, rather than banish them to his unconscious mind. With his analyst's help he can understand the ways in which he reacted to the traumatic events of his early life, he can come to know and understand the person he became and can begin to feel greater freedom to be himself, less inhibited by his fears of murder and violence towards those he loves.

Who are the patients?

Alan sought help for his agoraphobia, his severe eating problem and his depression. He had suffered for years and had received psychiatric help during crises. If you met him you would no doubt recognise that he was housebound and overweight yet you would also admire him for his intelligence, his wit and his many accomplishments in the arts. Only he and his close family would know of his private suffering and mental torment.

Frank, a man in his mid-twenties, had made it into young adulthood, but emotionally felt completely unable to cope with the world of jobs, responsibility and relationships. He had trained as a graphic designer but could not use his talents commercially. When he drew he became obsessively preoccupied with his designs, feeling 'pulled into' them. He functioned below his potential, remaining an office assistant. Often he found his mind taken over by glamorous daydreams or furious, repetitive grievances. At other times he would be flooded by panic or dread, and have to deaden himself with excessive alcohol in order to be able to carry on at all. In relationships he clung desperately and possessively to women who would complain that he did not really seem there for them. Inevitably these relationships floundered once the time came for commitment. He felt his life spiralling downwards, experiencing himself watching as though through a glass screen as his friends established themselves at work and started to settle down into family life.

For someone like Frank, psychoanalysis provides a safe space in which warded-off, nightmarish fears, provoked by becoming a fully active, competitive and sexually alive adult, can be named, faced and understood. Frank was helped to tackle the hard but exciting realities of adult life.

Nasima, a 16-year-old girl from a close family, became unable to go back to school after a half-term break. She felt too afraid of the other girls. Her parents were concerned and took her to an adolescent centre for help. It emerged that Nasima had become deeply confused in adolescence and feared what was going on in her mind. Her fear of becoming a sexual adult was so great that she felt compelled to remain childlike, frozen in time and stuck to her mother. After initial work at the centre, which gave her hope that she could be helped, she went into analysis.

For Nasima and other young people for whom adolescent development feels like an impossible passage, analysis offers a way of understanding the thoughts and feelings which can make a young person feel completely mad and without hope for their future. In many cases it is a way of preventing suicide or long term mental illness. Without analysis, someone like Nasima would enter adulthood having dissociated herself from her adult sexuality and be forced to live a restricted and phobic life; her capacity to love, her many talents and ambitions remaining hidden and wasted.

Mary's adoptive parents sought help for her when she was seven because of her frequent and unpredictable violent outbursts, her impulsivity and general insecurity. Mary hated change of any sort and she tended to rush headlong into things without thinking. Her awareness of her body seemed rather poor. She often bumped into things and fell. When distressed she attacked herself violently, picking at scabs, tearing at her clothes or pulling her own hair. She longed for friends but found sharing difficult. She needed to control other children and to be the centre of attention. When frustrated she could lash out at them. She was friendly to adults, when not in a rage, indeed she could often seem rather inappropriately over-friendly to relative strangers. She hated ever being on her own and night-time separation was almost impossible, leading to fraught bedtimes and disturbed nights for everyone.

Mary had been adopted when she was four and a half. Her birth mother had herself had a very difficult childhood and was a drug addict. She spent six months in a psychiatric hospital shortly before Mary's first birthday. During this time Mary was passed among a number of relatives and friends with no consistent carer. This was the first of Mary's many disruptions. Shortly after her mother's discharge the health visitor referred Mary to Social Services because of concern about her mother's ability to care for her. There were various reasons for the concern for Mary at that time. One concern was that her mother's partner could be violent. It was thought that he did not actually hit Mary but that he regularly assaulted her mother in front of her. Soon after the initial referral Mary was taken into emergency care and then placed with foster carers just before she was three. Eighteen months later she was moved to her adoptive family. The reliable and patient care of her adoptive parents had helped Mary to settle somewhat, but her distress and worrying behaviour continued and increasingly caused severe strain on her, her parents and all the family relationships.

On first meeting Mary her therapist saw a little girl with big black shadows round her eyes, who talked non-stop in rather an empty way and yawned frequently. At the end of their first meeting Mary asked her therapist if she would be wearing the same clothes next time. On their second meeting she described her worry that she had forgotten what the therapist looked like. Mary was offered intensive treatment five times a week.

So in answer to the question: 'Who are the patients?' we find that they are a wide range of different kinds of people: children, adolescents, young adults and older adults. They are people who come to know that they need help, for whom it matters sufficiently to commit to a fairly lengthy treatment and who have some capacity for thoughtfulness and reflection. In the case of child patients they are children whose carers can commit themselves to supporting the analysis by bringing them to their sessions consistently over a long period of time. They are people whose internal world interferes with their development, inhibits their full enjoyment and involvement in their external world; people whose capacity to be involved in creative work, play and loving relationships is seriously impaired. Some are very ill, others less so.

What is psychoanalysis?

The setting for psychoanalysis is designed to allow both analyst and patient to focus on the patient's inner world, with minimal interference from outside. The patient comes to the analyst's consulting room, at pre-arranged regular times, with sessions always the same length (traditionally 50 minutes). There are no phone calls or other interruptions; the setting has to be safe, predictable, consistent. Readers familiar with chemistry will recognise the analogy of a 'controlled environment' in which you can examine a reaction between chemicals in a test-tube by making sure temperature, pressure and pH are controlled and that there are no contaminating chemicals around.

The **analytic stance** includes respect and alert attention but overall non-intrusiveness. Although the analyst's personality is bound to come across in many ways, he or she aims as far as possible to stay in the background and let the patient take the foreground. Thus analysts avoid wearing very loud or provocative clothes, or giving political opinions, or talking about themselves. Ordinary social chat is avoided. This can seem very odd to the patient at first, even rude and bad mannered since we are so used to being put at our ease by the other person, being reassured that they are benign and friendly. However, when you think about it, we often chat socially to a stranger to fend off their suspicion, and make them like us and trust us. It is comfortable to be liked, but analysts aren't there to have a comfortable time; they are there to uncover the patient's deepest feelings and anxieties and to understand and help with these. Chapter 8 compares psychoanalysis in this respect with other forms of therapy that involve a more ordinarily supportive relationship between therapist and patient.

In adult analysis, the traditional use of the **couch,** with the patient lying down and the analyst behind, is customary. Most of the cartoon portrayals of analysts get it wrong. In reality the analyst is completely out of sight, and rarely if ever has a notebook and pencil; writing would interfere with proper listening and involvement. The rationale of using the couch is to free both patient and analyst from the inhibitions and distractions of sitting and watching another person's reactions and expressions. Lying down helps the patient to relax his or her social guard and be more in touch with the inner world, and with more childlike feelings. The patient is asked simply to say whatever comes into their mind, to report their thoughts, feelings and images, without censoring them or trying to make them logical. This is called **free association.** In practice it is very difficult to do. One quickly comes up against things that feel irrelevant or embarrassing, and finds oneself wanting to disobey the rule by censorship and alteration; sometimes one's mind goes completely blank. These reactions are important in themselves and the patient is encouraged to report them too. **Resistances** to free association are as valuable to the process as the relatively uncensored contents of the mind itself.

In child analysis, play takes the place of free association, and the child plays and interacts with the analyst, occasionally using the couch if he or she chooses. Through the child's play, and sometimes through the lack of it, the unconscious inner world is graphically brought to life in the consulting room.

The intensity of **full analysis,** four or five sessions a week, may seem surprising, until the nature of the enterprise is understood. Psychoanalysis involves emotionally based learning, altering deep structures in the mind that have formed over many years of relating to significant others. A deep trust and familiarity with the setting needs to evolve if the most private passions and worst nightmares are to emerge. Many people can only truly expose their vulnerable side when there is a short wait for the next session; Monday and Friday sessions often tend to be more 'closed up' and hard going for both patient and analyst, but useful times to explore the disruptive effects of separation. The length of an analysis is not set in advance, unless there are unusual external constraints. If it is allowed to take its natural course, an analysis typically lasts years rather than months. Usually analyst and patient agree on an ending date a year or more in advance, as the ending is an important phase to be worked through.

By convention in the UK we use the term **psychoanalytic psychotherapy** to describe treatment three times a week or less.

(The relationship between psychoanalysis and psychoanalytic psychotherapy is discussed further in Chapter 8.) Patients seen only once or twice a week may not necessarily use the couch, although many do. Endless circular and unproductive arguments can ensue about what is and isn't 'real analysis'. A few patients make remarkable use of once a week treatment and seem able to launch themselves into a deep and productive analytic involvement with the therapist, and some four and five times a week patients remain aloof and untouched by their analysis for years. It is vital to assess what a patient can manage and use at the particular point in their lives when they come for help. However, the authors would like to stick their necks out and say that in their experience the differences are very noticeable. When it is possible, more intensive work with most patients deepens more quickly and is more effective.

The value of definitions is also partly to give us a baseline for study and debate. If we are referring to discoveries resulting from psychoanalysis as a method of investigation, it makes most sense if we all know what we mean by psychoanalysis and what the precise parameters are. Full psychoanalysis is often the seedbed for new discoveries, which then inform the work of colleagues doing less intensive work.

The psychoanalytic process

To return to the process itself, an important source of resistances to free association from the beginning are unbidden thoughts about the analyst him- or herself. You rather like her dress, and she has an amazingly sexy voice. That picture in her waiting room is a bit lifeless and twee, and you remember how you wondered if she was embarrassed when you first spoke to her on the phone. These are all things you surely can't possibly be expected to say to a relative stranger! It would only be all right if you knew her well, if she had told you quite a bit about herself, and if you were confident that she liked you. You have a feeling that she might feel hurt and offended, then subtly take it out on you later. Or she might get flattered and seduced and things would get out of control.

Such thoughts and worries are part of the immediate **transference** to the analyst and the whole analytic situation, which give valuable insight into each individual's unique way of seeing and relating. There are always little hooks to hang transference on, real features of the analyst's appearance, tastes and personality, but sometimes it involves a huge misinterpretation of the other. With adults, use of the couch with the analyst out of sight encourages the development of the transference. The patient's particular expectations in relationships, based on personality and previous life experiences, quickly begin to emerge. With little real information about the analyst, preconceptions crowd in to fill out a picture. Outside the consulting room, our customary transferences to everyone we meet are modified by their responses which show us when we are right and wrong in our expectations. The analytic setting is unique in deliberately existing to concentrate, observe and make sense of transference, rather than modify and dispel it. The analyst's position and function mean that he or she quickly tends to become clothed with maternal and paternal transference. Examples of other situations where this can happen vividly are with teachers, seniors at work and doctors.

The psychoanalyst's job is to act as a **participant observer**, listening to the patient, but trying at the same time to listen beyond the words, to what is being hinted at or evaded. We find that free association, or in the case of children in the consulting room their play, reveals startling patterns and links in the mind that the patient doesn't know about. It is filled with **unconscious communication**. There are many things about people, too, that can only be seen by other people. An analyst with no axe to grind except a wish to help can enable us to see some of the things our best friend knows but could never tell us.

The analyst does not and cannot remain a neutral observer. He or she has to really take in what the patient is saying, and become affected and involved, all the while trying to keep on observing and thinking. Self-observation is crucial for the analyst; monitoring the real emotional effects of the patient, a willingness to be on the receiving end, the better to understand the patient's ways of relating. This experience of the analyst is referred to as the **countertransference**.

Two examples will help to show the subtle interplay of the transference and countertransference.

> Doug reproaches his analyst angrily when she gives him notice of a week-long break in the analysis. She feels guilty but also defensive, and wants to justify herself. She has to be able to feel the strength and particular quality of his rage directed towards her personally, over something real in the analysis. She has to hold on to the experience without discharging it in action, in order to make proper sense of it.

The analyst in this situation needs neither to take the moral high ground nor to retreat into a quick apology and explanation (which would be the easiest thing), but to think: 'Why this?' 'Why now?' and 'What does this feel like for me and what does it feel like being Doug at this moment?' The analyst, on the basis of what she knows of Doug, and what the present situation feels like, tries to identify with him in her mind. She might wonder, 'What internal image of me is Doug talking to and reacting to? Is it a parental figure who leaves him unthinkingly, and never takes justified complaints on board? Or am I, at this moment, someone who enrages him by reminding him that he is not the centre of the universe? Or do I feel like one of a couple, off on an exclusive holiday, flaunting my couple-ness and sexuality in front of him?' If she can pinpoint the image and feelings accurately, and make a suggestion to Doug about what is going on and why, she may engage his interest and curiosity about his upset and furious reaction, giving him some relief and new understanding. She takes care not to be defensive or intellectual when she does this, or it might seem to Doug that she is just trying to get out of any real responsibility for his distress and can't acknowledge that her break really does cause him pain.

The analyst thus tries to hold on to the distress, her own and the patient's, and tries to bear it and make sense of it rather than pushing it back defensively, or relieving herself of it quickly by apology and explanation. If she were to do this she would be relaxing the neces-sary tension of the analytic stance, and reacting more as one might in an ordinary social situation. The sometimes uncomfortable but often productive process of holding on to the tension, bearing the way the patient is feeling and seeing one, while one finds a helpful way of talk-ing to the patient about it, is called **containment**, and the process of making a link in the analysis which invites the patient to think about it is an example of an **interpretation**. Interpretations made by the analyst aim to bring out the unconscious or latent meaning of the patients' behaviour. They examine the defences in play at the time and often link the past and the present. A **transference interpreta-tion** concerns the live experience in the room between analyst and patient. It has the advantage that it addresses the here and now, some-thing that is emotionally 'hot' and immediate in the relationship. A closer look at another session with Doug illustrates all these points.

Doug arrived late for the session following his analyst's announcing her forthcoming break. His explanations for his lateness were all perfectly plausible. Yet at the same time there was a slightly sulky nonchalance in his manner, suggesting 'So what if I'm late; what's it to you?' She was aware of this but didn't comment.

After a silence in which he sighed and shifted around on the couch, he reported a situation at work in which, yet again, his female boss had let the whole team down by agreeing to two big projects at once. His group had worked flat out on the original project and just as they were likely to get this big order she was effectively withdrawing support and resources, pulling the rug out from under them. His analyst knew that Doug cared deeply about this project. It was a big one for him; a chance to show what he could do. Doug continued, sounding furious and at the same time impotent, almost like a child unable to affect his situation. He spoke about the details of his work situation, the helpless rage of his team, the complaints of his client and the humiliation he felt when telling the client of the delay which was beyond his control. Listening to his distress and complaints his analyst became aware of Doug's fantasy that his boss, a powerful woman, was secretly pursuing her own interests. There was even a suggestion that she had a flirtatious relationship with the other client which had been at the root of her prioritising that project.

Doug spoke at length and really wasn't interested in his analyst's opinions at the moment. He left no space for her to speak and half an hour passed. His analyst, meanwhile, though silent, was working hard. Recognising his hurt, his rage and his humiliation at work she felt sure that he also felt those things towards her at the moment. It was unlike him to come late and not be interested in what she had to say. She had to stop herself from defending herself; she wished she could tell him that she didn't want to have to take the week off either. She found herself wondering what it might have been like for Doug as a small boy when his father had left and his mother had protected herself from her grief with a string of brief affairs, often leaving him in the care of her sister.

She found a moment when Doug had paused to think, and said that she thought that he was letting her know how upset and angry he felt with her today, about the unexpected week's break. Doug was in no mood for this and expostulated: 'huh! You always think it is all about you, don't you!' She suggested that he felt very humiliated by her high-handed decision as if he was unimportant, and as if she didn't recognise how important all that's going on in his analysis at the moment really is. He listened intently. She continued that she had the impression that he was experiencing her like a mother figure who loses interest in him when there is an interesting man on the scene.

Doug was noticeably calmer and in a softer, more reflective voice said, 'It's funny, when I left here yesterday I saw a man in the street outside your house. I haven't seen him before and I had the passing thought that he was waiting to see me go before coming in here.' He went on to tell his analyst about a difficulty with his girlfriend. He can get very hurt and humiliated if she talks to other men when they are out. It developed into a big row last weekend, with him accusing her of being self-engrossed and loving all the attention she was getting.

He was wondering if it was the same thing, whether in fact he creates these situations. There was a long silence, and right near the end Doug said, quietly, and movingly, 'I wish my dad had stayed around, then I could have just got on with things without having to keep an eye on my mum, looking out for what she was getting up to all the time.'

In the process of arriving at the **insight** that his confusing, hurtful and humiliating experiences in the past are making him behave in destructive ways in the present, the patient has also had a new experience. He has been understood by someone who can really know about and bear his distress and his anger towards her, someone who goes on trying to understand and help him even in the heat of the moment. In his mind he adds a new figure to his internal figures. Alongside the old expectation of a maternal woman who is preoccupied with her man and doesn't wish to know how that hurts him, there is now an experience of another kind of maternal woman who while having a life of her own also has concern for how that affects him.

Here is our second example showing the interplay of transference, countertransference, containment and interpretation.

Katherine had experienced considerable deprivation and abuse, including some sexual abuse, in childhood. As a young adult her problems were compounded by sexual abuse by a therapist who was 'helping' her.

Her analysis was characterised by periods of utter despair in which she lay silently, unable to speak, yet conveying a desperate feeling that something must be done as she could do nothing for herself. Her analyst felt impotent and useless, as without any associations from Katherine she was hampered in being able to make sense of this terrible experience.

In a session well into the analysis Katherine talked graphically about the way in which her mother used to shut her up when she was deeply distressed and complaining by giving her food. In the session Katherine and her analyst were thinking again about why the therapist had abused her. In the past Katherine had felt either unbearably guilty herself or filled with hatred and rage against him. Now her analyst, drawing on her own frequent experience of helplessness in the face of Katherine's despair, speculated that perhaps he had found Katherine's damage, pain and helplessness quite intolerable and had felt that he must at all costs find some magical way of shutting up her distress, perhaps in some ways similar to her mother's feeding. The session had continued with further exploration of this idea.

In a session soon after this, Katherine was again plunged into a deep depression, unable to offer her analyst anything with which the analyst could help her. Her analyst experienced almost unbearable feelings of guilt at not helping her patient in her terrible distress, but stayed in role as her analyst, listening, thinking and trying to make sense of things. Near the end of the session, Katherine said scathingly to her analyst: 'So I suppose you haven't got a magic wand to help me, then.' The analyst replied that it was terrible for Katherine to feel that her analyst could do nothing to ease her desperation. When she felt this bad she wanted anything, however drastic or destructive, to relieve her misery and felt furious that her analyst would not take action. And yet, in the light of their discussion a few days ago, she thought that there must be a part of Katherine that was relieved that the analyst could bear her painful state without recourse to a magic wand.

Katherine returned the next day, thoughtful and less depressed. She said that she had thought a great deal about what the analyst had said. The thing that stayed with her most of all was the idea that it might be terribly hard for the analyst to be with her when she was like this and that the analyst might be feeling the pain and the helplessness. The analyst remarked that on previous occasions Katherine had imagined that, because the analyst did not DO anything, she was just sitting there untouched. If her analyst didn't take some kind of action, then maybe she didn't feel Katherine's pain. It had felt to her that there was nothing between jumping into action and complete unconcern. Katherine said with surprise in her voice that that was right.

In this example over the period reported, the analyst talked to her patient in different kinds of ways. When talking about the therapist's abuse they were thinking together about a new way of understanding his actions. This was a helpful part of their discourse; it was not a transference interpretation but did draw on the analyst's countertransference that she had struggled with and thought about over many sessions. The transference interpretation a few days later, when they were back in the thick of the familiar and impossible experience, drew on the hypothesis that had been made in the earlier session. It was in the transference interpretation that everything came together for Katherine and in which she experienced change. She came back reporting the entirely new experience she had had with the analyst. She had experienced the analyst as a person who, in spite of feeling under extraordinary pressure to shut up her pain, went on thinking and trying to help in a constructive way.

The psychoanalytic relationship may appear from the outside to be an artificial one. In fact it comes to contain all the complexities and passions of any close human relationship. The unusual feature of it is the analyst's restraint, his or her attempts all the time to think rather than spill out an immediate reaction to the patient. This is only completely possible in theory though, and in practice the analyst will often tend to be pulled a bit without knowing it, into reacting, fitting in with what the patient wants or expects. The patient's customary relationship patterns will thus tend to be **enacted** in small ways. It cannot be stressed too strongly, here, that we are not talking about gross acting out by the analyst such as lapses in confidentiality or inappropriate boundary violations. But subtle enactments are inevitable as the analyst picks up unconscious cues from the patient as to how to respond.

Mark, who was very stuck and restricted in his life, would come to a session enthusiastic about a possible new job, and his analyst would feel pleased for them both that things were moving. Then over the following days he would lapse into passivity, mentioning vaguely that he had forgotten to phone for the job application, or had lost it. The analyst found herself disappointed and restless, wanting to prod Mark into action, and would notice she was making slightly bossy-sounding comments about his inaction. He would become more passive while she would become more active, all the time trying to hide her irritation. At times she would find a sharp edge had entered her voice, in spite of her efforts to go on thinking and containing. In response, Mark would sound a mixture of meek and subtly mocking. It would start just a bit to resemble the sado-masochistic way Mark and his authoritarian father related to each other.

The analyst needed to find a way of standing back for a moment and reflecting to herself on the parts she and Mark were both playing. Only then could she make an interpretation that engaged Mark's curiosity, showed her understanding of his predicament and had a chance of helping him to alter rather than just go on repeating a lifelong pattern.

It is tempting in analysis to make intellectual links without a real connection to powerful wishes and feelings. But intellectual links on their own are not nearly as effective.

Beth knows intellectually that she always defers to older men and loses her clarity of thinking because her father liked to prove he was cleverer than women, and she couldn't bear to humiliate him. On many occasions on which she has deferred to her analyst, he has pointed out to her that she is doing just that and Beth has come to recognise the pattern. The fact that he seems interested that she is doing it, doesn't just go along with it but questions why, suggests to Beth that he isn't the vulnerable father figure she thought he was at first. She begins to show an argumentative and keen intelligence and finds that her analyst, far from putting her down or becoming humiliated, engages with her as an equal. Father remains in her mind as vulnerable but he comes to fill less of her horizon. He becomes simply himself rather than a template for maleness.

Soon Beth reports that when she visits home she tends to feel sometimes tender, sometimes irritated with her father about his vulnerabilities, but is no longer inhibited by him. She also finds herself getting to know him in a deeper way and finds that he is not quite as intolerant as she had thought. Her image of him had been limited and caricatured; the development of their relationship had been stifled by their repetitive and stereotyped reactions to each other. Her self-justifying and time-consuming internal dialogue with him ceases to intrude on her life. Her world becomes a bit larger and freer.

It should have emerged by now that analysis seems to work in a number of ways. We have spoken of the importance of **containment** and of experiencing and of internalising a new figure. Patients also come to own, sometimes reluctantly at first, previously disowned feelings and thoughts, parts of the personality that don't fit easily with how they would like to see themselves. By disowning unwanted features, one stunts one's whole personality. For example, Nasima's terror of her developing sexuality, and her fear that as she became a sexual person in adolescence she would become uncontrollably promiscuous, meant that she could not develop any adult sexual identity at all. She was inhibited and held back in her whole development. Gradually in analysis she could reclaim her sexual feelings and fantasies, re-experiencing them in relation to her analyst in the transference. Through the work she could be helped to understand her fears and could begin again the developmental process of adolescence, this time with the hope that she wouldn't be overwhelmed by impossible and forbidden sexual wishes.

Psychoanalysis can help to moderate what Freud called **the compulsion to repeat**. This unconscious tendency can lead us to re-enact situations which have previously caused distress, despite our conscious wish to do things differently next time. Alan, the patient who was exploring his dream in our first example, restricted his life in response to his unconscious fear of his own murderous violence. Yet he would find himself constantly feeling belittled and driven to a violent response, his worst and most feared situation. Nasima, whose inhibited behaviour served to guard her against sexual promiscuity, tried to move forward and to come to her sessions in a cab rather than requiring her mother to drive her each time. But on her first attempt she found herself accidentally getting into a car which she 'thought' was her cab, with a strange man who was actually waiting for someone else.

Through the experience of analysis Alan and Nasima both came to recognise the ways in which they created an external situation to enact and elaborate their internal view of themselves in relation to others. Once this was recognised and understood through many enactments in relation to the analyst, it slowly became possible for both of them to see their part in the constant re-creation of distressing life events, and to engage more actively in different, more constructive ways of relating.

Internal relationships re-create and distort the relationships of our daily life. For example, Beth's deep conviction that *all* men were vulnerable and had to be deferred to showed itself in the way she related to her male analyst. He became the externalisation of her internal picture of the father of her childhood. Through analytic interpretation of the numerous occasions when there was a live expression of this internal picture, change came about. It could be described as reality-testing the internal world and modifying it in the light of new information.

Change is also facilitated in a more general way through the provision of a safe and consistent setting for blocked development to unfold. The analytic stance is one of enquiry. It is a non-moralistic, non-judgemental attitude that over time and with interpretation comes to be internalised by the patient. It tends to modify or replace the harshly judgemental, mocking or contemptuous superego with which the patient comes to treatment. For example, over time Alan began to understand some of the aggressive and overbearing behaviour which he exhibited towards the analyst and others and which he despised in himself. He could see how he had responded to traumatic losses and separations in his early life with fear and a self-preservative omnipotence and aggression with which he hoped that he would hold on to his loved ones, and force them to stay with him. Recognising this, and experiencing his analyst's understanding of it despite his attacks on her, meant that he could be more understanding of himself and soften his need to act cruelly. Put another way, he had internalised a more supportive, understanding and encouraging conscience and guide to his behaviour.

It may seem from reading the examples above that, following an insight, the work is done. In fact there is the long process known as **working through** to be achieved. Psychoanalysis takes years rather than months. Following moments of emotional and intellectual understanding, old resistances reappear under the sway of the compulsion to repeat. The same situation, now in a different setting or guise, comes into the analytic encounter as freshly as if it had never been worked on. Working through requires the patient to understand how the meaning in the present situation is another version of one that has already been understood. Gradually the patient begins to spot it for him- or herself and starts to feel and experience things differently.

The activity of working through is intimately linked with **mourning**, a central concept in psychoanalysis. Mourning and working through both involve the gradual relinquishment of loved but lost people or ideals. Both involve psychic work and pain and both take time. Analysis involves the giving up of wished-for but unrealistic views of ourselves and patterns of relating. Old positions are mourned so that we become free to gain new ground. We also have to realise that we cannot become different people; through analysis we become more deeply and fully ourselves.

Suffering is part of the human condition – it is as much through losses, conflicts and failures as through success that human beings develop. But for those whose suffering dominates, whose internal conflicts inhibit development and whose failures get repeated, psychoanalysis can modify destructive patterns and offer the possibility of greater freedom to take control. As Freud himself put it, when asked how psychoanalysis can help if illness is connected to early experience which itself cannot be changed: 'much will be gained if we succeed in transforming your hysterical misery into common unhappiness. With a mental life that has been restored to health you will be better armed against that unhappiness' (Breuer and Freud, 1895: 305).

In this chapter we have tried to show something of what psychoanalysis is, how it works and the kind of people it can help. Since our aim was to give a flavour we have not included references for the multiple sources of the theories and ideas. Two other useful introductory texts which the reader can consult are Bateman and Holmes (1995) and Sandler, Dare, Holder and Dreher (1992). In the next chapter we will describe some of the major theoretical linchpins of psychoanalysis which inform and direct our work.

2

BASICS OF PSYCHOANALYTIC THEORY

Psychoanalysis is a branch of psychology particularly concerned with subjective experience. It has three aspects. First it is a body of knowledge about the mind, which has been discovered partly through the sort of work described in the last chapter and partly through studying ordinary human phenomena such as dreams, slips (like slips of the tongue) and jokes. Second the word 'psychoanalysis' refers to a method for investigating the mind, and third it refers to a form of psychotherapeutic treatment.

Psychoanalysis takes a **dynamic** rather than static view of the mind, seeing movement, energy, and in particular **conflict**, as intrinsic to mental life. For example, a person may want to do something his or her conscience doesn't allow, or may be pulled in different ways by love and hate for the same person. He or she may want to know the truth but also be frightened and reluctant to find out.

Central to psychoanalytic theory is the idea that much of our mental life is **unconscious**. Unconscious thoughts, feelings and wishes form the mental bedrock, with conscious experience the tip of the iceberg. Unconscious processes cannot, by definition, be known directly but have to be inferred from their effects, in a way analogous to the powerful but invisible effect of gravity.

Psychoanalytic theory offers a **developmental** perspective. Although there are a number of partly overlapping and sometimes conflicting psychoanalytic theories of development, all emphasise the formative effect of early relationships. Early experience is seen as interacting with innate endowment in determining the way the mind forms. Normal development involves acquiring an increasingly clear and stable sense of self, and an increasing capacity to relate to others as separate and unique. The lifelong maturing process is seen by psychoanalysts as involving successive mourning of earlier stages of life and former illusions, with the gradual achievement of a more truthful and realistic picture of self and the world.

This chapter will look at psychoanalytic conceptions of the inner mental world. We discuss unconscious processes, conflicts and defences in ordinary life. We will show how the study of dreaming and of psychological symptoms can illuminate the unconscious workings of the mind. Finally we will discuss various ways in which psychoanalysts have understood the developmental process.

Psychoanalytic perspectives on the 'inner world'

Freud was by no means the first to point out unconscious aspects of the mind. Our blindness to ourselves has often been poetically expressed, as in the seventeenth century Pascal's 'The heart has its reasons of which reason knows nothing'(1923–62). Freud found in his patients that 'the heart's reasons' could be shocking or frightening, needing to be hidden from consciousness.

Freud's models of the mind

Freud was interested in the ways people dealt with their intrinsic sensuality, sexuality and aggression. He saw these as drives which became channelled and controlled as the person grew from a ruthlessly pleasure-seeking little creature into a civilised, mature adult. His first conceptualisation of the mind's structure and function came to be called the **topographical model** (Freud, 1900). In this model the **conscious** mind is seen as the tip of an iceberg, with the **unconscious** the repository of a 'cauldron' of primitive wishes and impulses, kept at bay and mediated by a **preconscious** area, or function, where selection and processing of what is useful and acceptable to consciousness goes on.

Although the topographical model is still useful, Freud later developed a more complex and flexible **structural model** (Freud, 1923) of the mind containing the entities **id**, **ego** and **superego**. These are of course not concrete entities or locations, but ways of conceptualising important mental functions. The id encompasses primitive, bodily based wishes and impulses, pushing towards fulfilment. The superego represents the moral demands and prohibitions coming not just from external people like parents, but from one's own natural love of important others, and the wish to protect them from one's own more ruthless side. The ego is the executive part of the mind concerned with adaptation; when internal conflict occurs the ego mediates between the demands of id, superego and external reality, deploying a variety of **defence mechanisms** in the process. Id and superego are unconscious and much of ego functioning is as well. The evolution of these Freudian models has been explicated in detail by Sandler et al. (1992).

Symptom formation

Freud's patients came to him with a variety of neurotic symptoms. He grew to understand these as unconscious compromises between wishes and defences or, putting it a different way, between the dictates of id and superego. One of his own earliest cases (Breuer and Freud, 1895) will illustrate this.

The young, unmarried and dutiful pillar of her family, Elisabeth von R came to Freud with thigh pains and difficulty walking, for which no physical basis could be found. The disability, it much later emerged, first appeared when she gave up a possible romance in order to nurse her beloved father, who subsequently died. It worsened after an enjoyable walk one day alone with her brother-in-law, and still further when her sister, to whom she was consciously devoted, died in pregnancy. The symptom evoked much solicitude in the family, and Freud noticed that Elisabeth seemed to find an odd relief from the discomfort when he applied electrical stimulation to the affected muscles. (In these early pre-analytic years he was still using some physical treatments.)

As Freud turned wholly to psychological investigation, encouraging Elisabeth to let her mind run freely over the events and feelings of the last few years, particularly times when the pains had worsened, connections started to appear which she at first fiercely denied, then with horror and ultimate relief accepted. She had managed very comprehensively to hide from herself her passionate feelings for her brother-in-law and her envy of her sister. Most of all, she had forgotten a split-second thought on first seeing her sister's dead body: 'Now he is free again and I can be his wife.'

The published case history of Elisabeth von R is a moving one which, as Freud himself comments wryly, reads 'like a short story' and seems at first sight to 'lack the serious stamp of science'. However, reading it today one still gets a sense of connections being made in the work which resonate deeply with Elisabeth, and in fact lead, after initial deep distress, to great freeing in her feelings and her life. After an initial setback on parting from Freud, we hear of the symptom-free Elisabeth seen at a ball to 'whirl past in a lively dance' and subsequently to leave home and marry (but not the brother-in-law!). The site of Elisabeth's thigh pain turned out to be the place where her invalid father used to lay his leg for dressings, although she had not consciously made this connection at first. The electrical stimulation of the thigh produced an effect that seemed part pleasure, part pain. Freud's finely observed description of it suggests to the reader something erotic, but perhaps simultaneously a guilt-relieving punishment as well. This early case highlights the dynamic nature of symptoms. The neat way Elisabeth's symptom both fulfils and punishes sexual wishes, particularly if related to family members, without the wishes ever coming into consciousness, is characteristic of this sort of **hysterical** symptom (see Chapter 3). The symptom's **primary gain** is to allow the id and superego to reach a compromise. There is also a **secondary gain**. This is that Elisabeth remains an invalid, comfortingly close to the bosom of her family, although she is unable to separate and develop as a sexual woman. The case also shows some examples of psychic defence mechanisms.

Psychic defence mechanisms

We are driven from birth by a need to discover and make sense of ourselves and the world. In an important sense, learning truth about the world nourishes and expands the mind. At the same time, we need to protect ourselves from overwhelming feelings or frightening contradictions. How much reality we can bear at any moment is a matter of the balance of cost and benefit in the psyche; the balance between the need to know and understand, and the need to preserve a tolerable **psychic equilibrium**.

Today's young woman is less likely than Elisabeth to need to hide her attraction to her brother-in-law from herself. However, we do still need to see ourselves in a good light, as reasonable, decent people by our own and our society's standards, and the superego function of our minds constantly works to ensure this. People are troubled by knowing too much, not only about their sexuality, but also about their hatred and aggression. A trauma, particularly an early one, may also have to be 'forgotten' or remembered in an unemotional way.

A defence mechanism (A. Freud, 1936) is an automatic, unconscious mental operation, taking place in the ego, which has the function of helping the person to retain a psychic equilibrium. These psychic phenomena were first described by Freud and Anna Freud and have been confirmed and further elaborated by analytic work in subsequent generations. A central defence is **repression**, in which unacceptable feelings and thoughts are pushed from consciousness; for example both Elisabeth's sexual feelings and her fleetingly triumphant thought at her sister's death were repressed. The repressed material remains in a sense 'under tension', pushing towards expression, so that other defences may have to be deployed to allow it to emerge in an acceptable, disguised form. Repressed content may be given a coded disguise, in the form of a symptom, as with Elisabeth's leg pain and paralysis, which expressed both her desire and her defence against it. It may also be turned into its opposite, as in **reaction formation**, for example when someone finds themselves being exaggeratedly nice and helpful to someone they don't want to admit to themselves they really despise.

In **negation** the individual unconsciously draws attention to something repressed, by stressing its irrelevance or its opposite. In Freud's paper on negation (1925a), this is exemplified by a patient who says, 'You ask who this person in the dream can be. It's *not* my mother.' Freud, noticing that the idea of the mother was introduced by the patient himself, and by no one else, takes the mention of her, albeit in negative form, as an unconscious indication that it *is* his mother. **Projection** and **identification** are defences whereby parts of the self are attributed to the other or those of the other to the self.

In projection disliked aspects of the self are disowned and attributed to another. Projection always involves a **denial** of reality. This often involves polarised **splitting**, with both **idealisation** and **denigration**. For example, one may idealise oneself or one's own group, at the expense of someone else, or another group, becoming denigrated. This is the basis of patriotic fervour during a war, or racism, where the hated group may be seen as dirty, violent, ruthless, over-sexed, mean (in fact anything bad or feared), while oneself and one's racial group, or one's country or football team, seem wholly virtuous. To work best, projections need to be hung on pre-existing small 'hooks' in the other person or group, ways in which they may have some aspect of the disliked characteristic, which then becomes greatly enlarged. Projection may be done in such a way that the recipient is unconsciously stimulated into enacting the projected impulse. An example is when a person who might otherwise envy others boasts smugly to a friend about a piece of good fortune, thus making the friend experience the envy.

Identification is a normal part of development. Witness a child who has the mannerisms of his father. It is also a common part of the mourning process; the bereaved person unconsciously takes on, say, some of the characteristics of the dead person, or becomes fearfully convinced that they are suffering from the loved one's final illness. When intense and prolonged, this sort of identification may be a defence that impedes the natural mourning process. In a less intense form it is an ordinary and comforting way of keeping something of the loved person inside one. **Identification with the aggressor** (A. Freud, 1936) is a variety of identification, shown for example by previously under-confident and vulnerable children who cope with bullying at school by becoming bullies themselves (See Sandler, 1988).

Defences are a necessary part of mental life, but they can become troublesome if extreme, or if rigidly set into the personality. Some people find it unbearable to experience needs and vulnerabilities and to tolerate the independent separateness of other people's minds. Instead they protectively create a **narcissistic** picture of the world, in which they are the **omnipotent** centre. Such a defensive structure is a serious impediment to the development of relationships. Since others are merely experienced as two-dimensional bit-part actors in their own drama, they may feel able to use them heartlessly and contemptuously. These narcissistic mental worlds have been called **psychic retreats** (Steiner,1993). People often develop them in response to serious childhood trauma and neglect, but what is initially a sanctuary can then harden into a psychic prison, distorting and impoverishing later relationships.

Parapraxes and jokes

Unconscious thoughts and feelings can protrude like tips of icebergs in the form of **parapraxes**, popularly known as 'Freudian slips': slips of the tongue, bungled actions, forgettings or mis-rememberings (Freud, 1901). A nutritionist giving a lecture intended to say 'We should always demand the best in bread', but transposed the 'r'. We may forget to attend a dreaded meeting or call a friend's new partner by the name of the previous one, whom we liked better. A patient who was nervous about starting psychoanalysis, but trying not to know just *how* nervous, went to ring the clinic bell and mis-read the adjacent bell (which said 'caretaker') as 'undertaker'.

Freud wrote extensively about parapraxes. He showed (Freud, 1905c) how **jokes**, in the same way, often revealed shocking or worrying thoughts and impulses, disguised in humour to make them acceptable to both the teller and the listener. This makes humour a form of defence, often quite a helpful one. We become wry and affectionately tease ourselves and others about the things people are afraid or embarrassed about viewing too soberly, such as selfishness, intolerance, murderousness or ruthless sexuality.

Dreaming

Dreams were referred to by Freud (1900) as 'the royal road to a knowledge of the unconscious activities of the mind'. Modern-day psychoanalysts still agree with Freud that the study of dreams and dreaming gives us an important window on the way unconscious mental processes work.

Freud believed that the main function of dreaming was to prevent sleep from being disturbed by primitive sexual and aggressive impulses. The sleeper reached a compromise: he or she had some satisfaction of the wish in a disguised dream-form while continuing to sleep. In addition psychoanalysts today tend to think that part of the reason for sleep is *in order* to dream, because dreaming includes important processing and integration of the new psychic data that has flooded in during waking hours. Dreaming is vital, creative and integrative, not only a means of discharge.

In sleep the mind's daytime 'censor' and sense of rational logic is relaxed. Dreams recalled in the waking state can seem absurd or disturbing. Dreaming involves **symbolisation** so that one thing can stand for another, with images often condensed or displaced so that disconnections and odd new juxtapositions are made. When we dream we become more poetic, and more like Impressionist or abstract artists. The dreams of serious people may reveal quite a humorous capacity, and mild placatory people who have repressed their aggression may dream about being violent.

Phantasy

All psychoanalytic theories include the idea that unconscious thoughts and feelings are central in mental functioning. The mind is seen as progressively arising out of the body, so that bodily based impulses are primary, and gradually become transformed into thoughts and wishes located in the mind. Unconscious wishes, when blocked and frustrated, generate wish-fulfilling phantasies, also usually unconscious, which then feed into the construction of dreams, symptoms, slips and jokes. The 'ph' of phantasy denotes an unconsciously generated process as distinct from a consciously con-structed daydream, or **fantasy**.

Melanie Klein broadened Freud's conception of phantasy into an idea that all sensation and experience is represented in the mind in animistic and relational terms (see Hinshelwood, 1994). Thus **unconscious phantasy**, in Klein's terms, is the primary, continu-ous content of the unconscious. Examples would be the representa-tion of hunger sensations as someone frighteningly gnawing away inside, or experiencing feelings of love for mother as putting lovely things inside her.

These ideas, about a sort of animistic, unconscious accompani-ment of experience, arose partly from Klein's observations of children's play in analytic sessions. Children, particularly those she saw with emotional problems, would play out their own disturbing versions of family relationships in terms of sex between parents or child and parent, lovely feeding, angry cutting up, nurturing or killing babies, and so on. Violent themes were frequent whether or not children had been treated kindly by their parents. Klein emphasised the importance of Freud's idea of the **primal scene**. This was that, whether or not the child had actually witnessed parental sex, there was an innate template in the mind for representing parental coupling. This could become a source of jealousy and fear but also of fascinated preoccupation, from early in a child's life. The form the coupling took in the child's imagination would chime with the child's current preoccupations, whether predominantly oral, anal or genital.

Four-and-a-half-year-old Jane was very inhibited in her development, clingy and babyish with her mother, and made a great fuss if she was not allowed to sleep between her parents at night. She was not able to explain to her parents what her worries were, but in the first week of her analysis played in a way that graphically represented her phantasies and fears. The little people and animals in the playroom clashed together violently, with noses going into mouths and bottoms, and there was talk of knives going into tummies in bed. Play babies appeared and might be cherished and then attacked and thrown into the bin.

Gradually Jane's analyst was able to speak to her about her fears of what mummies and daddies did together, and of how Jane both longed for and hated the idea of a baby brother or sister. Vivid play with imaginary crocodiles and lions was interpreted as Jane's own biting fury about being little. Her analyst suggested to Jane in various ways that her furious jealousy and envy of the powerful grown-ups was fuelling her fears of fierce retaliatory punishment. As her analyst tuned into the underlying phantasy meaning of her play in this way, Jane showed great relief, started to sleep calmly in her own bed, and caught up with her peers developmentally.

Phantasising can also be seen as an ongoing process of hypothesising about the world and the relationships between people. Becoming aware of bizarre and disturbing underlying phantasy versions of reality can make sense of seemingly irrational fears in conscious life. Phantasies are gradually transformed as a result of actual experience, and generally become less intrusive or accessible in healthy adults than in children. However, in adult waking life underlying bodily phantasy persists in language as in 'a biting retort', or 'drinking in what she was saying'. It can also come to the surface in people with severe disturbances, for example in psychotic illness, where it forms part of delusions and hallucinations.

The idea of early body relationships and phantasies coming to imbue the world in a rich and complexly symbolised way also gives us a way of thinking about many attachments, superstitions and fears we carry through life, and can be given expression through art.

Mental representations and internal objects

Mental representations of the relationships between self and others are laid down in the mind from infancy onwards. Psychoanalytic theory, starting with Freud, has emphasised the way in which such internal 'templates' affect the way we perceive and react to other people in the present. This is the basis of transference, discussed in Chapter 1.

Internal representations are not merely faithful copies of external experience but are modified by the person's own wishes and impulses. For example a parental figure may be represented either as more benign than was really the case, or more hostile. In the latter case it might be that some of one's own hostility is attributed to the other, and one's self-representation is thus kept more benign (see the earlier discussion of projection).

The term **internal object** is also often used when describing internal versions of people. The word 'object' in this context means not an inanimate object, but the human object of one's love, hate, longing and so on. An internal object is usually seen as having a psychic existence which is more than representation, a more active or even autonomous 'figure' in the mind which interacts in various ways with other objects and the self. In the theories of Melanie Klein, the process of phantasy (see above) is intimately connected with the formation of internal objects, certain of which may thus be imbued with primitive, nightmarish or magically good qualities.

Internal objects (see Sandler and Sandler, 1998 for a review of the concept) are formed, in part, from the internalisation of external relationship experience and they in turn influence the way we experience relationships subsequently. People with largely benign and reliable internal pictures of others generally find it easier to recognise and relate well to loving and reliable people externally. Hence the observation that a loved and secure child is more likely to make relationships that lead to a loved and secure adult life, and to be able to provide love and security for others. A sense of fundamentally loving and good internal objects allows the child to play alone confidently, or to wait for comfort, or food, or understanding. This is not only because the child learns that these things are reliably available *outside*, but, more than this, there is a growing sense of being related to a good object who sustains one *inside* in the meantime.

By the same token, a child with, say, an unpredictable, sometimes violent parent will internalise a **primary relationship** with an unreliable and threatening figure, and thus come to inhabit an internal world where danger accompanies love and dependency. He or she may then grow into an adult who is drawn automatically towards similar experiences, and/or mistrusts and thus misses out on whatever good experiences might have been available.

Although early experiences are importantly formative, these templates are rarely set in stone, but function as active, dynamic parts of the personality open to gradual alteration with experience. In some, though, the distorted version gets stuck. The experience of psychoanalysis can help to make the internal world of objects more realistic and stable.

Psychoanalytic perspectives on development

A mature individual has a coherent and stable sense of self, and a capacity to perceive the other as existing separately, outside oneself, with his or her own unique mind and sense of self. You could say that the individual who is relatively mature lives mostly in a three-dimensional, complexly populated world, rather than a self-centric one in which the rest of the world simply provides scenery and actors, full of the person's projections. Maturity includes a capacity to manage one's emotional states. The mature individual can manage and enjoy intimate relationships and also tolerate being separate and alone. He or she is able to be productive and creative in some way. Freud summed all this up once as the vital abilities 'to love and to work'. There is of course no ideal, once and for all achieved, mature state; neither do psychoanalysts think of maturity in terms of normative external behaviours or ways of living one's life.

Different schools of psychoanalytic thought put emphasis on different aspects of the process of psychic development, but a number of basics are shared. It is agreed that early experiences, particularly relationships with mother, father and other important caretakers, interact with the child's innate endowment to shape the personality. These experiences structure the child's modes of relating, and his or her conscious and unconscious perceptions of the world. Psychoanalysts see normal development as a progressive unfolding of capacities and especially emphasise emotional and relational capacities, and changes in subjective experiences.

The centrality of mourning

Psychoanalytic theories all see mourning as central to development. Development always involves both gains and losses. For example the protected intimacy of babyhood has to be given up if the wider world is to be explored in toddlerhood. Development can become derailed when the stage needing to be given up has been unsatisfactory in some way, not equipping the individual properly for the next stage, as in the case of Joan, below.

Three-year-old Joan seemed angrily and despairingly to 'turn her face to the wall' when her little brother was born, and in family photographs of the time her face looks vacant and empty. Her mother, a deprived woman herself, could not provide enough support and understanding, and Joan's tendency to turn away, rather than vigorously to demand and compete for attention, added to the problem. Joan managed school, though she never did as well as expected. However, she became seriously depressed soon after she left home to go to university and had to be hospitalised.

Psychoanalysts see development as cyclical as well as sequential; **regression** to earlier stages of emotional development often occurs. Sometimes this happens in a repetitive way; sometimes it allows reworking of previous difficulties, and a new move forward.

After entering analysis in her thirties Joan would become withdrawn and depressed during breaks in treatment, or following sightings of the analyst's other patients. This time round though, the detailed understanding and support provided by the analysis enabled Joan gradually to work through this familiar predicament. She was finally able to recognise, mourn and give up her unattainable longing for blissful union with a perfect mother figure, accept the failings of the past, and come to terms with the satisfactions and disappointments of current ordinary life and relationships.

We will look now at four major psychoanalytic theories of development. We will start with Freud's original theories and then, arising out of these, the theories of Anna Freud, Melanie Klein and Donald Winnicott. Although there are a number of others, and some will be mentioned briefly in other parts of the book, we have selected these three, given our limited space, as being the most influential in British psychoanalysis. These perspectives all have different emphases and languages of description, which the reader may find somewhat confusing, but it is necessary to outline them to do some justice to the current diversity within psychoanalytic developmental theory.

Freud's theory of development

Freud's developmental theory is mainly about the development of **libido**, a non-specific sensual drive for bodily gratification which, at different stages becomes predominantly focused on particular bodily zones. Preoccupation with the more infantile zones never disappears completely but persists in normal adult sexuality as well as in perverse sexuality and in other ways (Freud, 1905a).

In the **oral stage** infant libido is centred around the mouth and pleasure in sucking. The infant, Freud thought, is largely auto-erotic. Living by the **pleasure principle**, the infant is able to achieve hallucinatory gratification, for example through sucking his own finger. However, such a mechanism will not work indefinitely and even the most attentive of mothers is not always able to satisfy her baby at once. In this way the infant becomes aware of reality. In his key paper, 'Formulation of the two principles of mental functioning' (1911), Freud highlighted the importance of coming to terms with the non-occurrence of wished-for satisfaction. This is needed for the development of the capacity for thought, which in turn is necessary in order to bring about action in the real world, and is an important step in the development of a mature ego. Although in 1911 he did not link this idea to the need for mourning, mourning of unrealistic wished-for ideals is, of course, intimately related to the development of the capacity for containing emotion and dealing with reality in a realistic, rather than phantastic, way.

In the **anal stage**, occurring at a time when the child is learning bowel control, the small child often finds anal activities pleasurable and absorbing. This stage also involves the negotiation of holding on, and letting go, of faeces but in other ways as well. Control issues during the 'terrible twos' can include many things besides the sphincter, for example battles over eating or dressing. Problems here may mark the beginning of persisting difficulties over 'give and take' within relationships. Underlying anal preoccupations may become unconscious but re-emerge symbolically, for example in dreams. An example from Mark, described in Chapter 1, will illustrate this:

> At a time when Mark was still stuck in an angrily passive relationship with both his mother and his analyst, and was unable either to leave home or get to work, he once dreamt that he was inside a mine, fascinated by digging deeply for jewels in dark, shitty mud.

From around the age of three children become increasingly aware of their genitals, finding they can be pleasurable to touch. They start to show off their bodies, and become curious about other children's, especially those of the opposite gender. Freud called this the **phallic stage**, as he thought that the penis was the central organ of interest for both sexes.

The **Oedipus complex** is the centrepiece of psychoanalytic developmental theory. While psychoanalysts since Freud may have disagreed about the timing or exact nature of the Oedipus complex, all have thought of it as of fundamental importance in development. Freud named this complex after the hero of the Greek myth. The Delphic Oracle predicted that Oedipus would kill his father and marry his mother, and due to an unfortunate set of circumstances this prediction came true.

Freud found that all the adults he studied, including himself, showed evidence of a more or less deeply buried attachment to the parent of the opposite sex and concomitant hostility to the parent of the same sex. He thought this originated somewhere between the third and fifth year of life and speculated that the theme had become embedded in the Greek myth, and also in other literature, for example in Shakespeare's Hamlet, because it struck a universal chord for humanity. Freud was clear that both homosexual and heterosexual versions of the complex were ordinary and universal, in both men and women, usually panning out in favour of adult heterosexuality, but leaving most of us with the potential for deep attachments both ways.

Freud thought that Oedipal wishes were given up as a result of fear; for example the boy fears that his father may punish him by castration, a belief that may be stimulated by the observation that a girl does not have a penis. We can sometimes observe the wariness of small boys about their genitals:

> James aged four, coming into the kitchen where father was chopping onions for lunch, instinctively clutched himself and asked nervously 'You're not going to chop my willy off, are you, Dad?'

Because of this fear, according to Freud, the little boy gives up his ambition to take his father's place with his mother. In so doing he internalises his father, accepting his father as both an external and an internal authority. In this way the **superego** is formed. Thereafter incestuous desires are forbidden and the whole affair is repressed and lost from conscious memory.

Not only fear but also mourning – the coming to terms with what cannot be had – play a part in resolving the Oedipus complex and this aspect has been more strongly emphasised by theorists following Freud. Love for the parents goes alongside fear and rivalry. Annie (below) had found an ingeniously bloodless solution to her Oedipus complex:

> Annie, aged three, explained apologetically but firmly to her mother that she had decided to marry Daddy. To her mother's query, 'But as I'm already married to Daddy, what will happen to me?' she replied confidently, 'You'll be all right Mummy, I've thought about that too. You can stay on as the maid.'

For the girl, in fact, Freud believed the situation to be more complicated, with the discovery of the penis leading to envy and a feeling of inferiority, and hostility to the mother for not giving her this organ. This gave way to the wish for a man's penis and the wish for a baby. With advanced understanding, psychoanalysts now think, the girl has an instinctive though subtle awareness of the precious things inside that she must protect and nurture. The existence of a penis stands out in a way that the phantasy of precious inside things can never do, though, and little girls may indeed go through a stage of being quite angry and upset about a perceived lack. Now, however, we would see a woman whose personality becomes organised around the conscious or unconscious idea of being a 'failed man' as in a developmental cul-de-sac, rather than following the typical female pattern, as Freud put forward. Although girls and women may sometimes envy men their physical power and phallic potency, men may equally envy women their capacity for motherhood, and may remain unconsciously in awe and fear of the power their mothers had over their early lives.

After the fears and passions of the phallic/Oedipal phase, Freud saw the child of school age as entering a **latency phase** in which there was a desexualisation of the child's interests, and libidinal energy was directed to the development of social, intellectual and other skills through the mechanism of **sublimation**. Latency, when the precursors of adult sexuality must be laid down, is a time for serious play and experiment. However, for sound biological reasons, actual sex within the family has to be taboo, and the erotic aspect of these childhood loves needs to be forgotten or obscured. Puberty brings about an upsurge in sexual and aggressive feelings which make a demand on the young person to begin putting feelings and fantasies into practice in relationships with peers. One of the vital tasks of **adolescence** is to shift erotic attachment away from the family into the outside world, so that sexual development can finally progress to Freud's **genital stage**.

The task of parents is to provide safe boundaries while allowing their children to separate. Elisabeth von R, Freud's patient described earlier in the chapter, was an example of someone unable without help to move beyond her intense Oedipal involvement with father in her adolescence. She may well have been disturbed by her emerging sexuality and needed to hang on to a secure place in the family as father's adored confidante, perhaps in her secret mind his 'real partner'.

Perhaps Elisabeth's parents colluded with her difficulties by allowing her to be father's nurse at such a sensitive time of her life. The brother-in-law too sounds like a barely displaced Oedipal object, an exciting but unattainable man within the family, attractive partly *because* he belonged to someone else. All this had to be hidden from herself, because the fulfilment of her desires would entail the death of her sister, leading to the intolerable conflict which was expressed through Elisabeth's illness.

Developmental lines: Anna Freud

Anna Freud was concerned to understand the many interacting strands of a child's development, the constitutional givens, the innate developmental processes and the environmental influence. She was strongly influenced by the theories of Sigmund Freud but to these she brought her own detailed observation of both normal and derailed development. She was interested in normal development as well as pathology; her therapeutic goal with children was to restore the child to the path of progressive development.

Anna Freud's theory of development gives due weight to all stages and areas of development from infancy to adolescence, allowing the analyst to distinguish between these and to view pathology against the background of normal development. She also drew attention to the fact that regression of functioning in a child was often a normal and temporary response to stress, whether caused by external factors or from internal ones.

Anna Freud and her co-workers in Hampstead (see p. 53) developed a tool for the assessment of development and psychopathology in children and adolescents, known as the **Provisional Diagnostic Profile** (A. Freud, 1965). This is a mental framework for thinking about the assessment of a patient; its aim is to prompt the diagnostician to think about all areas of the child's life and development, external and internal, so as to arrive at a balanced view of normal as well as pathological functioning. From its initial clinical use the profile developed into a research tool which could be used to compare cases and to assess changes during treatment. Anna Freud's theory of development was different from that of Melanie Klein in its attention to qualitatively different developmental stages throughout childhood and adolescence. Klein tended to focus on the early years of life.

Anna Freud also devised a method of assessing development known as **developmental lines**. A developmental line examines in detail a sequence of drive and structural development in a particular area of functioning. 'Whatever level has been achieved by any given child represents the results of interaction between drive and ego–superego development and their reaction to environmental influence, i.e. between maturation, adaptation and structuralisation' (A. Freud, 1965: 64). Originally Anna Freud described six developmental lines:

• From dependency to emotional self-reliance and adult object relationships
• From suckling to rational eating
• From wetting and soiling to bladder and bowel control
• From irresponsibility to responsibility in body management
• From egocentricity to companionship
• From the body to the toy and from play to work

Each of these lines is elaborated in detail, some more than others. Although the emphasis is on observable behaviour, the internal psychological developments required to achieve each step on each line is also spelt out. The lines can be used by non-analysts as well as analysts to examine a child's readiness for various life experiences, for example attending nursery, and to see in detail where there are developmental deficits, delays or distortions. It can also be seen if a child's development is uneven along the various lines.

In assessing pathology Anna Freud differentiated between **neurotic difficulties** (due to internal conflict) and **deficiencies**. The latter may be either of an organic nature or due to early deprivations, which delay or distort development. For the former condition she thought psychoanalysis the treatment of choice but for deficiencies she advocated what came to be called 'developmental help', a treatment which was differentiated from psychoanalysis because it did not necessarily emphasise the interpretation of intrapsychic conflict and defence. Edgcumbe (2000) has described how in Anna Freud's day the view was maintained that the developmental help offered to autistic, borderline and other children with atypical developmental disorders was not 'proper analysis' even if carried out five times a week. However, what almost invariably happened was that after a time interpretable conflicts started to emerge and the treatment would gradually transform into something closer to classical child analysis.

The struggle between phantasy and reality: Melanie Klein

Klein did not view developmental stages (oral, anal, etc.) in so clear and sequential a way as Sigmund Freud, finding in her analysis of small children that oral, anal and genital preoccupations and phantasies could co-exist in complex ways. She viewed development from a new angle, with her concepts of the paranoid schizoid position and the depressive position. These describe two basic oscillating mental states experienced throughout life (see Klein, 1940, 1946). In the **depressive position** an individual is able to see both herself and others more or less as they really are. Humans are complex, with both positive and attractive characteristics and other less positive or even unpleasant ones. To see another, or oneself, in this multi-dimensional way requires an acceptance of human frailty and also of the inherent separateness and autonomy of others.

You might wish for your mother (or wife or child) to be perfect in every way but if you actually see her that way then you will be seeing your wished-for fantasy rather than a real separate person. Similarly you might feel furious with your ex-husband, but if you see him as the embodiment of everything evil with no good characteristics of any sort, you are simplifying a complex picture. Your entirely negative view may serve the purpose of protecting you from the sadness you would otherwise feel at the loss of a person who in reality has some characteristics you once loved. It may also be protecting you against guilt about your part in the break-up, maybe even attributing some characteristics to him which you are disowning in yourself. The 'depressive' of depressive position does not means depression as an illness, but refers to mourning for lost illusions and certainties, and guilt and regret about one's attacks on loved ones.

Klein called the state in which people are seen as all good or all bad in a cardboard cut-out way, the **paranoid schizoid position**. The word 'schizoid' refers to the split between good and bad and the word 'paranoid' to projection by means of which good or bad qualities are disowned and attributed to others, who are then either idealised, or feared or hated. Negative feelings boomerang back, so that the *hated* object appears threateningly *hateful*. The paranoid schizoid state of mind is ruled by the principles of self-preservation, with no concern or mercy for others. Klein's work is sometimes easier to approach at first via secondary sources (e.g. Segal, 1973; Anderson, 1992; Hinshelwood, 1994).

Klein thought that the small infant's mental world had the qualities of the most primitive version of the paranoid schizoid position, in which he experienced two quite separate versions of his mother. His good experiences (like being fed, securely held or comforted) were attributed to the loved good mother, and his bad ones (like being cold or hungry) were attributed to the hateful bad mother. The infant phantasised lovingly taking in the good one, and hatefully ridding himself of the bad one, perhaps at first by screaming or vomiting her out. In Klein's schema, the angelic mother appears more lovely through being loved, while the nightmare version is made even worse by the infant's hatred and phantasised attacks. These vividly opposing versions of mother are perhaps the ultimate source of monstrous legends and fairy tales. Klein saw envy as an additional factor; the infant sometimes hating not just the bad frustrating breast or mother, but also the good, nourishing one which he cannot possess and control.

The child's primitive phantasies can be seen as first approximations to reality, makeshift constructions which are continually projected out into the world, tested against reality, and taken back in a modified form. If all goes well, extreme phantasy meets ordinary reality, and is gradually modified. The child begins to have an inkling that he has a loving but imperfect three-dimensional mother, and feels the beginnings of guilt and concern about his attacks on her, real and imagined. It is now that the depressive position sets in for the first time, and the two mother-images come together, so that mother begins to be perceived as a whole, more complex person. An ill-treated child will have more difficulty doing this, as his environment tends to confirm his worst phantasies. Rather than bringing opposites together, he may be forced to redouble splitting, so as to preserve some image of goodness somewhere.

The depressive position is never attained once and for all, either in childhood or beyond. We regularly lose it under stress and have to work and rework to recover it. Each new step or challenge tends to provoke anew a split between good and bad, a somewhat paranoid watchfulness and sensitivity, and a tendency to idealise and blame. Working through the experience will then allow a softening of certainty and self-righteousness, and the emergence of a more complex and sympathetic perspective, including seeing one's own failings. This work is intimately related to the work of mourning. Klein stresses the importance of **reparation**, repairing the damage done (in both imagination and external reality) to loved others by one's hate. Each time the task of mourning is achieved and the depressive position is regained, the personality is strengthened a little more by the reparative work done.

When Marjorie's elderly father had a stroke alone at home and died, she became furious with his general practitioner for not visiting him in recent months. She became preoccupied with self-righteous criticism of doctors generally, whom she saw as lazy and negligent, victimising helpless patients. During the next few weeks her anger softened, as she became overwhelmed with grief, and with guilt about not visiting her father very often herself. Over the next few months she remembered how difficult he had been, how often he had refused help, but how his independence had also been part of his strength and pride. As she mourned him she thought about both her exasperation with him and her love for him over the years; they had tried to do the best they could by each other.

After the loss of her father, Marjorie is at first in an angry and persecuted (paranoid schizoid) state, seeing things in a cardboard cut-out way, and allied with righteously good people against totally bad people. As she mourns, she is able to relinquish the simple view of things that initially buoys her up, and see the sadness and complexity of the situation. Her guilt and self-examination lead on to repair of her internal world; she is finally able to hold the memory of her father inside her in a loving but realistic way.

The attainment of the depressive position in Kleinian thinking is intimately related to the working through of the Oedipus complex. To come to terms with the fact that your parents have (or had) a relationship from which you are excluded requires an acceptance that others are outside your control. We might have an illusion of being the centre of the universe, all powerful and needing no one. However, three inescapable 'facts of life' (Money-Kyrle, 1971) are that we are not self-created but the product of an earlier coupling, that we were dependent on another to feed us, and that time is finite. Chasseguet-Smirgel (1985) similarly points out that we cannot belong to more than one sex or one generation, although we may try to deny such differences. Accepting these basics means giving up one's narcissism, one's solipsistic and timeless view of the world, in which one is the central actor and others are really one's property, simply there to play bit parts on one's personal stage.

When I contemplate the separate and independent existence of a couple who created me, I also have to face the idea of being observed and thought about by other minds that I cannot control (Britton, 1989). There were, and are, places in the world which I can never occupy. These exist not simply in space and time, but also in the form of others' private mental space, of which I cannot be a part. Taking this fully on board, and mourning the loss of omnipotence, helps me to form my own internal vantage point, from which I can reflect upon myself. I need this space to be able to observe and reflect on my own and others' reality, and if I lack it, I will be significantly handicapped in being able to think about and know the real world.

The facilitating environment: Donald Winnicott

Although all psychoanalytic traditions see the individual as a complex product of nature and nurture, some have put more emphasis on innate factors in development while others have been more concerned with understanding environmental influences.

Donald Winnicott, a paediatrician, child psychiatrist and psychoanalyst, was interested in Klein's ideas, but later his thinking diverged from hers, with more emphasis on the maternal environment and the emergence of the self, and less on the individual's conflict between love and hate (see Winnicott, 1958, 1965). From his numerous observations of mothers and babies, as well as his work with deeply disturbed regressed patients in analysis, he developed his ideas concerning the beginnings of mental life and the emergence of the self. His famous statement: 'There is no such thing as a baby – meaning that if you set out to describe a baby, you will find yourself describing a baby and someone' (Winnicott, 1964: 88) describes the starting point of his theory.

In the last part of pregnancy, the mother usually enters a period of **primary maternal preoccupation**, which continues for the first weeks of the baby's life. It is a state of heightened sensitivity to her own self, her body and her baby, coupled with a withdrawal of interest from the external world. In this state of sensitivity the **ordinary devoted mother**, sometimes referred to as the **good enough mother**, intuitively fits in with her infant's needs, expressed through what Winnicott calls his **spontaneous gestures**. So when the hungry newborn's gesture is towards the breast, the immediate response of the good enough mother is to offer the breast and for the milk to flow. The baby thus experiences a natural state of **magical omnipotence** having, in his mind, 'created' the breast with his wishes.

Winnicott believed in the vital importance of a phase in which the baby relates to the **id-mother**, the object of instinctual impulse satisfaction, and is unaware of the **environment-mother** who responds to his need. Over time the real mother needs gradually to disillusion the baby as to his omnipotence, so that he can begin the developmental work of differentiating the 'me' from the 'not-me', inside from outside. As this gradual differentiation occurs, a third, transitional space is created, in which the move from illusion and omnipotence to a shared reality can be mediated. Transitional space is closely associated with play and with the creation of symbols. Many children have **transitional objects**, which may remind them of mother's smell or have a texture associated with her comfort. He possesses the transitional object and plays with it until it is gradually discarded as no longer necessary to him.

With appropriate disillusionment and the mother's survival of the baby's muscular attacks on her, the 'I am' state emerges. The infant can start to use his mother, who is now 'out there' as one who helps, protects, feeds and plays with him and on whom he is dependent. This developmental stage in which the infant grasps a notion of reality requires psychic continuity, which will be derived from the good enough mother's predictability and reliability.

A crucial element of the mother's role is what Winnicott called **holding**. The ordinary devoted mother holds her infant securely and unobtrusively both physically and mentally, through her empathic holding of him in her mind. With these good conditions the **true self** can develop. Emotional or physical impingements rather than receptivity and responsiveness to a baby's needs, can lead to a false maturity and the development of a **false self**, in which defences of the vulnerable true self become the personality of the individual. With the failure of holding, the integrated development of the self is hindered. Winnicott speculates that '**dwelling-in-the-body**' and **feeling real** become impossible. Separation of the psyche and the soma (body) with a predisposition to psychosomatic illness may result.

Winnicott saw all disorders of the self, including infantile and adult psychotic illness and autism, as **environmental deficiency disorders**, resulting from failures of the **facilitating environment** provided by the nursing mother or carer. It is interesting to note that with such intense focus on the mother's role, Winnicott also wrote and spoke about the part played by fathers in these early weeks of the infant's life. Father's role was to support the mother and baby unit and to negotiate with the external world during the phase of primary maternal preoccupation.

It is often suggested that Winnicott underplays the role of aggression, relating its genesis solely to failures in the environment. In fact Winnicott's views on aggression and hatred are complex. In the first instance innate aggression is expressed in the infant in muscular movement which meets restraint against the inside of the womb or in the mother's arms. It is present too in eager, greedy sucking and chewing. The mother's survival of his attacks is vital to the infant's recognition that she is not a part of him and is not under his control. So aggression is an important developmental force.

Winnicott understands rage as a response by the infant to environmental impingement. It protects the true self. If the child is more mature, then hate is the response to impingement. Hate can be catastrophically overwhelming, especially if the child fears that the mother's love will not survive his hatred. Once the infant has discovered a shared world of reality, he can begin to relate through **cross-identification** or the capacity to think how the other might feel. With cross-identification comes a capacity for concern. Only at this point, when the object's separateness is recognised, can we think of someone as being **ruthless**. The stage of omnipotence when attacks are magically destructive, Winnicott calls a **pre-ruth** stage. In cases where the mother is unable to cope with her infant's attacks on her, particularly when she retaliates, then actual destructiveness becomes a feature of the child's personality. The child may defend against this by inhibiting his aggressiveness or by turning it on himself. It is in this context that Winnicott suggested that, in the clinical situation, the more aggressive child is the healthier one.

Making sense of theoretical diversity

These brief overviews of the developmental theories of Freud, Anna Freud, Klein and Winnicott give some sense of the diversity of perspectives within psychoanalysis. Freud's theories were the starting point for later developments, but different psychoanalytic 'schools' have evolved which have built on or rejected certain aspects of Freud's work, based on their own clinical observations. Given the complexity and diversity of human experience, and the difficulty of making entirely definitive statements about it, this is perhaps inevitable, particularly in a discipline which has, after all, only so far existed for 100 years. Some differences are merely in language, or emphasis, but others are more substantive, and time should enable us to discover which are most accurate and useful. Chapter 6, on research, will show how psychoanalysts continue to try to do this.

3

A BRIEF HISTORY OF PSYCHOANALYSIS

Sigmund Freud was born in 1856 in the village of Freiberg in Moravia, now part of the Czech Republic. He lived his later childhood and nearly all his adult life in Vienna. He was always a great Anglophile, with a love of English language and literature, and had briefly considered emigrating as a young adult. The circumstances under which he finally arrived in London, suffering from advanced cancer of the jaw, were sad and terrible. Obstinately refusing to leave his home until the danger could no longer be denied, his international stature in old age gave his friends a lever to help him and his immediate family escape the Nazis in 1938.

Having had his money seized and his books burned, before he was allowed to leave, Freud was made to sign a paper saying that he had been well treated. He added beside his signature, 'I can most highly recommend the Gestapo to everyone.' Freud was welcomed in London with a warmth that Vienna never allowed him. He died a year later, in 1939, fortunately never to know that the four younger sisters who stayed behind, Rosa, Marie, Adolphine and Pauline, all died in concentration camps in 1942.

By the time of Freud's death, psychoanalysis had become a world-wide phenomenon. Besides a method of research and treatment, it was a whole new way of understanding the workings of the mind. It started with one man, then a small group of followers in Vienna. As it spread through the world, the form it took locally depended both on the particular people who seeded it, and the culture in which it took root and grew. Paradoxically, the attempts of the Nazis to stamp out this 'abhorrent Jewish practice' only served to accelerate what Anna Freud in an unpublished letter (quoted in Steiner, 2000) called 'a new kind of diaspora'.

Many good biographies of Freud and of psychoanalysis exist (see for example Jones, 1964; Gay, 1988; Robert, 1966). Drawing on these sources, this chapter will give a broad overview of the development of Freud's ideas in the context of his life. It will then briefly describe how different psychoanalytic schools have taken different parts of Freud's thinking as a springboard for their development.

The next chapter will then go on to look at some of the distinctive forms psychoanalysis has taken in different cultures.

Freud's shift from 'brain' to 'mind'

Freud made his discoveries about the mind while working as a private neurologist, from the late 1880s onwards. Vienna was an exciting and creative city, to which he became deeply attached. However, its class-ridden and anti-Semitic culture angered and frustrated him. Freud was seeing the sorts of patients who today might consult their GP; frightened and unhappy people with ill-defined maladies of body and mind. Often these were patients whose complaints had been dismissed as unclassifiable and incurable by more illustrious physicians. Freud had not originally planned a career with patients. His original passion had been laboratory study of the brain. However, he came from a poor family and such work had earned him a pittance, offering little chance of professional advancement. He was desperate to be able to afford to marry his fiancée of five years, Martha Bernays. His almost daily love-letters during their engagement in the early 1880s give a vivid impression of the man, his passion and possessive jealousy, his continuous generation of ideas, his bursts of both arrogance and self-doubt, his wry humour, and his unusual capacity for self-observation.

A polymath and an energetic thinker, Freud had strong literary interests. He had a gifted prose style, and had translated a work by John Stuart Mill into German in his early twenties while a medical student. Medical training was less formally structured in those days, and Freud chose to spend most of his time studying physiology and neuroanatomy with Ernst Brücke, an inspiring teacher and one of the Helmholtzian materialist school of thought which believed that all living phenomena must (and should) be reducible to physics and chemistry. Among other original and inventive contributions, Freud developed an important staining procedure for microscopic work on nerve tissue, and went on to do innovative research on speech disorders and on cerebral palsy in children.

Freud's reluctant move from the laboratory to the consulting room was to result in a major shift in the emphasis of his thinking from 'brain' to 'mind'. In the nineteenth century parts of the body other than the brain were often held responsible in quite a concrete way for mental distress, partly because the body was often the medium of its vivid expression. The dramatic disorder called hysteria, at the time common, is a case in point. Hysteria was to play a key role in Freud's discoveries. The modern word 'hysterical' describes extreme, rather dramatised emotionality. This was not quite its original meaning, and this is because not only our language but also our very ways of expressing distress have evolved, partly thanks to Freud himself.

Late nineteenth century hysterics would often come to the doctor with a limb paralysis which did not follow the pattern typical of a stroke or other known neurological disease. The area paralysed corresponded not with the actual nerve supply of the limb, but with the mental *idea* of the limb. Other presentations included suddenly becoming unable to speak or to see, or having bizarre convulsions resembling the symptoms of demonic possession of earlier centuries. Hysteria was, and is, very different from malingering; these patients were not 'putting it on', although often accused of doing so. They genuinely believed themselves paralysed, or dumb, or blind, though often they appeared strangely calm, as if relieved of something, putting themselves passively in the hands of their families and doctors to be cared for. Freud hypothesised that their symptoms had symbolic meaning, and were a subtle communication. For example, unconsciously a hysterically blind person was saying something like: 'There is something I cannot bear to see', or underlying hysterical dumbness might be a fear of the potent and damaging things the sufferer might say if she could speak.

The 'shell shock' of the First World War was also a form of hysteria. Men who had been pushed past their emotional limit by fighting in the trenches would sometimes collapse into a mute or paralysed state. Although children may still produce symptoms like this, many Western adults are now too psychologically sophisticated. In particular the altered freedom and independence of women means that they can verbalise their passions, conflicts and distress to themselves, and thus to others, far more directly. However, there are often circumstances when direct expression of distress is not possible, and subtle forms of hysteria still occur.

Hysteria had always evoked powerful, even cruel reactions in doctors. An early attempt at cure was to cut off the clitoris, and this sort of approach had not entirely gone out of vogue in Freud's time. Even as late as the First World War, while some shell-shocked soldiers were beginning to benefit from psychoanalytically informed approaches (as is described in the novelist Pat Barker's 'Regeneration' trilogy), others, if they escaped being shot for cowardice, were treated with cruel procedures, like electric shocks to a mute tongue or paralysed limb, to try to force them back to normal. Again with the benefit of psychoanalytic hindsight we might see how a traumatised and oppressed individual (whether Hausfrau or soldier), driven to extremes and unable to communicate desperation and rage directly, collapses in such a way that these powerful aggressive feelings are projected into, and enacted by, the other (see Chapter 1). When Freud left Brücke's laboratory he set up as a neurologist, not a psychiatrist. In the 1880s, much of what we now recognise as symptoms of anxiety and depression were considered part of degenerative brain disorder. Hysterics were either seen in the same way, or dismissed as malingerers. Neurologists used physical treatments like electrical nerve and muscle stimulation, massage and hydrotherapy. As well as hysteria, Freud saw many patients, again often women, in the mentally and physically exhausted state known as neurasthenia.

Neurasthenics and hysterics would traipse miserably from doctor to doctor, often evoking hopelessness and impatience. Freud by contrast was full of humane interest in, and curiosity about them. He prescribed the customary physical treatments, which he soon suspected were useless, but was from the first, unusually for his time (perhaps even for ours), interested in listening to his patients, encouraging them to talk about their lives and their families and to tell their stories. In this he had been partly inspired by an important early mentor, Jean-Martin Charcot.

The French approach to neurological disorder was more thoughtful and advanced than in other parts of Europe at that time, and at the age of 29 Freud worked hard to win a six-month travelling scholarship to study under the controversial but charismatic neurologist Charcot at the Sâltpetrière hospital in Paris. Charcot dedicated himself to detailed observation and classification of neurological disease. Charcot demonstrated, often to large, admiring audiences, that hysterical symptoms could be temporarily induced or abolished by hypnotic suggestion, a purely psychological procedure. He believed that hysteria could be triggered by trauma, hinted that sexual problems were often involved, but held to the traditional view that the main cause was underlying brain weakness or degeneration. For Freud, the seeds sown by Charcot's work led him eventually to the realisation that hysteria was a fundamentally psychological disorder, with psychological roots and the possibility of permanent cure by psychological means. He had also seen it demonstrated that the conscious mind could dissociate itself from unwanted ideas and feelings.

The birth of psychoanalysis

Another vital thread in the story at this point is Freud's longstanding friendship and collaboration with an older mentor, the eminent physician Joseph Breuer. Breuer told Freud how, while treating a severely hysterical woman, he and she together had discovered the value of catharsis. The patient (the now famous Anna O) would gain relief and temporary stability from pouring out all her thoughts and recent memories concerning the origin of a symptom, what she came to refer to as 'the talking cure' or 'chimney-sweeping'. Stimulated by this new idea, Freud made a radical move from using hypnosis in the traditionally authoritarian way, to suggest away symptoms, and experimented instead like Breuer, encouraging the patient under hypnosis to reveal everything that came to her mind about a particular symptom. Where hypnosis failed, he would use the technique of simply instructing the patient to say exactly what was in her mind, without censoring it, at the moment he pressed on her forehead. He would continue with this pressure technique until the patient started to reveal material that seemed to make sense of the symptom.

As his experience increased, Freud began to drop the hypnotic and pressure elements of the treatment, discovering more and more that he could trust important patterns to emerge if he simply encouraged the patient to talk freely. In a way this represented his radical new version of Helmholtzian determinism, but in the sphere of subjectivity. Freud came to believe that the underlying elements of the neurosis formed a template deep in the mind, linked to the surface by chains of associative ideas, and that the truth would be bound to bubble up to the surface, given a chance. The modern psychoanalytic technique of free association evolved gradually as Freud was able more and more to relinquish control over the patient, and ask his patients to do the same with their thoughts, and to try to say simply whatever came to their minds. He soon discovered how difficult this was; how quickly resistances to free association appeared ('This is irrelevant, I won't bother to say this', or 'This is too embarrassing or childish, he can't really want me to talk about this'). Once Freud had moved beyond a simple catharsis model, where the sole aim of treatment was to 'get things off the chest', like releasing pus from a boil, he came to see that occasions of resistance themselves were interesting and significant. He came to associate resistance with the repression that seemed to have led to certain memories being replaced by symptoms.

Freud discovered that his patients' chains of thought habitually moved back from the difficult adult situations around their symptoms, towards childhood difficulties and preoccupations. He also discovered that his patients' associations would often move hesitantly but inexorably towards sexual matters, things that women in particular simply did not talk about then, even to their physicians. At first as appalled as his patients by the direction things were taking, Freud characteristically then became interested in this discovery. Already he was regarded as eccentric in Viennese medical circles for his new ideas on hysteria and use of the suspect French technique of hypnosis. His developing theories on the sexual origins of neurosis finally put paid to the prospect of a traditional career, and by the late 1890s he had become largely isolated from the medical establishment.

Breuer supported Freud loyally at first, and together they published the landmark *Studies on Hysteria* (1895). Freud's co-author however finally balked at the sexual direction in which things were pointing, and decided not to collaborate in further work. It later emerged that Anna O's treatment had been ended abruptly by Breuer when she had suddenly revealed an intense passion for her attentive physician. Freud, unlike Breuer, was not frightened and repulsed when similar things started to happen in his own consulting room. On the contrary, he became curious and intrigued at this further layer of discovery. Not only did patients come to talk about their intense and disturbing memories, fears and passions to Freud, but they were starting to re-experience them in the room with him too. A version of the past seemed to be re-experienced in the present: that is, the transference was beginning to be noticed.

The seduction hypothesis

Freud, too, characteristically 'fell in love', both with people and with discoveries and theories, becoming temporarily blind to more sober views. His infatuation with the therapeutic possibilities of cocaine in his late twenties, with initial blindness to its addictive dangers, had been a case in point. He also had a way of becoming deeply attached to, and sometimes overly influenced by, a series of older male mentors and friends throughout his life. What characterised him also, though, was a tremendous capacity for learning from mistakes and being prepared to change his mind. By 1893, Freud had become passionately convinced on the basis of a number of cases that hysteria was always the result of sexual molestation in childhood, often by the father or another close relative. This is because he was finding more and more references to childhood sexual feelings within the family, in dreams, slips, daydreams and other material, and this led him to surmise actual sexual contact between children and parents.

Although shocked at this discovery, Freud was also enthusiastic about the prospect of now helping many patients and finally making his name, so that he could securely support his growing family. There is evidence from his correspondence (and he suggests as much in his autobiographical study (Freud, 1925b)) that he went through a phase when he was so convinced of the idea that he often influenced his patients to believe it about themselves.

However, as he moved further and further from hypnosis and the control of patients' thoughts by suggestion, and more and more towards truly allowing the unknown and unexpected to emerge, Freud realised that his theory did not always quite ring true, and his certainty started to abate. Some letters to his friend Fliess in 1897 (see Masson, 1985) show how crestfallen he was at the loss of a theory in which he had invested so much.

Childhood sexuality

It is untrue, though sometimes stated, that Freud abandoned the so-called seduction hypothesis. He went on believing that sexual abuse of children happened and was harmful, but what he did abandon was this rather simplistic causal theory of hysteria. In a similar way, he also gradually let go of other mechanical sexual theories, such as the idea that neurasthenia was the result of inadequate sexual release, and that anxiety was sexual tension that had been dammed up and converted into another form. What he discovered in the place of these 'hydraulic' theories was something much more subtle and complex. He realised that children did not simply register and react passively to external happenings, but filtered and interpreted reality through their own rich inner world of exciting and fearful fantasy. Ultimately Freud, far from ignoring the damage caused by parental sexual abuse, has helped us to see much more clearly *why* it is so damaging.

Freud was aware that he was by no means the first to challenge the innocence of childhood. His evidence came from his patients but also importantly from his self-analysis, started in 1897 and probably continued on and off throughout his life. He felt compelled to do this, not just by scientific curiosity, but also because of the way he suffered following the death of his father. He had always been subject to highs and lows; after the bereavement he was depressed and blocked in his work, had various psychosomatic symptoms and was more than ever preoccupied with fears of dying.

Dreams and self-analysis

We know most about Freud's self-analysis from his correspondence with Wilhelm Fliess. Fliess was one of Freud's series of idealised male mentors who at the time played an important role, receiving the outpourings of Freud's thoughts and feelings in long daily letters. Freud decided to use his dreams as the best starting point, a way into his hidden inner world. Many of these were then to figure in his major work *The Interpretation of Dreams* (1900). He tried himself to associate freely to his dreams, just as he asked his patients to do, following his trains of thoughts as far as he could, trying not to shy away from anything seemingly absurd, shocking or distressing.

Characteristically, Freud approached this enterprise determinedly and found it personally relieving, while also a source of new and confirmatory data for the theories he was generating from work with patients. Freud was, of course, working on himself in a pre-Freudian era, and discovered things that thanks to his work would seem familiar now. Many fragmentary childhood memories and feelings emerged. For example he found (with his characteristic mixture of shock and interest) that his emerging idea of the Oedipus complex also applied to him. Realisation of his hidden childhood passionate feelings about his mother and wishes to get rid of his father started to make sense of the burdensome guilt he was experiencing over his father's death and the seemingly irrational fear of his own impending death. He became intrigued by the idea that great authors, from Sophocles to Shakespeare, had been artistically driven to communicate their own unconscious knowledge of fundamental human truths, for example in the stories of Oedipus and Hamlet.

Self-analysis cannot go nearly as far as analysis by another, because there is so much about oneself that, by its very nature, only another person can observe. However, by using his dreams Freud was giving himself the best chance of finding something unknown. Dreams, as we have seen, are a way of thinking when asleep. Thoughts are freer from censorship and from rational, systematic organisation. They are full of strange but meaningful juxtapositions and densely packed symbolic images, which connect present and past in unexpected ways. When analysed, they often emerge as more sharply clever and humorous than our careful and guilty waking selves. They can reveal what we really feel, think and want; things that are often shocking, silly or distasteful to our conscious selves.

As he worked on his self-analysis in the years around the turn of the century, and built up his experience with dozens of patients who had different sorts of problems, Freud was in a very creative phase. He was theorising not just about dreams and childhood sexuality, but about such apparently widely differing subjects as the mechanisms of various neuroses and the nature of jokes. A readable and engaging book he wrote around this time was *The Psychopathology of Everyday Life* (1901). As well as a clear account of dream mechanisms, Freud gives a compelling description of the many sorts of slips we make that give windows into the unconscious mind. We have seen some examples of these in Chapter 2. Freud showed how normality and pathology often differ in degree rather than kind. We all use neurotic mechanisms to protect our peace of mind: our psychic equilibrium. These latter sorts of findings of Freud's seem to have become almost a commonplace in our culture.

The early circle

At this stage Freud was largely working alone, discussing ideas in letters and conversations with a very small circle of friends and colleagues, and giving weekly lectures at the university to a small audience. He had begun to publish his new ideas, which were met mostly with indifference and hostility locally, though there was beginning to be some interest outside Austria. Freud was also involved with his growing family. Although he protects their privacy in his public writings, his letters show how interested he was in his six children. From time to time a child's dream appears as an illustration in his writings.

In the first few years of the twentieth century, a small circle of local colleagues began to gather around Freud, and meetings of what was later to become the Vienna Psychoanalytic Society began. These took place on Wednesdays in Freud's waiting room. Others started to experiment with psychoanalysis and contribute findings to the growing body of knowledge. Visitors from further afield started to attend. The German, Karl Abraham and the Hungarian, Sandor Ferenzci both first visited in 1907, and the Welshman, Ernest Jones, who was to establish psychoanalysis firmly in London, and to become Freud's biographer, first visited in 1908. Freud was particularly pleased at the interest shown by some physicians in Zurich, among them Carl Jung. He was drawn to Jung, who was to become the next in his succession of close confidants.

Jung and his colleagues were among the first gentiles to want to study psychoanalysis seriously, and this was very important to Freud. The early psychoanalysts were all Jewish, and anti-Semitism sometimes fuelled outrage against the new ideas. In these early years, psychoanalysis was creating a public furore. Although there was admiration and enthusiasm for the new ideas, not infrequently some listeners would storm out of scientific meetings when psychoanalytic ideas on childhood sexuality were put forward. Jones reports that at a neurological congress in Hamburg in 1910, a Professor Wilhelm Weygrandt banged his fist on the table and shouted, 'This is not a topic for discussion at a scientific meeting; it is a matter for the police!' The problem was not so much the topic of sexuality itself, which had to be admitted to be of scientific interest and importance, but the way that Freud had abolished the usual strict demarcations between normal and perverse sexuality, and between adult sexuality and the alleged innocence of childhood.

Conflict and dissent

The reaction against the new ideas, and the courage and persistence needed by the early psychoanalysts to maintain them, also helps to explain why certain followers who started to diverge fundamentally from Freud were disowned by the embryonic psychoanalytic establishment. The ideas were so new, so hard won and at times so strongly attacked that they generated a fierce protectiveness. Often it felt to the beleaguered pioneers as if the dissenters amongst them were giving way to both their own and the public's resistance and distaste by dropping central psychoanalytic tenets: the existence of unconscious psychological processes, the phenomenon of resistance and the existence of childhood sexuality and the Oedipus complex. To deny, dismantle or qualify any of these seemed an undoing of the new discoveries, a return to a more comfortable and familiar psychology.

The passionate Freud did not disguise his favouritism, his hunger in particular for devoted brothers and sons. His position as founder of a movement which required him to analyse many of his followers, to become privy to their innermost secrets, attracted intense transferences both positive and negative. Biographers also suggest that some early followers were unstable, talented but troubled people who gravitated towards a discipline, as yet open to all, which might explain and relieve their unhappiness.

The youthful and energetic Jung was at first hailed by Freud as his 'son and heir'. This led to disappointment when Jung recast the idea of childhood sexuality as symbolic rather than literal, and became increasingly drawn to mystical and religious ideas. It is of course impossible to do justice to the depth and complexity of Jungian thinking and practice here, which came to be called **analytical psychology** rather than psychoanalysis. One way of trying to capture a fundamental divergence between Freud and Jung in the early days is to say that Freud saw psychology as ultimately rooted in biology, and thus as deriving from the evolutionary forces which Darwin had recently described. Human beings might produce all sorts of mystical and religious ideas, they might generate primitive and crude beliefs and rituals, or artistic and cultural developments of the highest order, but underlying all these would be basic, ultimately bodily based passions which had been subjected to sublimation or defence.

Jung believed, by contrast, that there were 'higher' or mystical forces that transcended human experience. His followers conceptualised the analytic process and relationship in a very different way from Freud. Jung for example came to see transference as something more mystical than a system of projections requiring understanding and interpretation. Today a branch of Jungian psychology (the 'Zurich school') has remained 'classically' Jungian in this way, while the thinking and work of other Jungians, sometimes known as the 'developmental school' (see Alister and Hauke, 1998) has tended in a number of ways to converge with that of contemporary psychoanalysts.

The final break between Jung and Freud came in 1913. An early Viennese follower, Alfred Adler, had broken from Freud two years previously. Adler, like Jung, eschewed the importance of sexuality, and he also came more or less to dispense with the idea of unconscious processes; psychology's traditional primacy of the conscious mind was reinstated. For Adler, neurosis was based on the vicissitudes of innate aggression, the 'will to power', and a tendency to overcompensate for feelings of inferiority. His **individual psychology** was based on the primacy of the ego and of conscious forces of aggression. Freud was initially interested in both Adler and Jung's ideas, and encouraged their development, but the problem ultimately seemed to be that both new theories dispensed with and replaced, rather than deepened and enriched, the existing ones.

Freud's evolving ideas

Freud's thinking went through many shifts and developments during his 40 years or so of psychoanalytic writing. Many contradictions and loose ends remain, various terms remain unclear or have evolved in meaning, and new theories are layered upon old ones which have not been fully discarded. Although later footnotes correct and expand on some of his earlier work, Freud was on the whole too eager to express new findings and ideas to be concerned about later scholars who would worry over ambiguities, or critics who would seize triumphantly on inconsistencies.

A good deal of Freud's thinking has stood the test of time, and has remained unmodified or been built upon; some has been completely discarded or else greatly adapted. Reading Freud a century on, we have to surmount some language difficulties based on the contemporary hydraulic and mechanistic scientific conceptions. The Strachey translation of Freud's works (Strachey, 1953–74) also creates some barriers for readers in English, through its use of some clumsy and pseudo-scientific terms in place of the more evocative and open-ended ones of the original German. Freud was wide-ranging in his interests and enthusiasms. He wrote about certain of his cases, such as 'Dora' (1905b), the 'Rat Man' (1909a), 'Little Hans' (1909b) and the 'Wolf Man' (1918). He also wrote about his theories of mind and clinical technique, as well as looking at how basic mental processes were expressed in the arts and in group processes, mythology and religion.

Freud's underlying working model of the mind evolved considerably over the years. He would find a particular conception more and more stretched and deformed by new data, culminating in the need for a leap of his imagination into a new, more complex formulation. His first model, from the 1880s up to 1897, was the simple one of sexual trauma leading to blocked memories and feelings which had to be released like pus from an abscess. Next came a richer and more complex conceptualisation, laying greater stress on what the mind itself was capable of creating. Rather than just registering and having to deal with external events, Freud came to see us as driven from within by all sorts of primitive impulses and wishes, inhabiting a rich world of desire and phantasy which somehow has to be managed so that we can live and function in the real world.

Finally, as described in Chapter 2, the topographical and then the structural models of the mind were developed. The ideas in the structural model (Freud, 1923) of ego and superego allow expression of the increasing importance in Freud's thinking of the individual's relationship to others in their own right, rather than just as objects at which to discharge drives. It marks the beginning of what psychoanalysts rather clumsily call object relations theory rather than simple drive theory. That is, emphasis moved towards the *objects of* drives, and our innate need to relate to others, rather than a need to discharge tensions *per se*. We then have in our mind representations of significant others, and actively relate to them internally, with important mental consequences.

Thus the superego in Freud's new model is formed from the gradually internalised moral strictures of the parents, (and ultimately *their* own parents, and the wider society) and is also coloured in a tit for tat way by the child's aggressive impulses towards these loved ones. The internal experience of one's superego can then have significant effects without anyone else being present. This makes sense of Freud's frequent observation of the activity of an unconscious sense of guilt, leading to self-sabotaging of success.

Freud contrasted two conditions, mourning and melancholia, or depression as it would now be called (Freud, 1917b). A person may be very attached to someone, say a partner, but in an ambivalent, hostile way. If this partner leaves, or dies, he or she will be particularly hard to mourn, and to let go of. Instead, he or she will be 'taken inside' the self, and unfinished business in the relationship will continue. Tormenting reproaches of the self will now occur, which unconsciously are really meant for the lost, disappointing other who has now become installed inside the self. This model has proved very useful in understanding the angry self-reproaches of people with depression, and this paper of Freud's is one that remains widely read.

Throughout both the topographical and structural phases of Freud's thinking, aggressive impulses and desires emerged as increasingly important. Freud struggled to decide where to put aggression and went through different formulations. Was it an intrinsic part of sex? Was it connected with self-preservation? Was it essentially a destructive impulse that had to be kept under control? Freud's growing pessimism about human nature following the horrors of the First World War (Mitchell and Black, 1995) shifted the tone of his implicit political philosophy from a Rousseauesque to a more darkly Hobbesian one. His final formulation, which has remained contentious, was of a lifelong conflict in all of us between the so-called **life drive** (or life 'instinct', which is not such a good translation of the German 'Trieb') and **death drive**. The life drive is the drive towards union, growth, new creation, while the death drive represents an innate tendency towards giving up the struggle, moving towards fragmentation and quiescence, rather similar to the idea of entropy in physical systems. Aggression was then seen as a turning outwards of this dangerous, lethal force, in order to protect the individual.

There has been much argument and scepticism about Freud's death drive notion, particularly regarding its biological plausibility. It has also been pointed out that it makes no sense to equate aggression with destructiveness in a blanket way, as aggression is a broad and complex entity which can clearly work for both good and ill. Melanie Klein was the main follower of Freud's to take up his notion with any enthusiasm, as it seemed to her to make sense of some of her clinical findings. Post-Kleinians use the life and death-drive dialectic mostly as a clinical concept. They perceive a basic human conflict between the love-based pull towards knowing, understanding and making contact with the other (however fraught or angry this contact may be) and on the other side an apparently hate-based, nihilistic opposition to the essential different-ness and independence of the other. The death drive ultimately seeks to negate the disturbance of having feelings or thoughts at all; it is an opposition to the continuance of life itself. (For a good clinical article about this see Segal, 1997b.)

Some key historical figures

To complete this brief history of psychoanalysis, we will mention briefly some key 'historical' figures (some still living) who made important contributions between the turn of the century and the mid-1980s. Many of these individuals and their ideas are referred to in more detail elsewhere in the book. The list is in birth date order. It is inevitably very selective, and is also biased towards developments in the UK.

Sandor Ferenczi (1873–1933)
An early follower, the Hungarian-born Ferenczi is now best known for the experimentation with analytic boundaries which he documented in his clinical diaries (see Dupont, 1995). He was particularly interested in the role of environmental trauma in psychopathology.

Karl Abraham (1877–1925)
Abraham, who founded the German psychoanalytical society, was an outstanding clinical observer who died young. He was the second analyst of Melanie Klein, and his observations of primitive and psychotic mental processes (Abraham, 1924) were developed further in her work.

Ernest Jones (1879–1958)
A Welshman who established psychoanalysis in London, Jones was Freud's official biographer. He remained a friend and correspondent, and helped bring Freud to safety in London at the end of his life. Jones was a major political figure in British psychoanalysis for decades. His scientific views started to diverge from those of Freud, for example concerning female sexuality, and he become interested in the ideas of Klein, whom he encouraged to settle in London.

Melanie Klein (1882–1960)
Klein was inspired by discovering Freud's early writings, and had analysis first with Ferenczi in Budapest and then Abraham in Berlin,

before coming to London in 1928. Like Anna Freud (below), she worked directly with children, including some who were very young. Where earlier analysts had mostly inferred childhood mental life from work with adults, Klein observed directly how troubled children expressed their deepest fears and phantasies through their play (Hinshelwood, 1994). She extended Freud's discoveries in important ways (including his concept of the death drive). Her work was controversial and led in the 1940s to a crisis within the British psychoanalytical society (see Chapter 4).

Anna Freud (1885–1982)

Anna Freud came to London with her father as a refugee in 1938. She was already trained both as a teacher and as a psychoanalyst and, unlike her father, had psychoanalysed children. Her contribution to psychoanalytic theories of development evolved both from her commitment to her father's theories, especially his structural theory of the mind, and from her direct experience of children. During the Second World War she established the Hampstead War Nurseries, residential homes for children separated from their families because of the war, and innovative, for example, in their emphasis on preserving the child's attachment to his parents by any means possible, and on giving him other stable attachment figures. Anna Freud and her co-workers went on to influence practice and policy in many areas of child care, for example social care and the law. Anna Freud trained her young co-workers, some themselves refugees, in the art of detailed observation of the children. These observations have been movingly documented (A. Freud, 1944). In 1947 she organised training in child psychoanalysis, together with a clinical and research centre, known as the Hampstead Child Therapy Course and Clinic. This was renamed The Anna Freud Centre after her death, and it continues to provide clinical work, research work and training.

James Strachey (1887–1967)

James and his wife Alix Strachey were part of the 'Bloomsbury' connection of psychoanalysis, James being the brother of Lytton Strachey. James and Alix's letters to each other while Alix was away having analysis with Abraham in Berlin in 1924/25 give a fascinating glimpse into the analytic culture of the time (Meisel and Kendrick, 1986). James Strachey was the main translator of Freud's works into English. In 1934 he wrote an innovative paper about how he thought psychoanalysis worked (Strachey, 1934) which is still frequently referred to today.

Ronald Fairbairn (1889–1964)

Fairbairn was a key figure in the development of **object relations theory**, which moved from Freud's emphasis on discharge of drives and pleasure-seeking, towards seeing people as primarily relationship-seeking. The thinking of Fairbairn and Klein had some early similarities and Klein borrowed and modified Fairbairn's concept of a 'schizoid' mode of being. In Fairbairn's view, the internal world did not consist of innate phantasy, which influenced how external reality was perceived from the start, but developed as a substitute and compensation for inevitably unsatisfying experiences in external relationships. Fairbairn saw maternal indifference, caused for example by depression, as significantly traumatic for infants. The child would feel that he had destroyed the mother's feelings either by his hate (a depressive reaction) or by his love (a schizoid reaction). See Fairbairn (1952).

Heinz Hartmann (1894–1970)

Hartmann was a refugee from Vienna who settled in New York. Together with Kris and Loewenstein he founded the **ego psychology** school of psychoanalysis which dominated North American psychoanalysis until around the 1980s (see Chapter 4). As Mitchell and Black (1995) put it, while Freud the archaeologist dug for the deeply buried relics of infantile sexuality and aggression, followers such as Hartmann became interested in the more ordinary features of mental life Freud had unearthed and set aside. Hartmann's work has a central focus on the ego; its structure, defences and its adaptation to reality, and greatly broadens psychoanalysis to overlap with the concerns of traditional psychology. Hartmann recast Freud's view of the dreaming, pleasure-seeking baby who is finally forced to face unwelcome reality, into a creature designed to seek adaptation to its environment.

Donald Winnicott (1896–1971)

Winnicott brought his long experience and perspective as a paediatrician to psychoanalysis. Initially deeply influenced by Klein, he later developed his own distinctive views on infant and child development, concentrating less on internal phantasy life, and giving greater weight to environmental influences than did Klein. There were significant differences between Winnicott's and Klein's thinking on the origin and role of aggression and hatred in development. Among Winnicott's many concepts are those of the transitional object and transitional space, the holding environment, the good enough mother, and the true and false self, mentioned in more detail in Chapter 2 (see Winnicott, 1958, 1965).

Michael Balint (1896–1970)

Balint came to England from Budapest in 1938, having worked with Ferenczi. A lively and independent thinker, he was interested in the cross-fertilisation of psychoanalytic ideas with other disciplines. He is famous for his group work with general practitioners ('Balint Groups') in which he helped GPs to examine and learn from the doctor–patient relationship, however brief the consultation (Balint, 1957). Balint also worked with deeply disturbed patients, and coined the term **basic fault** (Balint, 1968), which referred to a deep layer of unintegrated psychic deprivation.

Otto Fenichel (1897–1946)

Fenichel was a physician who attended Freud's lectures at the University of Vienna from 1915, and later became a committed member of Freud's group of psychoanalysts. He was elected to membership of the Vienna Society in 1920 and made contributions as clinician, scholar and teacher of psychoanalysis. He systematised classical theory and technique in a wish to establish 'the correct application of psychoanalysis', based on Freudian theory (Fenichel, 1945). As a historian he was the first to write a consistent social history of the psychoanalytic movement. After moves to live in Norway (1933) and Prague (1935), he emigrated to Los Angeles.

Wilfred Bion (1897–1974)

Bion was analysed by Klein. He worked as an army psychiatrist in the Second World War, and his early psychoanalytic discoveries were about group processes first observed amongst soldiers. The 'Northfield Experiments' involved innovative psychiatric rehabilitation of soldiers using group work (Bion, 1961). Bion later went on to work with psychotic patients and to make seminal discoveries about primitive mental processes in normal and psychotic individuals and about the nature of thinking itself. His description of maternal (and analytic) containment was an important addition to Kleinian theory in that it showed how the environment interacted with the individual's personality and internal phantasy. Bion is often hard reading, but some of his more accessible papers are collected in *Second Thoughts* (Bion, 1967).

Marion Milner (1900–1998)

Prior to her analytic training in the early 1940s, Milner had already published the first of several influential books, *A Life of One's Own* (Milner, 1934) which was based on a diary of her inner experience and attempts to free her unconscious thinking. Analysed by both

Sylvia Payne and Donald Winnicott during her training, Milner became an influential member of the Independent group. She made contributions in the field of aesthetics and creativity, informed partly by studying her own artistic creativity and the blocks she encountered to it. (For collected works see Milner, 1987.)

John Bowlby (1907–1990)

Trained in the British society, Bowlby formed an important bridge between psychoanalysis and ethology through his observational work on attachment and loss (Bowlby, 1969, 1973, 1980). Although Bowlby moved away from psychoanalytic work into ethological research, his legacy has kept psychoanalysis connected with what is seen from the outside, and with our mammalian nature. The work of Bowlby and subsequent researchers into attachment theory provides scientific support for many object relations ideas. His work was also sociologically significant in its stress on the traumatic effects of premature and prolonged separations of mothers and children, for example during hospital admissions.

Herbert Rosenfeld (1910–1986)

Rosenfeld was a physician who emigrated to London from Germany in 1936, to escape Nazi persecution. He became interested in understanding and helping the psychotic patients he met in psychiatric hospitals, for whom little could then be done. He was aware of the importance of organic processes in psychosis, but discovered that accurate empathy and understanding of how patients were thinking and seeing the world could often mitigate their disorder. He was analysed by Klein and, together with Segal and Bion, made seminal contributions from a Kleinian theoretical perspective to the psychological understanding of psychosis, and hence to the understanding of abnormal primitive processes that could occur to a degree in all human minds (Rosenfeld, 1965). He is noted also for his work on **pathological organisations** of the personality (Rosenfeld, 1987). A popular and dedicated teacher, both in England and abroad, he made a big contribution to repairing the psychoanalytic culture in his native Germany after the war.

Betty Joseph (b. 1917)

Joseph came to psychoanalysis from social work, and like many psychoanalysts, was influenced by her professional work with mothers and babies. She became interested in Klein's ideas, and has been a major figure in the post-Kleinian development in the UK. Her main area of work is on clinical technique. She has been particularly interested in how the intricacies of people's internal worlds are displayed in the minutiae of the moment to moment clinical interaction, where they can be understood and gradually transformed (Joseph, 1989).

Hanna Segal (b. 1918)

Segal was born and medically trained in Poland, but it was from Paris that she and her parents fled to Britain at the beginning of the Nazi occupation. Like Bion and Rosenfeld, her contributions to psychoanalytic theories about psychosis began in her work on the psychiatric 'back wards', in her case helping sick Polish servicemen who had little English. Initially inspired by Fairbairn in Edinburgh, she was analysed by Klein, and became a distinguished writer and thinker in the Kleinian tradition. She has made contributions to fields as diverse as symbol formation, aesthetics and literature (Segal, 1981). She has been a leading critic of the madness of nuclear weapons proliferation (Segal, 1997a).

Heinz Kohut (1923–1981)

Kohut founded the American school of **self psychology**, which insists that psychological deficit rather than conflict is at the heart of many human ills, and was a major challenge to classical American ego psychology from the 1970s onwards. Some of his work converges with that of Winnicott and other British Independents. Reacting to what he saw as the blind spots of the dominant model, Kohut emphasised the need for parents, and by extension analysts, to **mirror** the child/patient, understanding his/her needs for narcissistic expression such as idealisation and omnipotence, without hasty interpretation which could be experienced as condemning and moralistic. Kohut was particularly interested in preoccupied or narcissistic parenting, in which an inauthentic self developed with a pervasive sense of disconnection from others. He did not see hatred and aggression as primary, but as secondary responses to trauma. Kohut suggested that empathy and attunement, rather than interpretation and insight, were the key factors in treatment (Kohut, 1977).

Harold Stewart (b. 1924)

Stewart began his medical career as a general practitioner and explored the therapeutic use of hypnosis before training as a psychoanalyst. Concerned with clinical issues and problems of technique, his contributions range from dream interpretation within the psychoanalytic process to the technical challenges of working with very disturbed and regressed patients. He stresses the value of work outside as well as within the transference (Stewart, 1992).

Joseph Sandler (1927–1998)

Sandler studied both psychology and medicine, and trained in the classical psychoanalytic tradition with his unusual combination of clinical and research skills he became the first psychoanalyst in Europe to achieve full academic recognition: he held several chairs in psychoanalysis. An international figure, he served terms as president of the International Psychoanalytic Association (IPA) and editor of the *International Journal*. His theoretical contributions built bridges between classical drive theory and object relations theory (the inner representational world) which contributed to the revolution in American ego psychology. He engaged in active dialogue with different theoretical orientations, and was at pains to encourage theoretical precision. (See Sandler, 1987.)

4

PSYCHOANALYSIS ACROSS CULTURES

In the 1920s and early 1930s interest in psychoanalysis was already spreading. A steady trickle of foreigners was coming to Vienna, Berlin and Budapest to learn from, and be analysed by, Freud or a member of his circle. These early analysands often returned home fired with enthusiasm to join or found local psychoanalytic societies. Many others, who read Freud with interest but balked at personal analysis, incorporated bits and pieces of analytic thinking into their clinical approach. In each new country psychoanalysis developed its unique flavour. This depended both on the nature of the founding pioneers, and on the local politics, culture and language in which the new ideas germinated and grew.

The rise of Hitler in the 1930s had a dramatic effect on the history of psychoanalysis. It caused the scattering of the, mostly Jewish, early analysts from their centres in Budapest, Vienna and Berlin to all corners of the globe. Ironically, Hitler could be said to have contributed to the rapid dissemination of something his regime feared and hated. Some at least of the heat and bitterness of the early conflicts and splits within many psychoanalytic societies might also be laid at Hitler's door, because of the sudden, forced co-existence of local and refugee analysts. The local analysts either felt secure enough to be experimenting with new analytic ideas, or had adopted a diluted and eclectic version of analysis. The refugees, in contrast, traumatised and dispossessed, were often fiercely protective of the more traditional psychoanalytic thinking they felt they had rescued from an inferno.

In this chapter we will give some examples of this 'psychoanalytic diaspora' (Steiner, 2000). We will start with the enthusiastic embrace of psychoanalysis, and its complex evolution, in the USA. Next will come Britain, where psychoanalysis has always been a small, ambivalently regarded discipline, but where many creative thinkers have lived and worked. Then we will consider French psychoanalysis, which has its own unique flavour, linked more directly with the political left wing and with academia than in many other countries.

Lastly, we shift from a geographical to a political perspective, and examine the problems of psychoanalysis during and after conditions of social and political repression in Germany, Argentina and former Czechoslovakia. In these countries the psychoanalytic profession has responded in different ways to totalitarianism and we consider the question of whether real psychoanalytic work can take place under totalitarian conditions.

Enthusiastic embrace: psychoanalysis in the USA

In 1908 Freud was invited to give a course of lectures by Stanley Hall of Clark University, Massachusetts. This was to be Freud's only visit to America. He told Ernest Jones that he had found his cabin steward on the ship reading *The Psychopathology of Everyday Life*, which began to bring home to him how his fame was spreading.

Although now under challenge there as elsewhere, psychoanalysis had striking early success in the USA, meeting American needs at a crucial historical moment. The USA quickly became, and remains today, the country with the largest number of psychoanalysts (although Buenos Aires is currently the city with the largest number per head of population). Psychoanalysis soon became medically dominated, and this provided the main frame of reference within psychiatry, influencing the whole American way of classifying and treating mental illness well into the 1970s. In the middle years of the century it was a wealthy and exclusive profession of mostly male physicians. The situation was, from the first, intriguingly different in Britain. Here, psychoanalysis was never a wealthy profession, and was freely open to women and to non-physicians. It has remained more on the margins than in the USA, with an uneasy and contentious place within psychiatry and psychology. What happened in the USA for things to evolve as differently as they did?

In the early twentieth century, challenges arose in North America, as they did elsewhere, both to a puritan sexual morality and to the uninspiring model of mental illness based on inherited defect. At the same time, this relatively new land lacked the constraint of an ancient medical establishment run from a few august institutions. Medicine was decentralised, and freely given to borrowing and adapting ideas from Europe. Young progressive physicians seized upon psychoanalysis as liberating and optimistic. It easily became part of an eclectic and pragmatic psychotherapeutic approach with a strong emphasis on challenging societal and family restrictions. Freud himself was suspicious of its ecstatic welcome, and feared from the beginning that psychoanalysis would be tamed and watered down, and become a 'handmaid of psychiatry'. The profession's development was however to be far from smooth (Hale, 1995). In the crucible of the USA different waves of émigré analysts, with their home-grown counterparts, were mixed into an explosive brew, leading to what Ernest Jones in England ruefully referred to as the 'American psychoanalytic civil wars'. The early American analysts were mostly physicians interested in Freud's ideas, but without training. They were struck by the proven usefulness of various psychoanalytic ideas in the human laboratory of the First World War; the meaning of words like catharsis, symptom formation, defence, conflict and repression (see Chapter 2) had come alive through experience with shell-shocked soldiers.

Famous amongst these early eclectic physicians were William Alanson White and Harry Stack Sullivan. They applied the new ideas in their own practice and teaching, liberally sprinkled with commonsense notions, and often taking a very environmentalist position that downplayed sexual and aggressive drives. This environmentalist position was congenial to North American culture, holding as it did apparent promise of benefit through social change.

From the late 1920s the early analytic immigrants from Europe came in search of a larger, freer place to live, work and make their mark. Examples were Helene Deutsch, Karen Horney and Otto Fenichel. They had often had brief analyses with Freud or one of his immediate circle. Some were invited over to help set up and develop psychoanalytic training institutes along the lines of those in Berlin or Vienna, as Sandor Rado was in New York, and Franz Alexander in Chicago. At the same time, young American physicians could afford to go to Europe for training. In 1938, 12 of the 23 trainees in Vienna were American. The later émigrés to the USA came in flight from Hitler, in several waves following his rise to power in 1933. They included Heinz Hartmann, who was to found the school of American ego psychology.

The 'psychoanalytic civil wars' started in the 1930s, when the economic depression exacerbated pre-existing rivalries. The conflict was over professional standards, and especially over who were fit to be trainers in the new institutes. Initially it expressed itself across generational lines. As was to happen in Britain around the 'Controversial Discussions' (see below), the analysts involved on both sides were passionately protective of their ideas. The refugees who had left so much behind suffered anguish over perceived threats to the psychoanalytic culture they had rescued from Hitler.

The young American psychiatrists who had been keen enough to spend time training in psychoanalysis in Europe, aligned themselves with these refugee analysts, and challenged their eclectic, untrained, local elders over positions of leadership in the new institutes. Although Freud himself had been strong in support of lay analysis, the young psychiatrists were also eager (in this case to the dismay of non-medical refugees) to make psychoanalysis and themselves respectable in the eyes of their peers by restricting the discipline to those with medical training.

In the event, the young Americans won the day and made psychoanalysis both medical and respectable in the USA. Trainings became lengthy and stringent. Lay analysts were relegated to lower-status research or teaching posts, or to the treatment of children. They were to continue to earn less and to suffer in competition for patients with the medical psychoanalysts until 1986, when a representative of the psychology profession successfully sued the powerful overarching professional organisation, the American Psychoanalytic Association, for unfair discrimination. This landmark case ultimately opened the doors to officially approved psychoanalytic training of other professionals.

The disputes continued through the 1940s and 1950s: mostly centred in New York, they had echoes and repercussions elsewhere, importantly the West Coast. A series of dramatic splits occurred in institutes on both sides of the USA. The chief protagonists on one side were the traditional psychoanalysts such as Hartmann, who passionately wished to preserve the legacy of Freud. On the other side were the powerful eclectic elder statesmen, such as Harry Stack Sullivan, and their younger followers, including Karen Horney and Erich Fromm, who gave rise to the **neo-Freudian** movement.

The American Psychoanalytic Association came to play an important part in regulating and guarding the standards of the new profession. It had to steer a course between the Scylla of over-rigid orthodoxy and the Charybdis of an eclecticism gone wild, unrecognisable as psychoanalysis. Orthodoxy tended to win the day in these early decades, with the APA going through what some have seen as quite a vigilant phase over lay analysts and unorthodox trainings in the 1960s and 1970s. Revisionist ideas, which included those not just of the neo-Freudians but of others like Melanie Klein, were often deliberately excluded from the teaching syllabus of traditional institutes, and it has taken a long time for such ideas to spread widely.

After the Second World War there was a flood of applications for psychoanalytic training in the USA, and of patients wanting to be analysed. Psychoanalysis began to take centre stage in psychiatry. By the 1960s the majority of psychiatric trainees were entering personal analysis and more than half were doing formal psychoanalytic training, often with the support of substantial government funding. Major psychiatric textbooks and classification systems became heavily influenced by psychoanalysis.

Along with this huge popularisation and medicalisation came inevitable attenuation. Many clinicians adapted their analytic training to inform a humane, generic sort of practice involving therapy and advice-giving, and often drug prescribing as well. This gave rise to the screen image of the fatherly 'shrink', which although far from typical of psychoanalysis proper on either side of the Atlantic, has contributed to the popular image. Something originally challenging and iconoclastic often became, in American medical practice, comfortable and paternalistic, reconciled with conventional values and with conformist sexual conventions.

In the late 1960s and 1970s American psychoanalysis finally became a victim of its own success. Complacency had diminished its iconoclastic appeal, and efficacy claims were inflated. There was a demand for psychotherapy, including behavioural and cognitive therapies, and insurance companies started to withdraw funding for lengthy treatments. The turbulent counter-culture of the 1960s including the anti-psychiatry movement made its mark, for example in the form of feminist challenges to classical conceptions of female sexuality, and the burgeoning of other anti-Freudian critiques (discussed in Chapter 5). The development of psychotropic drug treatments and new discoveries about the brain made somatic psychiatry exciting again; the wheel had come full circle. The American psychiatric classification system now excluded psychoanalytic explanations and reverted to being simply descriptive.

Challenges, however, also stimulated much creativity in American psychoanalysis. The last few decades have seen a burgeoning of research, both quantitative and qualitative. Side by side with many developments in ego psychology has come a new interest in object relations theories. A huge range of different theories now jostle for position. Some see the current American situation as representing fragmentation of the discipline, and fear a loss of common identity in psychoanalysis. Others (Wallerstein, 1992) see psychoanalysis as passing through a phase common to all young disciplines which will lead eventually to a healthy diversity with broad agreement on the essentials.

Schism avoided: psychoanalysis in Britain

Early in the history of the British Psychoanalytical Society (BPAS), in the 1920s, reports of Melanie Klein's novel experiments in Berlin with the analysis of small children were beginning to interest British psychoanalysts. Klein's approach contrasted with that of Anna Freud and her associates in Vienna. In her early thinking Anna Freud believed that the child could not form a transference that could be made use of and interpreted as it could in the adult, because the experience that would later be able to be 'transferred' was still in process. The analyst had instead, especially initially, to reassure and guide the child in a parental way. Only when trust had been established should careful discussion of the child's worries about sex and aggression be initiated (A. Freud, 1926).

Klein in contrast thought of transference as immediate, even in children, and observed that sometimes the child seemed to experience her as a negative or threatening figure. Rather than trying to win the child's trust by explaining the real situation, Klein interpreted what she saw as the child's expression of primitive phantasy through play and behaviour (Hinshelwood, 1994). Thus she would for example interpret the child's fear and jealousy about the lurid versions of parental sex they imagined. Or she might interpret the child's fears of retaliation for the intrusive and violent things they wanted to do to separate the parents and 'get in on the act', and their intense conflicts between love and hate. Klein not only used a very different technique from Anna Freud, but was demonstrating a new conception of unconscious phantasy, and of the nature and chronological development of both the Oedipus complex and the superego.

Klein was glad to accept Ernest Jones's invitations, first in 1925 to lecture to the BPAS, and then in 1926 to live in London. Klein was grateful for the warm and generally open-minded reception of the British, somewhat distanced as they were from the analytic fray of mainland Europe. Over the next decade she became an important figure in British psychoanalysis. Her powerful and determined personality and her copious new ideas alike created both friends and enemies, but the overriding atmosphere was one of tolerance.

Meanwhile a number of native British psychoanalysts, such as Winnicott, Payne, Sharpe and Bowlby, were making valuable contributions. These analysts were to play a central part in giving stability to the theoretical and political divisions which were soon to follow. Other key figures of British psychoanalysis were also starting their work in these early years. From 1933 many European refugee analysts were helped to settle in London, culminating in 1938 with the arrival of Sigmund and Anna Freud themselves, and the relative peace of this creative phase of British psychoanalysis was disturbed. Fierce debates concerning the technique of child analysis, the nature of phantasy, the development of the superego and the nature of female sexuality were no longer conducted at a safe distance, but face to face. Under this pressure the BPAS now started to separate into three distinct groupings.

As in New York, the émigrés closest to Freud and his daughter, such as Dorothy Burlingham, Kate Friedlander and Willi Hoffer, felt they had to protect the legacy of their already mortally ill friend and teacher. For many of them Klein's ideas were not psychoanalytic at all; she was heretical in an analogous way to Jung or Adler. They objected also to her sure way of presenting things, and were dissatisfied with the evidence she provided for her theories. Klein and close supporters, such as Susan Isaacs and Joan Rivière, felt deeply that their developments were true to Freud's vision, and were dismayed at the prospect that they might even be expelled from the British society.

The émigré group was joined by some British analysts like Barbara Low. Their numbers were also swelled by Klein's daughter Melitta Schmideberg, who together with her analyst Edward Glover became bitterly hostile to her mother and her ideas. Many of the original British analysts, for example Ella Sharpe, Sylvia Payne and Ernest Jones, together with émigrés such as Michael Balint who were less directly linked to Freud, fell into a 'middle group', often with some passions and intellectual leanings one way or the other but providing something of a useful buffer. Donald Winnicott, for example, although influenced by Klein's thinking, was later to develop his ideas about the mother–baby relationship in a different way to Klein. John Bowlby too was to move away, and make important links between psychoanalysis and biology in his contributions on human attachment. James Strachey is best known and frequently quoted even today for his seminal paper on the therapeutic action of psychoanalysis.

The declaration of war on Germany in September 1939, closely followed by Freud's death, added to the ferment. A temporary calm descended when many British members moved from London to safer parts of the country, leaving the Viennese, whose freedom of movement was legally restricted, numerically dominating meetings. When members then returned in 1941, the intellectual and emotional atmosphere rapidly became unbearable and there was intense pressure for change. Demand grew for an improvement in the structure and distribution of power in the BPAS, and for better intellectual dialogue. What emerged was a plan both for a series of business meetings to try to democratise leadership and training in the society, and also for a series of academic meetings where differing theoretical views could be properly debated. The latter became famously known as the 'Controversial Discussions', in which the onus was on Klein's group to present and justify their new ideas.

Documents regarding the debates and differences of the war years have now been carefully collated (King and Steiner, 1991) and make dramatic, and often painful, reading. However, the work done during the many, frequently fraught academic and business meetings achieved something unique in the history of psychoanalysis thus far. This was a psychoanalytic society which was able to contain its differences and stay together, finally offering its students a training containing a rich mixture of contesting points of view, and forcing its members to go on encountering this too.

The three groups became enshrined in rules that remained paradoxically almost entirely unwritten, through what came to be known as the 'Gentlemen's Agreement' brokered in fact by three women: Anna Freud, Melanie Klein and Sylvia Payne. These groups, nowadays known as the Contemporary Freudian Group, the Klein Group and the Independent Group, contribute equally to the theoretical training of students in the British society, and are equitably represented in the political structure.

Although in some ways this tripartite structure has maintained the stability of the society, it may now be stifling creativity. This is because in many ways it represents 'family' or 'political', rather than truly intellectual divisions, which certainly exist but no longer unfold neatly along group lines. The society is currently in an important phase of self-examination where it is actively addressing such issues.

Individualism and authoritarianism: psychoanalysis in France

France was relatively late to embrace psychoanalysis, but when it finally took root it penetrated the culture deeply. Debate over the best way of translating Freud took place as a matter of course in the popular daily newspaper, *Le Monde*. The debate was not resolved and there is still no equivalent to the Freud *Standard Edition* in French.

It was the French literary world and the Surrealist movement which first welcomed psychoanalysis as a theory. Psychoanalytic method was introduced to France in the 1920s by immigrants: a

Pole, Eugenie Sokolnicka, a German, Ralph Loewenstein, and a group of Swiss, especially Ferdinand de Saussure. All trained in Vienna and Berlin, often supported and sponsored by Freud's rich and influential follower, Marie Bonaparte. These few were responsible for the training of a whole second generation of French psychoanalysts, including Jacques Lacan, Daniel Lagache, René Laforgue and Sacha Nacht.

This generation of analysts were all French nationals, unlike in other countries where the pioneers were refugees. Rather than needing to preserve the work of a master in a distant homeland, this generation took Freud as their starting point and developed their thinking in tune with French intellectual ideas. The sufferings of the French in the Second World War also contributed to a strong political, anti-authoritarian current. For the French, Marx and Freud remained connected when communists elsewhere had discarded psychoanalysis, seeing it as conflicting with Marxist theory.

French psychoanalysis has been strongly influenced by an intellectual, philosophical tradition rather than a clinical and empirical one. It has always been more associated with intellectual circles than with medicine and clinical psychology. This has often led to difficulties in dialogue and mutual understanding, between French- and English-speaking psychoanalysts whose thinking has developed on separate sides of a language and cultural divide. In recent years, however, study groups of French and British analysts have been meeting regularly to explore theoretical and clinical issues, for example in the annual Anglo-French Colloquium, founded in 1987, and the Anglo-French Colloquium on female sexuality, which was started in 1996. There is also a growing interest in the work and ideas of Lacan amongst intellectuals in Britain and an interest amongst analysts in the contributions of French analysts on psychosomatic illness and other issues to do with the body.

In her book on the history of psychoanalysis in France, Marion Oliner (1988: 7) comments:

Many French psychoanalysts...are not striving for scientific conciseness. Quite the contrary. The French prefer a style that will express the amorphous, open-ended, even ambiguous nature of the unconscious, a style that does not use expressions borrowed from the natural sciences but strives for poetic evocativeness.

She adds that the French are accustomed to judging an argument by its elegance rather than its usefulness, and that an Anglophone may search in vain for practical, technical applications of theoretical pronouncements in French psychoanalytic writings. Neither do the

French see the need to make psychoanalysis 'respectable' by applying the criteria of the natural sciences to its methodology. The French think of themselves as stewards of classical psychoanalysis, and their theories have tended to adhere to a classical drive model, and to stay close to the unconscious, and to the body.

In practice however, there are tangible differences from classical psychoanalysis, notably fewer sessions per week. While in this country we define psychoanalysis as four or five times a week, in France it is usually no more than three times a week. There are often differences in who would be considered suitable for psychoanalysis, the British taking a broad spectrum of people into analysis, while the French restrict themselves to the more neurotic patients, seeing more disturbed people in face to face weekly sessions.

Within French psychoanalysis we will highlight three important streams of thought: Lacan, the Paris School of Psychosomatics, and André Green.

Jacques Lacan

Psychoanalysis in Paris, the birthplace and continuing headquarters of French psychoanalysis, was subject in its early days to a series of schisms, as a result of which there are now two French psychoanalytic societies affiliated to the International Psychoanalytic Association (IPA), and many others of a more or less Lacanian orientation, which are not. The key controversial figure, Jacques Lacan, developed an idiosyncratic version of psychoanalytic theory which came especially to be taught in literary academic circles (see Chapter 7). Although Lacan never represented typical or mainstream French psychoanalysis, his charismatic authority put him in a central position, impelling colleagues to assert their stance for or against his work.

Lacan was a paradoxical figure who, while presenting himself as iconoclastic and anti-authoritarian, attracted many admiring adherents. A special feature of his analytic technique was variable-length, and often very short, sessions. Sessions would end at a point determined by the analyst, underpinned by his theory of 'logical time'. This became a focus of both fierce allegiance and official censure.

Lacan's theoretical writings, while containing many fascinating ideas, can be so obscure that for the non-specialist they are generally best first approached through secondary sources such as Benvenuto and Kennedy (1986) and Frosh (1999). Lacan re-interpreted what he saw as the essential Freud, particularly Freud's early work on the language of the unconscious as shown in dreams, slips and jokes. Influenced by turn of the century linguistic theory, Lacan came to see language as central, a matrix which fundamentally shapes and forms us.

For Lacan, we are formed by a series of splits and losses, which take us further and further away from a primary unified state with the mother, and establish irrecoverable loss and lack as intrinsic to human existence. The newborn is separated from something that cannot be represented, and will be driven to try to recover this loss throughout life, although there is at this early stage no experience of subjectivity, only an unorganised collection of drives. In forming a sense of subjectivity, we first enter an Imaginary order, in which a reassuring but nevertheless entirely false sense of identity and wholeness is formed by the images of ourselves we see mirrored by others. What we see through mirroring, though, is an image of us based on what the other desires, rather than, as Winnicott might in contrast say, something authentic about ourselves being reflected back to us. The mirror stage has the important function of bringing fragmentary drives together and creating some sense of identity, albeit a false and narcissistic one.

What is necessary next is for this narcissistic relationship with the mother to be interrupted, and for a social being to be created. For Lacan (following Freud) this happens when father interrupts the mother infant dyad with his prohibition of incest, buttressed by the threat of castration. Along with this 'third term' enter language and culture, a distinction between 'I' and 'you', and an enforced recognition of difference, particularly difference between the sexes. This 'symbolic order', the order of the subject's full constitution as human, thus causes further loss and alienation, as well as the important gains of the social world.

There is for Lacan no such thing as an authentic self or centre of being. The subject is not formed by a process of increasing integration; instead he or she is formed by a series of divisions and losses. The so-called ego is a false structure, merely a social creation, and Lacan was particularly dismissive of the work of the ego psychology school.

In analysis, Lacan believed, the ordinary falsely based subjectivity of the patient needed to be subverted and dispersed (for example by the analyst's unresponsiveness, or unexpected reactions) so that he became more in touch with his deepest unconscious desires; so that the linguistic meanings that predated him, into which he was born, could speak through him. Like the Surrealists, Lacan sought in analysis to decode and liberate the patient's deep and fundamental unconscious desire. This desire, though, is for something unrealisable, the obliteration of difference and separateness in a state of oneness.

The Paris School of Psychosomatics, and related others

While Lacan's ideas were derived from Freud's early work on the Unconscious, a very rich seam of thought arose from Freud's *Studies in Hysteria*. Although English-speaking analysts tended to place less emphasis on the body than the mind, the French stayed faithful to the importance of hysteria with its particularly intimate relationship between mind and body.

In Paris analysts such as Pierre Marty and Martin M'Uzan (1963) researched the nature of psychosomatic phenomena. Their work was based on interviews with hundreds of patients who came to their clinic with psychosomatic illnesses. These patients showed both a lack of words for feelings and a lack of capacity to symbolise. Marty and M'Uzan suggested that the dissociation between mind and body came about through a progressive destruction of loving attachment to important early objects linked with early trauma.

Joyce McDougall, Didier Anzier and Janine Chasseguet-Smirgel have taken the mind–body relationship firmly into the centre of psychoanalytic thinking. McDougall and Anzier, following Winnicott, are concerned with the very earliest separation of the 'me' from the 'other'. In this move from fusion to separateness the baby must gradually learn to inhabit his own body. McDougall shows how psychosomatic processes take over when we fail to deal with the psychic pain of separation and loss. Like Winnicott, she thinks both about the baby, and about the mother who fails to enable the infant to separate. In her extensive writing (e.g. McDougall, 1986) she shows how the body can become the theatre in which a whole psychosomatic language is elaborated.

Anzier, following closely Freud's idea of the sexual instinct being linked to, or depending on, the self-preservative instinct (anaclisis), was influenced by Winnicott and also by Bowlby. He focuses on the holding function of the skin 'envelope', both protecting from excessive excitation and 'holding' the psyche. In normal development, gradually the ego and the skin mutually hold each other.

Also rooted firmly in the body, Janine Chasseguet-Smirgel has made an internationally recognised contribution, particularly in the areas of perversion and the surprisingly under-studied area of female sexuality. Her book on female sexuality (1988) did much to bring this important area of psychoanalytic understanding back into serious consideration.

André Green

Though influenced by Lacan as a result of attending his seminar in the 1960s, Green remained affiliated to the Société Psychanalytique de Paris, the mainstream psychoanalytic society from which Lacan had broken away. As his very original and independent thinking developed he distanced himself more and more from Lacan. His significant contribution has been in the area of 'psychose blanche' (blank psychosis) and the work of the negative. His seminal paper, 'The dead mother' (1980) describes a clinical phenomenon in which the patient re-experiences in analysis an awareness of a depressed mother; mother is physically present, but is experienced by the child as dead and absent. The mother's depression is felt as a sudden loss of love. A catastrophic situation arises in the child; loss of love is followed by loss of meaning, with nothing making sense any more. The child cannot mourn the loss of the mother but instead disinvests in her and inevitably at the same time installs a disinvested, absent or dead experience of mother in his mind. The child's development may continue apparently normally but with a psychic hole or blankness within; in effect an identification with the dead mother. Clinically, the presence of the negative has become a widely valued concept.

Horatio Etchegoyen describes André Green (in Kohon, 1999) as 'a Freudian analyst who has managed to integrate in a lucid synthesis the influence of authors as diverse as Lacan, Bion, and, especially, Winnicott'. He has been a prolific writer since the 1960s on both psychoanalytic theory and applied psychoanalysis in regard to the work of Proust, Sartre, Borges and others. However, although he has spoken frequently at international conferences, it is only in recent years that he has been fully translated into English. This means that he has so far been less influential in the English-speaking world than in Latin America and the rest of the Spanish-speaking world.

Repression and after: psychoanalysis under totalitarian regimes

Though neither a political movement nor a belief system, psychoanalysis is bound to come into conflict with totalitarianism. The essential truths about human nature which psychoanalysis strives to discover will often prove at odds with the dogmas imposed by a repressive regime. A dictator who stresses the purity and superiority of his particular race will wish to crush knowledge about *universal* human struggles with sexuality, aggression and hatred, and about mechanisms of projection, idealisation and denigration. A regime which fears and denigrates individuality, and forcibly imposes an idealised collectivism will want to outlaw a practice which emphasises personal autonomy, self-discovery and self-expression.

Psychoanalytic ethics insist on strict standards of privacy, confidentiality and openness to the other, without prescription or condemnation of behaviour; all dangerous to dictators.

While psychoanalysis contains no explicit moral code, in the way that a religion does, it is centrally concerned with loving and hating, and with how our morality develops. It is also preoccupied with truthfulness: the search for knowledge about oneself and the world, however unwelcome or inconvenient that truth might be. Psychoanalysis has shown how a resilient sense of self is built upon the internalisation of loving relationships in which the separateness and individuality of the other is recognised and tolerated. Omnipotent wishes to control others run counter to this and are seen by psychoanalysis as regressive, even if inevitable from time to time.

In its short history psychoanalysis has frequently fallen foul of totalitarianism. Like many other disciplines it faces a dilemma. Should psychoanalysts in totalitarian regimes superficially adapt to the regime, working within it and accepting its restrictions, while trying to preserve essential tenets and beliefs for better days? Or should they make no compromise, but put their activities on hold and/or go 'underground'? We will think first about the situation in Nazi Germany, where psychoanalysts tried to preserve their discipline by adaptation. Then we will look at psychoanalysis as it struggled to survive in some form *outside* the jurisdiction of repressive regimes in a Latin American and a former Iron Curtain country.

Psychoanalysis and compromise: Nazi Germany

The first home of the German psychoanalytic society, Berlin, witnessed an early creative flowering. The society had many creative native members, such as Karl Abraham and Max Eitingon, and talented immigrants such as the Balints, Franz Alexander, Melanie Klein, Theodor Reik and Otto Fenichel. It was admired for its low-fee public clinic and its well-organised training. The Nazi take-over of 1933 had an impact from which German psychoanalysis took many decades to recover. What was to prove so insidiously destructive was that rather than being suspended or going underground, as in Holland, Hungary or Poland, an altered version of psychoanalysis became officially sanctioned by the state, and was even regarded as a valuable tool of National Socialism.

Post-1933 a beleaguered German psychoanalytic society struggled for its continuing existence. Psychoanalysis came under attack in the Nazi press as anti-religious and destructive to the German spirit. Described for example as Jewish-Marxist filth, it was frequently misrepresented as advocating morally lax, licentious behaviour. In 1933 Freud's books were amongst many burnt publicly in Berlin. The society had the choice either of disbanding, with analysts continuing to practise secretly, or of eliminating step by step whatever endangered it as an institution. Supported at first by the International Psychoanalytic Association and Freud himself, the German society embarked on the latter course, to try to preserve itself and psychoanalysis. First the Jewish board members had to be replaced, then all Jewish members of the society had to realise that their resignation was required. Most, but not all, escaped abroad. Following Max Eitingon's emigration to Israel, the new leaders Felix Boehm and Carl Mueller-Braunschweig strove to reassure the government that psychoanalysis posed no threat. Indeed, as it worked to give the ego mastery over the instincts, it could help to produce good citizens, they argued!

Efforts to obtain the required teaching licence for the society were in vain. Instead it agreed in 1936 to become part of a new Institute for Psychological Research and Psychotherapy set up under the leadership of Dr M.H. Goering (a cousin of Field Marshal Goering), which rapidly became known as the Goering Institute. The aim of this institute was to evolve a 'new German psychotherapy'. This would be given to 'socially and biologically valuable patients' who would be helped to realise meaningful and valuable lives as part of the great common destiny of the German people.

The Nazis had a highly ambivalent relationship to psychoanalysis. Although vilified by name, it seemed to be recognised as a powerful, potential weapon with which to combat time and energy lost to the war effort through neurosis. It was re-branded as 'depth psychology', and stripped of all dubious terms connected with sexuality. The psychoanalysts in the Goering Institute were forced to amalgamate their training with that of the Jungians (whose then desexualised and mystical ideals attracted the Nazis), Adlerians, and various eclectic schools of psychotherapy. A shared lecture course included instruction on heredity and race: this featured lectures by Herbert Linden, a psychiatrist, who was the chief administrative officer of the Goering Institute and a key figure in the Nazis' central euthanasia policy, which was aimed at ridding psychiatric institutions of untreatable patients.

Archival material collected for an exhibition in Hamburg in 1985 (Brecht et al., 1985) illustrates the gradual slippage of psychoanalytic integrity under these conditions, in spite of good intentions. Many psychoanalysts tried to carry on the true spirit of psychoanalytic enquiry in a quiet way, secretly holding the 'new German psychotherapy' in contempt (Chrzanowski, 1975). However, it is hard to see how this could ultimately have worked, given the degree of compromise required. Rather, what comes across chillingly in some of the archival material is a gradual move towards embracing National Socialist ideals among certain of the leading psychoanalysts.

Some German analysts did express brave opposition by getting involved in anti-Fascist underground movements. Edith Jacobsohn was arrested in 1935 and escaped a year later while having medical treatment outside the prison, going on to achieve valuable work in the USA. John Rittmeister, clinic director in the Goering Institute, was executed for his underground resistance activities in 1943. Both were disowned by their psychoanalytic peers who feared for their own safety. Rittmeister's final psychoanalytic writings were scribbled in note form on paper bags in his cell. They point out the false appeal of mystic fantasy ideals, and describe a reality-grounded maturity that recognises another individual as truly separate.

After the war, the IPA was reluctant to take the old German Psychoanalytic Society (Deutsche Psychoanalytische Gesellschaft: DPG) back under its wing. Debate focused on the drift towards eclecticism under 12 years of Nazi rule, and the prominence of the self-styled Neo-Analysis school of Schultz-Hencke (which in practice dispensed with most basic psychoanalytic concepts). The preoccupation with eclecticism masked deeper worries about compliance with the Nazis. The latter concerns were less easily expressed, as the larger psychoanalytic world also wished warmly to welcome back old German colleagues who had suffered much.

The IPA's dilemma was finally resolved in 1951 by the formation of a splinter group of the DPG, which called itself the German Psychoanalytic Association (Deutsche Psychoanalytische Vereinigung: DPV) and promised a return to analytic standards acceptable to the international community. Although this strategy appeared to solve the immediate problem, and to be in some respects importantly reparative (Eickhoff, 1995), it also gave DPV members a channel for disowning and projecting the evil and guilt associated with Fascism, as well as the bogey of 'poor standards', into the old society, the DPG.

As with the whole of German society, it was mainly the second post-war generation in the 1960s and 1970s who started asking their teachers and parents the difficult questions that would lead to a constructive facing of the past. This allowed the beginning of mourning, with freeing of blocked creativity (Ehlers and Crick, 1994). The pain of the whole international psychoanalytic community has also taken time to work through; the German invitation to host an international congress in Berlin in 1981 was fiercely rebuffed; the conference was later rescheduled for 1985 in Hamburg, which held fewer painful memories for the analytic Jewish community. The DPV was small, and struggled to grow and find its voice in the post-war years. Recent conflicts and traumas were often too painful to be thought about and tended to go underground, to the detriment of free and original analytic thinking. The association was helped greatly, however, in both practical and morale terms over the following decades, by the goodwill of colleagues from abroad who came to run regular supervision and discussion groups. British analysts – early examples being Willi Hoffer, Michael Balint and Herbert Rosenfeld – have particularly helped in this way, and the tradition still continues. Thriving psychoanalytic institutes now exist in many German cities.

Psychoanalysis in opposition: Argentina

Hungry for culture and ideas from Europe, Latin American countries took up psychoanalysis in the early twentieth century with as much enthusiasm as the USA. Early influences occurred via the universities, for example through the departments of philosophy and literature in the University of Buenos Aires. Then after the First World War, psychoanalysis became strongly identified with psychiatry. For example in Argentina there was a prolonged battle for official recognition of lay analysis. Latin American countries also experienced the early turbulence and schism over authority that has characterised psychoanalysis world-wide (Tylim, 1996).

Psychoanalysis in Latin America has always had a link with radical politics; two of the main founders of the Argentinian Psychoanalytic Association, Angel Garma and Marie Langer, were European émigrés who had been involved in the Spanish Civil War. This anti-authoritarianism also contributed to the popular appeal of Lacan's work, which appeared (at least superficially) to represent freedom and the avant-garde.

As in France, the language barrier led to a long period of separate evolution within these Spanish- and Portuguese-speaking countries, with separate bodies of literature evolving. Freud's works were translated into Spanish in 1923, but only since the 1980s have Latin American countries provided part of the editorial structure of the *International Journal of Psychoanalysis*, and taken their turn with North America and Europe to provide presidents of the IPA, and to host the biennial international congresses (see Chapter 9 for more about these international organisations).

In spite of this relative isolation in early years, Latin America has provided some leading international figures in psychoanalysis, such as Ignacio Matte Blanco and Otto Kernberg from Chile and Heinrich Racker and Horacio Etchegoyen from Argentina. A number of British psychoanalysts have been particularly influential in Latin American thought, especially those working in the Kleinian tradition such as Hanna Segal, Wilfred Bion and Donald Meltzer.

In the terrifying and turbulent times of military dictatorship in Argentina between the 1960s and 1980s and in the relatively unstable and lawless period which followed, psychoanalysts found it very hard to hang on to clarity of thought and to their boundaries. Pressure to collaborate with the oppressors is one problem for psychoanalysis under dictatorships, as we have seen; another is pressure to transform it into a crusade for social reform. Either way, if this attitude permeates clinical work, the analyst risks the loss of the neutral analytic stance. In the one case he or she sides with the oppressor, in the other with the oppressed. The patient is deprived of a real chance to find integrity and personal strength for him- or herself.

In Argentina, psychoanalysts were mostly not drawn into the service of the oppressive regimes, as they were in Nazi Germany; neither was their work forbidden. They continued to work in private offices, or hospital clinics for the poor. However, in a world where the courts no longer reflected any natural moral sense of justice, and where the worst paranoid phantasies became commonplace reality in torture and disappearances, mental health workers of all kinds no longer had the background framework of a relatively stable, rational and predictable world from which to work. Dr A, a junior psychiatrist, found herself unable to tell whether a patient's terrified account of persecution constituted a psychotic delusion or a true picture of reality. She was asking urgently to see the hospital director, who in those days was a member of the military regime. What was appropriate: to agree to this request or to refuse it? What might be the implications of either course of action for the patient and for Dr A herself?

An Argentinian analyst Janine Puget discusses how ethical confusions abound in the mind of patient and analyst when corruption is part of daily life (Puget, 1992). She describes a patient announcing triumphantly how he has smuggled a useful gadget through customs by bribing an official. Her countertransference impulse is to accept this commonplace act without comment; 'everybody does it', after all. However, braving the patient's initial caustic scorn, she takes this seriously as a communication about his relationship to authority, something he can 'slip through' not just in the prevailing social climate, but in the analytic relationship. A rich seam then opens up in the analytic dialogue and the patient is able to talk about his difficulties in transmitting clear-cut values to his son. The son habitually treats him in the same scornful way in which he has just attacked the analyst; there is a fearful taboo on discussing politics at home, and he has a dilemma over his son's recent request for a gun to defend himself with, thus taking the law into his own hands.

Argentinian psychoanalysis has flourished with the ending of the military dictatorship, and Buenos Aires has hosted one of the biennial congresses of the International Psychoanalytical Association. A freer political climate has contributed to an increased sharing of psychoanalytic literature and ideas between Latin America and North America and Europe.

Psychoanalysis underground: Czechoslovakia

Following on the heels of liberation from Fascist oppression, many psychoanalytic groupings, for example those in Hungary, Poland and Czechoslovakia, faced the problem of communist totalitarianism, another situation in which entitlement to free exploration and expression was threatened. The Czech situation will be used to illustrate the vigour and persistence of the Eastern European psychoanalytic movement in spite of this. The first Czech group to be interested in psychoanalysis gathered in the 1920s around the Russian Ossipov, who was in contact with Freud. A second group gathered in eastern Slovakia around a Czech psychiatrist, Jaroslav Stuchlik. By 1935 numbers in Prague were swelled by Jewish émigrés, including Otto Fenichel, who was instrumental in getting the group's initial acceptance by the IPA in 1936.

The German occupation in 1939 put a stop to these activities. Some analysts managed to flee, others died in concentration camps. One surviving member of the group, Bohodar Dosuzkov, continued to keep psychoanalysis alive, underground, during the Second World War. As soon as the war ended, Dosuzkov re-established an official IPA study group, only for it to be banned once again by the communist regime in the late 1940s. For the next 40 years, psychoanalysis continued underground in Czechoslovakia, with meetings and the training of candidates going on in private dwellings. It was only following the events of 1989 that a third study group could be set up, now in the Czech Republic. This led finally to acceptance of the Czech group as a provisional psychoanalytic society in 1999, well on the road to full membership of the IPA.

Michael Sebek (2001), a Czech psychoanalyst who worked during these years, discusses the problems of 'underground' psychoanalysis.

Could patients really risk free association in a society that placed such restrictions on what could be said – even thought? Furthermore, could analysts really risk interpretations and confrontations which would elicit the patients' rage? Could they insist on payment for missed sessions in a climate where to conduct a session at all was an illegal activity for which they risked imprisonment if the patient informed on them? Some collusion was bound to occur in which analyst and patient saw themselves as to some degree comfortably aligned against the state, with any 'totalitarian' part of the patient comfortably denied and projected. Once again, part of the freedom and depth of the analytic setting is compromised.

Conclusion

In this chapter we have described psychoanalysis developing in a number of different social and political cultures. We have seen how easily the task of discovery in psychoanalysis can be derailed; psychoanalysts may become too aligned with the aims of the prevailing establishment, too collusive with the patient or too identified with a repressive state. At the same time we can see how the power and authenticity of the underlying ideas help the psychoanalytic enterprise to survive even in the most inhospitable climate, and to evolve and renew itself.

5
CRITIQUES OF PSYCHOANALYSIS

By its very nature, dealing as it does with the instinctual, the irrational and the ambiguous, psychoanalysis is subversive and shocking. While psychoanalysts must not complacently dismiss all challenges as 'just defensive' on the part of the challenger, if psychoanalysis were never criticised we would know it was dead. Neither should psychoanalysts seek acceptance by too much compromise and conformity. For example, the flourishing of a conservative brand of ego psychology in the American psychiatric establishment of the 1950s and 1960s perhaps inevitably set itself up for revisionist criticism (see Chapter 4). Psychoanalysis also runs into problems when, a victim of its own success, it becomes confused in the public's mind, as it is in the UK currently, with the myriad other forms of therapy and counselling it has unwittingly spawned, some of which do not have well developed standards of training or ethics. This chapter addresses the critiques of psychoanalytic theory and practice. It cannot hope to do justice to this complex topic, so is generously referenced for further study.

Because people habitually study their own minds and those of others, everyone tends to consider themselves experts on the subject; the special expertise of physicists will never suffer from the same popular demotion. The permeation of our culture with Freudian ideas, often in palatable, banal form, is double edged, and Forrester (1997) comments ruefully that 'the process of writing about Freud must always be one of un-educating one's readers' (p. 12). Psychoanalytic critique is full of 'straw men', so distorted and misrepresented has psychoanalysis popularly become. A particular feature of much psychoanalytic critique is that it concentrates on Freud, often on his earliest theories, now over a century old. Lear (1998) points out that we can become stuck on Freud, as on some rigid symptom, idolising or denigrating him. Practising psychoanalysts frequently sigh to see yet another distorted and antiquated version of their theory and craft misrepresented and attacked in the media, as if the scores of lively and creative later thinkers had never been born.

We will group the many critiques of psychoanalysis into five broad categories. (The issue of therapeutic efficacy is not considered here, but comprises part of Chapter 6.) First, psychoanalytic claims to truth can be disputed philosophically, often centring around the scientific status or otherwise of psychoanalysis. Second come challenges to Freud's originality as a thinker: was psychoanalysis really something new and important? Various 'contextualisers' have sought to question this. Third are the political and ideological critiques of psychoanalysis. Some of these challenge the very idea of a therapeutic relationship in which there is an unequal balance of power; some object to the institutions which have grown around psychoanalysis; others, including the influential feminist critique of psychoanalysis, have specific objections to part of psychoanalytic theory. Fourth come critiques by patients who have written about their experiences of insensitive, even abusive treatment by their analysts or therapists. Lastly come what we have called 'global' critiques. These are openly hostile attacks on psychoanalysis, often centred primarily around Freud's moral integrity, then generalising this personal attack to encompass all aspects of psychoanalysis, methodological, theoretical and therapeutic.

Critiques concerning the truth and knowledge claims of psychoanalysis: Popper, Cioffi, Grünbaum and others

The truth value and explanatory power of psychoanalytic claims about the mind have always been fiercely debated. Underlying this, Gardner (1995) suggests, are radically different experiences of the intuitive acceptability of Freud's ideas. While some feel them to be far fetched and alien, others feel a natural affinity with them. This difference in basic gut feeling lends passion to the theoretical debate about whether psychoanalytic thinking is to be taken seriously or not.

Freud asserted that psychoanalysis was a branch of the natural sciences; a guarantee of professional respectability (as it remains today). An immediate problem with this is the nature of the science of psychology generally. We are dealing with an open system, with myriad variables, many intrinsically unobservable, where we are bound to have great difficulty in rigorously establishing causal relations between events. Except at the behavioural and neurochemical level of explanation, human psychology presents complex problems of testability. Strict empiricists using physics or chemistry as a model may accuse psychoanalysts of being slippery when the problem is at least in part the slipperiness of their material under study. So, unless we are broad in our definition of science, it is easy to accuse psychoanalysis of being unscientific, and a number of philosophers of science have done this.

Karl Popper (1969) and Frank Cioffi (1970), in particular, assert that psychoanalysis is not a science, because its propositions are not falsifiable. They go even further, saying that it is a pseudo science like astrology and phrenology; it wilfully employs defective methodology. For example it keeps adding bits on to its theories in order to accommodate new data, rather than discarding the theories. They imply also that psychoanalysts cannot be trusted to test their own theories: they are far too biased, and this must instead be done impartially by external observers.

Cosin, Freeman and Freeman (1982), in their detailed critique of Popper and Cioffi, consider that both have an odd view of the way scientific knowledge actually advances. It is unrealistic and counterproductive to expect any scientists to spend most of their time refuting and dismantling their ideas rather than building on them in a speculative way. They show that Popper and Cioffi also fail to distinguish overarching scientific theories and their constituent hypotheses. Psychoanalysis is not monistic, but like other sciences has a complex, changing structure with component concepts and hypotheses at different levels, many of which can, indeed must, be modified or discarded without nullifying the whole enterprise. The physical sciences themselves, whose theories are supposed *par excellence* to be falsifiable, discard theories only when alternatives emerge which fit the data better or are better at generating research problems.

Gardner (1995) points out that even theoretical physics is a pseudo science on Popper's criteria, as it is all the time finding strategies for accommodating apparently recalcitrant data. It makes no sense either to say that findings generated within the psychoanalytic setting can only be reliably tested outside it by non-analysts; after all, the equivalent would be laughable in theoretical physics. Every science can work only within its own frame of reference and methodology, using its own experts to test it. Ideas from other fields simply lend additional corroboration, doubt, or stimulus to research. Nor can facts be generated independently of theory. Pure observation, we know, is a myth. Having said this, it is clear that the phenomena of resistance, ambivalence, over-determination, reaction formation and so on can indeed tempt the analyst to 'have it both ways'. The very flexibility of psychoanalytic theory means that the analyst must be exceptionally disciplined in its application.

The concept of unconscious mental functioning seems to provide a red rag to scientistic critics. How, they say, can something by its very nature unobservable be truly tested? For psychoanalysis, the idea of unconscious beliefs and desires is required to conceptualise previously inexplicable phenomena such as dreams, slips and symptoms. Holmes and Lindley (1989) compare Newton's assumption of Galileo's principle of inertia. A body continues to move in a straight line unless acted upon by an external force. Even if this force is not evident it is assumed axiomatically to be present, and must be sought in the same way that the psychoanalyst observes the effect of unconscious motivation and then has to seek its precise nature. Much about the nature of gravity remains obscure in physics, but the concept is indispensable. The crucial question about such concepts is whether, when combined with other plausible assumptions and observations, they yield interesting or useful predictions and explanations.

We will look now at some specific examples of the arguments advanced against psychoanalysis as a science. Popper (1969) complains that psychoanalysis purports to explain everything about the mental world and thus really explains nothing: 'it is a typical soothsayer's trick to predict things so vaguely that the predictions can hardly fail: that they become irrefutable' (p. 37). Popper backs up this sort of complaint in a curious way, with an invented example of his own, thus: 'I may illustrate this with two very different examples of human behaviour: that of a man who pushes a child into the water with the intention of drowning it; and that of a man who sacrifices his life in an attempt to save the child.' Adler, he says, would interpret both as an act of self-assertion, so that he wins on both the swings and the roundabouts. On the other hand: 'according to Freud the first man suffered from repression (say, of some component of his Oedipus complex), while the second man had achieved sublimation' (Popper, 1969: 35). Cosin et al. (1982) point out how in this rather odd example (unrelated to anything Freud or Adler wrote) complex theoretical concepts (sublimation, the Oedipus complex) are taken out of context and presented as facile and empty jargon, which is then attributed to Freud so that he is made to look absurd. Popper and Cioffi often use such straw man arguments.

In another example, Cioffi is objecting to the use psychoanalysis frequently makes of 'explanations in the alternative'. Two separate quotations from Freud are juxtaposed as follows: 'If the father was hard, violent and cruel the superego takes over these attributes from him.' And: 'the unduly lenient and indulgent father fosters the development of a strict superego.' Cioffi condenses and reduces this to: 'if a child develops a sadistic superego, either he had a harsh and punitive father or he had not' and comments that 'this is just what we might expect to find if there was no relation between his father's character and the harshness of his superego' (Cioffi, 1970: 484). Thus Freud's explanation is concluded to be worthless. There are several points to be made about this. First, in his careless reading and understanding of Freud, by excluding the whole middle ground, Cioffi has obliterated all cases of *ordinary* leniency or strictness in fathers. Psychoanalysts do indeed tend to observe that either extreme of parenting can contribute to a harsh superego, and this probably makes intuitive sense to many readers from the 'commonsense psychology' viewpoint (to be discussed shortly). In the clinical situation the 'feel' of each superego is likely to be different. In the 'lenient parent' case for example we might often find it had a more guilty quality, because of the feeling the patient often has that he had 'got away with' his aggression and misdemeanours, rather than been punished unfairly, as in the other case. Also, every case will be unique, and strict (or lenient) parenting is neither a necessary nor a sufficient condition for development of a strict superego.

Freud gradually reached the standpoint of contemporary psychoanalysis: that there are no specific or consistent determinants of specific neurotic problems. In estimating the pathogenicity of an event for a particular person, Freud was concerned with its meaning for that person. Although very adverse childhood situations will mostly have adverse effects, the precise nature of the effects cannot be predicted, as there are so many variables in human life, not least the innate individual temperament and the set of phantasy beliefs with which one meets and interprets one's environment.

Cioffi radically misunderstands these facts about psychoanalysis. He combs through Freud's writings to try to show that there is no direct relation between 'cure' and recall of pathological sexual events and impulses from childhood, as if this underpinned theory and treatment. Cosin et al. (1982) draw detailed attention to the distorted and out-of-context way in which Freud's texts are once again used here, and show how Cioffi's endeavours in any case miss the point. In all but his very early (nineteenth-century) work, Freud stresses that it is the dynamic factors of repression, resistance and transference – ignored by Cioffi entirely – that form the essentials of psychoanalytic theory and practice. The simple cause and effect model which Cioffi spends so much energy trying to dismantle is not recognisably psychoanalytic at all; it might equally fit an old-fashioned behavioural model with the mind as a 'black box' between stimulus and response. Cioffi and Freud seem to pass one another by without recognition. Freud is concerned with the mechanisms and processes of the mind; Cioffi is stuck in his preoccupation with certain putative products of the work.

Adolf Grünbaum (1984) maintains, contrary to Popper (whom he criticises severely for sketchy and sloppy work), that psychoanalysis can be evaluated scientifically, and that Freud (whom he in many ways professes to admire) was intent on doing this. However, psychoanalysis fails its own scientific tests and is rendered invalid. To come to this conclusion Grünbaum homes in on a remark made by Freud (1917a) in one of his *Introductory Lectures*. In this particular passage, Freud is countering the argument that insight might be merely a result of suggestion. He tells us that the analyst's suggestion might have some effect on a patient at an intellectual level, but that emotionally, and in relation to the patient's illness: 'his conflicts will only be successfully solved and his resistances overcome if the anticipatory ideas he is given tally with what is real in him' (Freud, 1917a: 452).

Grünbaum uses this one sentence to set up a hypothesis (the 'tally argument') on which he believes (and he appears to believe Freud believed) the whole of psychoanalysis rests. That is, that the neurosis cannot be cured without insight, that only psychoanalysis provides insight, and hence the cure and only the cure proves the truth of the theories. Grünbaum then goes on to deduce at length that because psychoanalysis has not been proven to cure people reliably, and because cure can happen in other ways, including spontaneously, psychoanalysis is falsified.

The intellectual historian Paul Robinson (1993), like many others, feels that Grünbaum has selected a relatively casual remark of Freud's and 'made a philosophical mountain out of an expository molehill' (p. 217). He is puzzled at Grünbaum's tunnel vision about this, given that he has made such an extensive study of Freud; Freud frequently expressed pessimism about cure, and he clearly used many other sources of evidence for psychoanalytic ideas in both the clinical and non-clinical sphere, for example dreams, slips, myths, jokes, poetry.

Jim Hopkins (1988), Richard Wollheim (1993) and Sebastian Gardner (1995) are all philosophers who develop an important theme overlooked by Grünbaum and his fellow scientistic critics. That is that psychoanalysis derives from, and builds upon, 'commonsense psychology', the ordinary way in which we explain ourselves and others with reference to desires, beliefs, feelings, intentions, and so on, including wishful thinking and self-deception. Psychoanalysis contributes both breadth and depth to this by explaining hitherto irrational or inexplicable phenomena such as symptoms, dreams, slips, and by building up a picture of the underlying psychological structures upon which commonsense psychology rests.

Commonsense psychology can lend itself to scientific exploration, but cannot lend itself to the rigorous testing of causality possible in the physical sciences. Gardner points out that when a toddler says 'Drink!' and reaches for his bottle, we assume a causal connection between the action and the desire to drink. Following Grünbaum's strict requirements, such a causal relation cannot be assumed until we have proven inductively that 'utterances of "drink!" are indices of desires to drink' and 'drink-desires cause reachings for bottles' (1984: 108), which would be absurd. Gardner points out that although our causal hypotheses in psychology are bound to be provisional and fallible, that does not mean that we must abandon making them.

Both Hopkins and Wollheim demonstrate the faulty reasoning involved in Grünbaum's strong objection both to free association, and to Freud's use generally of thematic connections to explore underlying meanings and causes. Much everyday human understanding is based on such language connections, and Freud was extending this in an intuitively logical way in his methodology. Dreams and slips are formed, according to Freud, by associative pathways which free association unearths by reversing the process. Grünbaum seems not to grasp this aspect of Freud's thinking at all. He fails generally to do justice to the complex structure Freud attributed to the mind and, like Cioffi, instead becomes involved in debates about childhood aetiology of symptoms which are essentially peripheral matters in psychoanalysis. Wollheim also takes issue with Grünbaum's liberal use of the concept of suggestion to explain psychoanalytic findings, that the patient simply produces what the analyst wants to hear. Wollheim points out how grotesquely inflated this process becomes in Grünbaum's thinking; how helpless and gullible people are supposed to be, and challenges him to give a detailed, plausible and properly psychological theory of how and why so much suggestion occurs.

Robinson suggests that we should accept that ideas of the self can never achieve the rigour of ideas about nature, and that analysis thus necessarily exists on the border between science and the humanities. He compares Darwinian science as something

at once empirical and hermeneutic: it works by deciphering clues – such as the fossil remains of extinct species – in order to reveal a hidden reality, namely, the working of natural selection. Freud proceeds in exactly the same fashion when he deciphers the evidence of dreams, slips, and neurotic symptoms to reveal the hidden reality of the unconscious... Science is in fact a continuum, with psychoanalysis occupying an honoured place towards the Darwinian end. (1993: 262)

One way of escaping the debate about scientific status altogether is to assert (contrary to Freud's own view) that psychoanalysis is a purely hermeneutic discipline, concerned with plausible meanings and reasons, rather than mechanisms and causes. David Will (1986) points out that this stance tacitly accepts Popper's narrow view of science, and gives up any aspiration to find objective truths about subjectivity. Will points out that there have to be different investigative techniques in the human sciences and the natural sciences, and hence *epistemological* differences occur. However, the same test of truth should apply to knowledge in both the human and natural sciences; the *ontological* status does not differ. For a psychoanalytic hypothesis to be true it must correspond to a real mental process or event. The hermeneutic stance quickly collapses into relativism, with psychoanalysis losing its power to reveal the individual to herself and unmask self-deception. The whole concept of resistance, for example, dissolves. The concepts of self-deception, and ultimately of truth and falsehood, begin to disappear, so that finally we are only able to comment on what people are making of the world.

Critics who question Freud's stature and originality – the 'contextualisers': Roazen, Ellenberger, Sulloway

Ernest Jones's (1953–57) scholarly biography of Freud could be said sometimes to idealise its subject, so it is unsurprising that, given the modern tendency to topple heroes, there have been many challenges to this. Paul Roazen (1969, 1971) is an example of a biographer who takes a more critical view of Freud than Jones, without however seriously undermining Freud's genius and originality. Henri Ellenberger (1970) goes further in the direction of reducing Freud's stature. By the particular way he portrays Freud as heir to a long tradition of 'dynamic psychiatry' he explicitly and implicitly challenges Freud's originality. Ellenberger suggests that contemporaries of Freud such as Adler and Janet had as much or more claim to fame as Freud, and are remembered as lesser men only through accidents of history. A third alternative biographer is Frank Sulloway (1979), who is even more explicit in his 'damning with faint praise', and develops an ingenious thesis that Freud was not even really a psychologist at all, but a 'closet sociobiologist' who owed most of his apparently original thinking to Fliess and Darwin. These critics are all 'contextualisers' because of the way they use the context of Freud's life and work, the people and ideas around him, to question his stature and originality.

In any historical reconstruction, details can be legitimately disputed and alternative interpretations proposed. However, sometimes readers can notice idealisation or hostility to the biographical subject, and hostility to Freud is barely disguised in Sulloway. Roazen is a different matter. Psychoanalysis is a very new, and very personal, discipline; some people who knew, loved and revered Freud and his immediate followers personally only died in the last quarter of the twentieth century. Reactions to any biographical research are bound thus to be complex and at times impassioned.

Roazen (1971) uses, as one important source, interview material from over a hundred witnesses who were colleagues, family, friends or patients of Freud or who were otherwise involved in the early psychoanalytic movement. One irritated reviewer (Wolf, 1976) refers to the distinction between 'oral history' and 'gossip', depending on whether one uses such material in a scholarly way or not. Wolf thinks Roazen is deliberately trying to throw an unfavourable light on Freud, and John Gedo (1976) tends to agree, but also acknowledges 'a grain of truth that deserves serious attention'. The grain in question concerns Roazen's showing the psychoanalytic movement's unhelpful tendency to an apostolic relationship to Freud.

Kurt Eissler (1971) was furious at the way Roazen presented the story of the tragic relationship between Freud and Victor Tausk (Roazen, 1969). Roazen (1977) then strenuously attempted to refute Eissler's criticisms. Roazen certainly often draws attention to Freud's difficulties and weaknesses, but Freud emerges from Roazen's pages as a complex and brilliant man, and attacks on him are not on the whole used, as they are in so many cases, to attack the credibility of psychoanalysis itself.

Ellenberger's work in tracing the evolution of dynamic psychology over the last two centuries is widely admired for its comprehensive scholarship (e.g. Abrams, 1974; Mahoney, 1974). A central thesis is the question of why four men of (in Ellenberger's view) equal talent and importance – Janet, Freud, Adler and Jung – have been judged so differently by history. Ellenberger disputes much of the special originality attributed to Freud, in particular the discovery of the importance of the unconscious, though he acknowledges the innovative nature of the psychoanalytic method. Ellenberger's more double-edged praise relates to Freud's innovation in founding a 'school' that is 'a revival of the old philosophical schools of Greco-Roman antiquity'.

Ellenberger likens the training analysis to an 'initiation' and 'surrender of privacy and of the whole self' by which 'a follower is integrated into the Society more indissolubly than ever was a Pythagorian, Stoic or Epicurean in his own organisation' (1970: 550). Both Abrams and Mahoney are less impressed by Ellenberger's grasp of the essential nature of psychoanalysis than by his historical scholarship. They feel that through his detailed and piecemeal contextualisation, he has seriously failed to grasp the genius of the new gestalt, or paradigm, that Freud developed out of the raw material of ideas that was to hand.

Robinson (1993) mentions both Ellenberger and Roazen as significant precursors to the later, more full-blooded critics of Freud. He then addresses one of these latter critics, Frank Sulloway, in detail. Sulloway, a historian of science who studied with the sociobiologist Edward O. Wilson, sets out to place Freud within the tradition of evolutionary thought from Darwin to Wilson. He argues that Freud is fundamentally misrepresented by being regarded as a psychological thinker. He sets out to discredit the 'Freud legend' in a patently hostile way, which has been made much use of by other detractors, in spite of the eccentricity of Sulloway's claims. Part of this eccentricity is a claim that it was a 'brilliant political strategy' on the part of the Freudian establishment to disguise Freud's biological legacy and pretend that he was an original psychologist.

Sulloway's own strategy, according to Robinson, is to diminish Freud 'by association', exaggerating the influence of certain thinkers on him and downplaying others, in the service of his 'biological' thesis. Fliess, the key figure in Sulloway's reinterpretion, is presented as a crucial intellectual influence and thus as having to be vigorously rehabilitated from his usual position in the historical record as a lightweight, even bizarre thinker whose influence on Freud was mostly emotional. Fliess, according to Sulloway, provided Freud with the key evolutionary ideas (for example to do with the evolutionary importance of the nose, and of bisexuality) that form the hidden core of psychoanalytic theory.

Robinson shows how the evidence for this is laboured and unconvincing, with Sulloway going through tremendous contortions to make meagre facts fit his theories. At the same time, Sulloway almost entirely ignores key psychological aspects of psychoanalysis, such as the unconscious itself. Robinson feels that this shows a profound anti-psychological bias on Sulloway's own part, which seems to prevent him, for example, from seeing any significance in the Oedipus complex, which is mentioned almost in passing as a 'psychological correlate' of something fundamentally biological.

Sulloway has an even greater tendency than Ellenberger to talk as if the whole were the same as the sum of its parts. Because Freud was influenced by contemporary evolutionary biologists, sexologists and so on, apparently he could not have been original. Again, the genius of such thinkers as Freud and Darwin in synthesising what is already known into a new conceptual whole does not seem to be properly grasped; intellectual revolutions, Robinson reminds us, cannot occur in a vacuum, but as Thomas Kuhn (1970) has shown, are always richly prepared.

Political and ideological critiques of psychoanalysis: Millet, Timpanaro, Szasz, Rycroft

Since their inception, psychoanalytic theory and practice have been seen variously as liberating, authoritarian and conformist, a radical way of addressing the individual in society, patriarchal and sexist, revolutionary, reactionary or elitist. Stephen Frosh (1999) suggests that this depends partly on one's version of psychoanalysis; different approaches to psychoanalysis have different social implications and political standpoints. Different readings of Freud may also lead to very different conclusions. For example some feminists (e.g. Millett, 1970; Greer, 1971) see Freud's work as inimical to their cause; others (e.g. Mitchell, 1974; Chodorow, 1978) read him as essentially an ally. Some critics are not critical of the content of theory and practice *per se*, but deplore the politics of psychoanalytic institutes and societies as authoritarian and anti-creative.

The feminist critique of psychoanalysis took off in the late 1960s and 1970s, abhorring and disputing Freud's representation of women as physically and mentally inferior to men, fundamentally defined by their lack of a penis rather than by any distinctive attributes of their own. Particularly inflammatory was the concept of penis envy, and Freud's idea that women did not just *feel* themselves to be inferior to men (which feminists might accept and work with), but actually through their different biology triggering different developmental pathways, were destined actually to *be* inferior, for example in their intellect, ethical sense and capacity for mature relationships. Feminist critiques also came to encompass Freud's sometimes high-handed treatment of female patients like Dora (Freud, 1905b).

The irritation engendered by all this meant that much of what was radical and potentially liberating for women (and men) in the rest of Freud's writings tended at first to be ignored. Freud was after all a man of his time, and more respectful of, and thoughtful about women than many; also psychoanalysis was also one of the few professions where women were welcome from an early stage, and able to make seminal contributions. In addition, the writings of other psychoanalysts with alternative and more convincing views about femininity to Freud's (e.g. Ernest Jones, Karen Horney, Helene Deutsch, Melanie Klein) were often overlooked by the early feminist critics. Thus interesting new ideas about women, mothers and babies (in addition to fathers) were ignored. The concept of penis envy, for example, is less outrageous when placed alongside ideas about envy of the mother's capacity (the 'maternal breast') and of the parental couple.

In Frosh's view, feminists' disappointment with the humanistic and consciousness-raising therapeutic approaches they had turned to contributed to an eventual move back to psychoanalysis and its powerful conceptual tools for understanding how (for example) patriarchal and other norms of society might be internalised. Frosh sees this as the political strength of psychoanalysis generally: that it can analyse how the structures of the social world enter into the individual. With understanding, change becomes at least a possibility.

Frosh discusses how left-wing thinkers may be uneasy with psychoanalytic theories which stress biological instincts and drives, because they might encourage complacent views about the unchangeability of human nature, and hence the inevitability of social inequalities like patriarchy. The Marxist critic Sebastiano Timpanaro (1974), although not wholly critical of psychoanalysis, does in one passage accuse it of being 'a bourgeois doctrine...incapable of seeing beyond an ideological horizon delimited precisely by the class interests of the bourgeoisie' (p. 12). Artefacts of bourgeois family life can in Timpanaro's view be mistaken for biological facts. However, theories which eschew drives, like those of Fairbairn and Kohut, may run into different ideological problems. Their emphasis on maternal provision, and their location of all psychopathology in environmental (essentially maternal) failure, seems to idealise motherhood, and inexorably to pull women from the workplace back into the home. Frosh sees classical ego psychology also as politically compromised by its emphasis on an adaptation to society, which could encourage conformism.

Both Frosh and Michael Rustin (1991) politically favour a post-Kleinian conceptual approach. Bion's theory of containment, (see pp. 9 and 55), Frosh feels, reinstates the dynamic function of the environment implicit but often downplayed in Klein, and allows a dialectical encounter between individual and environment. Frosh and Rustin see this as appropriately addressing the human aggression which is anti-social and anti-change, while providing the powerful and optimistic concept of reparation to rescue at least the possibility of striving for a better society.

Jeffrey Masson's (1989) extreme view that all unequal therapeutic relationships encourage abuse will be discussed below (see p. 93). Thomas Szasz (1969) has a similar view about any psychotherapy provided by the state: that it will inevitably become a means of brainwashing and state control. Holmes and Lindley (1989) find Szasz's 'right wing libertarian' viewpoint unconvincing and quite patronising. Szasz seems happy for the more well-off to seek private therapy, but argues that the poor need jobs and money, and that the uneducated need knowledge and skills, not psychoanalysis. In Szasz's view, the kind of personal freedom that psychoanalysis promises can have meaning only for persons who enjoy a large measure of economic, political and social freedom. Holmes and Lindley assert that this superficially attractive polemic rests on a false dichotomy, between jobs and money on one hand and psychotherapy on the other. Why might an individual not need both? Psychoanalysts working psychotherapeutically in the public sector are often impressed at how patients are often freed to develop in all sorts of ways, not least to work (and earn!) more successfully.

The frequent criticism that psychoanalysis is elitist, available only to the relatively few who can afford it, might be answered in the form of a question: why do we accept this in Britain? Scandinavian countries include intensive psychoanalytic psychotherapy as part of the routine mental health care provided by the state. It would be interesting to see if more of a public outcry would have ensued if heart bypass operations were available only to the better-off in the UK, all other heart attack sufferers being given only superficial symptom relief. It is also worth noting that, in Britain at least, psychoanalysis is not an enormously wealthy profession, and most patients are not very wealthy either. They have usually sacrificed considerable material benefits in pursuit of improved aspects of their psychological quality of life.

Finally, certain dissenting psychoanalysts, an example being Charles Rycroft (1985), have criticised psychoanalytic institutions' tendency to factionalism, and choose to work outside them. Ironically, the problem may often reassert itself in the form of a new faction, this time a group of dissenters analysed by the rebel him- or herself. François Roustang's (1982: 34) challenging statement, 'there are no good psychoanalytic societies', applies particularly to the Lacanian school, which Roustang sees as especially fanatical and leader centred. However, it serves as a useful reminder of the difficulties people can get into when studying and practising such an intensely personal and emotional discipline.

Patient critiques: Sutherland, Sands and others

Patients such as Marie Cardinal (1975) have written in positive terms of life-changing therapeutic experiences. Others give accounts of treatments that went wrong, where they felt misunderstood or abused. Usually, such authors have assumed their experiences to be typical, and drawn the conclusion that the model of therapy their therapists espouse is fundamentally flawed. Stuart Sutherland (1976) writes as a sufferer from manic depressive psychosis who experienced a number of different psychotherapeutic approaches, none of which was very helpful, and who also spent many months on a psychiatric ward being treated with various drugs. He had short periods of contact with two people who apparently called themselves psychoanalysts, although their training and affiliations are not stated. Their behaviour as described sounds rather odd, with poor attention to boundaries and wild interpretations. We might also wonder at analytic treatment being undertaken so readily and casually as is described with someone suffering from a psychotic illness; this would usually be undertaken by an experienced specialist, with appropriate psychiatric support in place.

Although we do not know whether Sutherland's 'analysts' had received a proper training or not, Wynne Godley's (2001) experiences at the hands of the British psychoanalyst Masud Khan are clearly a case of professional misconduct on the part of a senior figure. Khan was eventually removed from the membership register of the British Psychoanalytical Society, but only after a number of individuals had suffered from his activities. Such experiences have been salutary for the profession, and have led to improvements in ethical and clinical governance procedures (see Chapter 9).

Anna Sands (2000) writes feelingly of two contrasting experiences of psychotherapy. The first is with a therapist who called himself 'psychodynamic' in orientation, whom she experienced as rigid and insensitive. Inaccurately, the author also refers frequently to her non-intensive therapy as 'psychoanalysis', and draws many negative conclusions about psychoanalysis itself on the basis of her painful experiences with this man. It is not stated what sort of training either he or her next therapist had in fact had. The second therapist, whom she experienced as helping to heal her from the hurt engendered by the first experience, is described as warm, sensitive, friendly and helpfully revealing of herself. (See Chapter 8 for a discussion of different approaches to psychotherapy). What Sands's book does do well is to show how powerfully and painfully a non-social therapeutic stance can evoke feelings of hurt and alienation in patients, if not adopted skilfully and flexibly, and if not coupled with very active and sensitive attention to the intense negative transference that can be revealed.

Global critiques: Webster, Crews, Masson and others

A number of critics mount extensive and intensive attacks on all aspects of psychoanalysis. Freud's character and integrity are called into question, as are his research methodology, his therapeutic claims and the whole body of his ideas. Where post-Freudian analysis is considered, this is with certain limited exceptions treated in the same way; the whole profession and institution of psychoanalysis, past and present, is explicitly or implicitly dismissed.

We will mainly consider the arguments of just three examples of this category of critic. Although there are a number of others (e.g. Eysenck, Fish and Gellner) we think the work of Richard Webster, Frederick Crews and Jeffrey Masson between them covers the important ground to be addressed. Webster and Crews were both before retirement university teachers of English, Webster at the University of East Anglia and Crews in Berkeley, California. Webster is the single author of the long and dense book *Why Freud Was Wrong* (1995), although this draws extensively on the work of most other Freud critics. Crews, as well as putting forward his own ideas, gathers and edits the works of other critics, which he introduces and links in his characteristically caustic style. *The Memory Wars* (1997) is based on two hostile articles Crews wrote for the *New York Review of Books*, and includes the lively correspondence for and against psychoanalysis that these generated. *Unauthorised Freud* (1998) collects 20 authors in various degrees hostile to, and critical of, Freud and psychoanalysis.

Although these critiques are global, one central theme or preoccupation is usually more or less evident for each author. Interestingly, the primary focus of Crews's disquiet about psychoanalysis is in polar opposition to that of our third example, Masson; both are concerned about memories of severe abuse, particularly sexual abuse, uncovered during psychotherapy, but concerned in incompatible ways. Masson, a Sanskrit scholar who trained in psychoanalysis in Toronto, left the profession deeply disillusioned. His books *The Assault on Truth* (1984) and *Against Therapy* (1989) reproach Freud bitterly for, as Masson sees it, suppressing his early 'seduction hypothesis' out of cowardice and deceit. Masson feels that, as a result, many adults seriously abused as children, by parents and others, have had decades of damaging disbelief from psychotherapists who see them as fantasising the abuse. For Masson, Freud's whole intellectual achievement crumbles because of his so-called 'abandonment of the seduction theory'. Masson's books are characterised by vivid and horrific catalogues of the abuse of helpless adults and children by various 'caring' professionals.

Crews, in contrast, reproaches Freud equally bitterly for ever suggesting that his hysterical patients had been abused by their parents. Although Freud later modified this belief, Crews feels that great damage had already been done. In his view, a recent wave of feminist therapists ('recovered memory therapists') have returned to Freud's earlier, discarded hypothesis, resulting in the persecution of many innocent parents whose gullible children have had suggestively implanted by their therapists the idea that they have been abused. Psychoanalysis is squarely to blame, Crews feels, and the psychoanalytic idea that one can repress or dissociate from a traumatic episode is highly suspect. Both Crews and Masson see it as their mission to discredit psychoanalysis totally, in the one case to protect parents, in the other patients. Thus Crews: 'Since the very ineffability of psychoanalytic theory allows a user to reassemble its parts so as to rationalise any number of new or revived enthusiasms, only a thoroughgoing critique can discourage further reckless attempts to disclose the purported contents of "the repressed"' (1998: xi).

Robinson (1993) remarks on how Masson 'writes in the charged language of moral indignation, his discussion of historical questions giving way easily and often to personal judgement and ad hominem attack' (p. 103). Robinson finds Masson's picture of the cowardly Freud giving in to peer pressure highly contrived and implausible. He impartially examines the documentary evidence relating to the 'abandonment of the seduction theory', showing how this became oversimplified, misrepresented and mythologised, certainly by Masson, and even latterly by Freud himself. In fact Freud changed his views about the aetiology of hysteria gradually, and remained confident that sexual abuse of children was psychologically damaging, and occurred regularly, though not as extensively as he had at first thought. Neither was the diminishing of Freud's belief in 'seduction' a necessary condition for developing his ideas about the Oedipus complex; his ideas about childhood sexuality became increasingly complex, with the emerging discovery of the close interplay of fantasy and (sometimes traumatic) reality that psychoanalysts recognise and work with today.

Another helpful rejoinder to both Masson and Crews emerges from Joanne Stubley's (2000) thoughtful and even-handed review article which covers Crews's *Memory Wars* and Philip Mollon's (1998) scholarly work on trauma and memory. Stubley stresses the need to tolerate the complex uncertainties and ambiguities of the memory debate, avoiding the temptation of polarised views or positions of false knowledge.

Webster's main objection to psychoanalysis is less clearly stated, but a complex central agenda emerges from his dense and discursive text. In Webster's view, Freud was largely unoriginal, claiming the ideas of the writers and poets (of Webster's own discipline) as his own, then fitting them into his Procrustean theoretical bed. 'Again and again Freud strangled in false science the very "poetic" insights which he had glimpsed in imaginative literature' (1995: xiii). Although he advertised himself as a 'fearless transgressor' figure, he was really a rigidly authoritarian, self-idealising and charismatic personality. Psychoanalysis is religion through the back door in a secular age, and has managed to fool many intellectuals. Intellectuals, Webster says, tend to be 'conformist by nature' (p. 9), and diminish themselves by the attribution of such riches to Freud.

Webster deprecates nearly all his fellow-critics of Freud, referring to them as unable really to shake themselves free of Freud's charisma. He refers to Masson for example as ambivalent for having a 'pre-lapsarian' view of Freud, and to Grünbaum as ambivalent for attempting to take psychoanalysis seriously at all. Webster implies that he himself is one of the very few real 'fearless transgressors' around, at times becoming grandiose in his claims, according to one thoughtful reviewer of Webster's book (Crockatt, 1997). Crockatt also points out a repeated and misleadingly out-of-context use of a particular primary source by Webster, to support his unusual idea that Freud had a repressive attitude to sexuality and set out to 'purify' people.

In what he calls a 'critical biography' section Webster also advances an unusual view of Freud's childhood (which has not emerged in previous biographical studies) to explain his behaviour, suggesting that he was a 'conditionally loved' child, with damaging expectations from his parents which left him with a deep sense of insecurity. Webster then catalogues chronologically many episodes of Freud's life which he feels illustrate his ensuingly flawed personality, from his interest in Charcot's ideas about hysteria (in Webster's view a spurious diagnostic category), through his championing of cocaine and his 'infatuation' with Fliess to his allegedly bullying attitude to his patients, and his analysis of his own daughter. This is presented in a relentlessly negative way which lacks the scholarly biographer's usual attempt to discuss and understand in context.

An oft repeated theme emerges then, in Webster's text, of a crass and corrupt authority figure who has annexed the riches of others and enslaved many good and well-meaning people. At various points Webster talks approvingly of certain 'rebellious' followers of

Freud (for example Fromm, Horney, Erikson, Kohut) who partially escaped the master's hegemony and made important and original contributions. From Webster's impassioned tone and polemical stance, one cannot help but wonder what personal significance this theme has for him. Webster freely uses psychoanalytic concepts such as unconscious motivation, projection, idealisation, denial and ambivalence in his critique, forestalling objection by his assertion that such concepts have always belonged to literature. Despite his protestations, Webster's uneasy oscillation between attacking these ideas and claiming them for his own discipline suggests complex and ambivalent feelings.

These 'global critiques' are especially notable for their colourful and iconoclastic tone. Thus Crews: 'Did Freud plumb the depths of the psyche....Or did he just clog *our conception* of the psyche with a maze of misaligned plumbing, leaving the effluent of his own strange imagination to circulate through our medical and cultural lore?' (1998: xxii) and '...our great detective of the unconscious was incompetent from the outset – no more astute really than Peter Sellers' bumbling Inspector Clouseau' (1998: x), 'the endlessly devious and self dramatising Freud', and finally, 'As for Freud's Promethean self analysis, which we will be slighting below, it was nothing more than a sequence of contradictory dreams and hallucinations that he entertained and overinterpreted with cocaine-enhanced feverishness' (1998: 7). An example from Webster: 'Freud made no substantial intellectual discoveries. He was the creator of a complex pseudo-science which should be recognised as one of the great follies of Western civilisation' (1995: 438). Crews's 'effluent' motif appears too in the work of Ernest Gellner, another 'global' critic, who contributes a chapter to Crews's (1998) book. Gellner fears that an invitation to free association is an invitation to 'let go the sphincters of the mind' and is like 'undressing on a day on which one is wearing badly soiled underwear'. Such statements may reveal an essential psychic truth in Freudian ideas about unconscious bodily phantasy more simply and clearly than might be achieved through laborious intellectual debate.

It emerges from these global critiques that their authors explicitly or implicitly accept many basic psychoanalytic concepts, indeed use them liberally in their attacks. Crews refers to the idea of unconscious mental functioning as 'uncontroversial' (1998: xxiii), and agrees that 'one cannot easily dismiss the proposal that "defence mechanisms" such as projection, identification and denial affect mental productions'. Webster, damning Freud with faint praise, acknowledges that 'his work is shot through, in a somewhat random manner, with real insights into human nature.' (1995: 12). Masson also, as a former psychoanalyst, has no problem with many of the ideas themselves.

However, what all three authors also share is a profound worry that psychoanalysts cannot be trusted with the mind. There is great concern about the power of the analyst over the helpless patient, in particular the danger of analytic suggestion amounting to brainwashing. Analytic treatment, Crews suggests, is a form of recruitment and control. The patient is made dependent, her critical judgement disarmed, and she is finally admitted into an elite community, full by now of passionate certitude about psychoanalysis. Crews wonders how psychoanalysts can know 'whether a given expression should be taken literally, or regarded as a compromise formation shaped by this or that unconscious defence against a wish or fantasy' (1998: xxv). This seems to speak of a despair that one human being can ever intuitively understand another. In Crews's view the concept of over-determination is particularly dangerous, giving the psychoanalytic interpreter even more arbitrary licence to grind the patient's material into his own sausage machine, 'playing a riff on a haphazardly chosen tune' (ibid.: xxv). Free association is a 'wild card' which the analyst can play in whichever way suits his theories.

Psychoanalysts can recognise these as concerns voiced by many patients before coming into analysis. They are after all being asked to enter a relationship by its very nature highly asymmetrical in terms of power and responsibility. Having experienced the ineffectual deadness of inaccurate or imprecise interpretations, however, analysts and patients are mostly reassured that suggestion poses more of a theoretical than a real danger. From the extent of the fears voiced in these critiques, one might wonder whether there can be any benign, workable human relationship when power and knowledge are asymmetrical. Such pessimism would preclude many professional relationships such as nursing and medicine and many non-professional ones, not least the fundamental relationship between parent and child. Hinshelwood (1997) has tackled this theme at length, showing how psychoanalysis seeks to alter the very 'inequality' it appears at first to foster; the patient ultimately achieves a new independence as he or she reclaims disowned and misattributed parts of the self.

If the psychoanalytic research and treatment method is so flawed, what should be put in its place? Crews implies that we are better off with nothing. A hope emerges in Webster's later chapters that some form of social and psychological Darwinism will eventually liberate all thinking human beings, replacing the need for such neo-religious observances as psychoanalysis. For Masson, 'the very *idea* of psychotherapy is wrong' (1989: 24). Formal psychotherapy by its very nature leads to abuse and exploitation, and the best hope is for leaderless self-help groups of fellow-sufferers. 'What we need are more kindly friends and fewer professionals' (ibid.: 30). This demonstrates an odd mixture of despair (that all 'unequal' human relationships are doomed) and idealistic naivety (that sufferers are 'good' and will not misunderstand, abuse or exploit each other). Most importantly perhaps, it means we forget the conceptions of the unconscious, transference and resistance, and will be doomed to discover them all over again.

Conclusion

All psychotherapists, including psychoanalysts, must engage with their critics in a respectful way, and be prepared to learn from them, as Feltham (1999) points out. However, there seems something unusual about the opprobrium generated by Freud and psycho-analysis that is worth trying to understand as a phenomenon. Why has psychoanalysis suffered such a fall from grace in the closing decades of the twentieth century? There is always the insult Freud represents to familiar and deeply held beliefs about ourselves, but it is clearly out of order for psychoanalysts smugly to blame all criti-cism on 'resistance'. One important factor is generally agreed to be a backlash from the earlier idealisation of Freud. Once the hero Freud was discovered to be flawed, for example a man of his time in sometimes seeming misogynistic and authoritarian, detractors could move in for the kill.

Psychoanalysis has betrayed us by not proving to be the panacea some over-enthusiastic early followers (but never Freud himself) hoped for and trumpeted. Linked to this, the recent advances in brain science and mood-altering drugs have led to hopes for a new panacea for human happiness; some feel it is only current limita-tions in brain technology that stand in the way, and there is no longer any need to bother with the mind.

At a deeper level, Robinson postulates that the spectacularly hostile attitude towards psychoanalysis in the 1980s represents a revolt against the modernist view of the mind espoused by Freud, and a return to positivist certainty. Robinson notices a 'curious resonance' between the 'conservative feel' of much opposition to Freud and the politics of the 1980s. Lear feels similarly that we are in a culture 'which wishes to ignore the complexity, depth and darkness of human life' (1998: 27). The enthusiastic way cognitive-behaviour therapy has been embraced in recent decades, to the detriment of psychoanalytic approaches, perhaps bears witness to this same cultural trend.

6

PSYCHOANALYSIS AND RESEARCH

To research means to investigate systematically and critically, in order to establish facts or reach new conclusions. The psychoanalytic *method* is itself a research tool for investigating the mind. Research using this tool is the main source of psychoanalytic *theory*. The psychoanalytic method is also a *treatment* and the most significant findings are made from inside psychoanalysis, using its own methodology. However, for a full picture it is also necessary to look at the psychoanalytic method and the theories it generates from an external position. Related disciplines (for example ethology, cognitive psychology, developmental psychology, neurobiology and genetics) can be useful as part of this. It is also important to examine psychoanalysis empirically as a treatment. Such research may concern both **outcome** and **process**. That is, it is necessary to find out whether psychoanalysis as a treatment works, and if so, the detail of how and why it works.

This chapter will first describe psychoanalysis as research in itself. It will then discuss some empirical tools psychoanalysts can use to research their own theory and practice. It will go on to look at interdisciplinary studies, involving neighbouring fields. Finally the question of the feasibility of researching the outcomes of psychoanalytic treatment will be addressed, looking at the challenges of applying standard outcome research methodology to a long-term and complex method of treatment.

Psychoanalysis as clinical research

By the very nature of the psychoanalytic method, the analyst's clinical observation, for example that an insight brings a particular patient relief, constitutes research into the unconscious. The patient's inner world is investigated using the trained mind of the analyst, within a setting carefully controlled to reduce external 'noise'. The analyst's understanding remains provisional, ready to be altered or deepened. Interpretations are hypotheses, to be tested against the patient's immediate responses and what later emerges in the analysis. As participant observer, the analyst tries to be objective about her own reactions to the patient, and to maintain an observing mental position while taking part in the relationship. Theory needs to be a framework for thinking, and should not influence observation in a distorting way.

These are of course ideal expectations. Psychoanalysts are human, and have prejudices and blind spots in spite of their best efforts to tackle these in personal analysis and supervision. This means that the research tool that is the analyst's mind is inevitably imperfect. However, the process of improving it, if you like 'calibrating' and 'validating' it, is something that a good psychoanalyst continues to try to do.

The analyst is in a position to observe many things the patient cannot see. The analyst in turn though will be blind to certain aspects of the relationship, and will intermittently need the help of a further layer of observation. This is where a supervisor or peer discussion group comes in. For this, the analyst will make from memory, in as much detail as possible, a **process recording** of what went on, verbally and non-verbally, to present to the other clinicians.

Clinical research may also be conducted through groups of colleagues meeting regularly to discuss particular sorts of patients whom they are treating, in order to develop aspects of theory and/or technique. Thus findings about a single patient may be found to generalise to others. In undertaking such study, it is of course necessary to read the psychoanalytic literature and that of relevant fields. Any psychoanalyst or group of analysts needs to be aware of competing psychoanalytic theories and conceptualisations, and should not be wedded immovably to familiar ways of understanding.

A psychoanalyst, like a surgeon or a musician, practises an evolving craft, which is passed on through successive generations. The published literature which clinicians find most useful on a day to day basis is therefore of a 'craft' type that deals with technique, and with the detailed understanding of particular psychological problems. A useful aid to learning and research of this sort recently has been the publication of a large cross-referenced psychoanalytic data base, the Psychoanalytic Electronic Publishing (PEP) CD-Rom (2001).

There are some problems with 'craft' literature, however. Fonagy et al. (1999) point out that clinical theory-building is usually inductive rather than deductive. The strategy of clinicians is to find patterns in their work which they can explain using existing theoretical constructs. As a result, pieces of psychoanalytic theory accumulate, with ideas overlapping rather than replacing each other. Psychoanalysis thus becomes full of partially incompatible formulations.

Although we need to some extent to tolerate ambiguity and fuzzy-edged theory, there is now a need for psychoanalysts to operationalise its concepts more clearly.

Conceptual research

Psychoanalytic concepts evolve out of clinical findings, hypothesised general principles grouped together from the study of a series of cases. Theory consists of a group of concepts. The evolution of a theory, and its conceptual parts, usually requires the development of a specialist vocabulary. One of the difficulties with psychoanalytic concepts, as the discipline developed, has been that the meaning of a concept may change while the vocabulary remains the same. As theory evolves there may also be disagreement between psychoanalysts as to the precise meaning of a given concept and sometimes, unless care is taken with explicit definition, the fact that there is a difference in how something is understood may not be readily apparent. Conceptual research in psychoanalysis addresses the development of theory by giving systematic detailed attention to concepts, their definition and the clinical evidence from which the theory is built. To challenge individual bias such conceptual work is often undertaken by a group of colleagues working together.

The Hampstead Index Project, started by Anna Freud and Dorothy Burlingham at the Hampstead Child Therapy Clinic, is an important example of such a conceptual work group. Each clinician was asked to index all the weekly notes of completed cases under conceptual categories, such as defence mechanism, superego or object relationships. This produced, on each case, a series of index cards each of which contained a concept and then a clinical example from the case which was thought to illustrate the concept. Manuals were written, giving definitions with which to assist the indexing. It was soon found that it was not easy to agree on the definitions or on how a given piece of clinical material should be understood conceptually. This led to a series of research groups who studied and refined a variety of concepts in relation to the clinical evidence that was available from the cases. Out of this work, the director of the project, Joseph Sandler, and his colleagues, produced a large number of important publications which made significant advances in psychoanalytic theory (see Sandler, 1987).

In working with a group of colleagues in this way, Sandler (1983) realised that psychoanalysts may sometimes hold mutually incompatible theories or part theories, often without being aware of this fact. Sandler suggested that, far from being undesirable, such implicit and elastic theories could often guide the analyst's clinical work in useful ways and that assisting an analyst to become more aware of the theoretical beliefs, through the use of probing and challenging group discussion, could result in clinical and conceptual developments. These ideas were used, for example, in the methodology of a conceptual project on trauma at the Sigmund Freud Institute in Frankfurt where Sandler was a visiting professor (Sandler et al., 1991).

Extra-clinical validation of psychoanalytic concepts

Some psychoanalysts believe it is impossible to conduct empirical research into psychoanalytic constructs outside the consulting room without trivialising or oversimplifying them (e.g. Green, 2000). From certain academics outside the field (e.g. Grünbaum: see Chapter 8), the corollary of this has been a suspicion that psychoanalytic concepts are untestable and have little truth value. Can psychoanalytic concepts and clinical phenomena be measured and evaluated outside the consulting room, in a replicable way? Can we, for example, design rating scales of psychic functioning which will be sophisticated enough to satisfy psychoanalysts, but robust enough to be used by independent raters?

In recent years, several psychoanalytic researchers have been tackling these problems. Hobson et al. (1998) working at the Maudsley Hospital, London, developed the 30-item **personal relatedness profile**, a scale designed to capture the complex ways of relating to others that are of relevance to psychoanalysts. In one test of this scale, the researchers used as their experimental material videotaped psychodynamic assessment interviews with two groups of patients. Using the standard American psychiatric classification of that time, *DSM III*, one group had been diagnosed as having the serious condition **borderline personality disorder (BPD)**, a condition characterised by extreme mood swings, self-harming behaviour, poor sense of self and disturbed ways of relating to others The other group contained less disturbed patients, diagnosed as having **dysthymia**, a mild form of depression. The researchers asked psychoanalytic psychotherapist raters, 'blind' as to diagnosis, to watch the video clips and assess interpersonal relatedness as shown in both the narrative and the way the patients were observed to relate in the interview.

One hypothesis, which was confirmed, was that it would be possible to differentiate in a replicable way between the two groups on the basis of the ratings. Further, these ratings fell into two distinct groups, distinguished on the basis of the theoretical division between Klein's paranoid schizoid position and depressive position states of mind/ways of relating (see Chapter 2). The borderline patients were rated high on the former and low on the latter, whereas the reverse was true for the dysthymic patients. Examples of the paranoid schizoid ratings were 'omnipotent, feeling no need of others', 'intense, univalent black-or-white exchanges, perhaps wonderful or awful'. Examples of depressive position ratings were 'a capacity for ambivalence, in which participants grapple with the complexities of relationships' and 'genuine, appropriate concern between participants'. Thus it was shown that a particular psychoanalytic frame of reference meshed meaningfully with a psychiatric frame of reference, where both had been developed in very different contexts, and from the different poles of subjective and objective description.

A similar kind of work, but on a more comprehensive scale, has been carried out at the University of Denver, Colorado, by a team led by Jonathan Shedler and Drew Westen, who have developed an instrument known as the Shedler-Westen Assessment Procedure (SWAP-200), discussed in Shedler (2002). The SWAP, like the personal relatedness profile, is able to capture the richness and complexity of psychoanalytic constructs about character and pathology, while providing reliable data for research. It contains 200 theoretical descriptive statements about the patient, informed by various psychoanalytic theories but free of the associated technical jargon. The items were refined over many years until clinicians testing them could affirm that they captured everything that they considered psychologically important about their patients. The rater must judge each of the 200 statements as to how well it describes the patient being rated. A clinician who knows the patient well will be able to order the statements into eight categories, according to how well or badly they fit.

The instrument is based on the Q-sort method, which has considerable psychometric advantage, as it asks the rater to rank, rather than give scores. Developing and using the SWAP proves in itself a worthwhile exercise, as it encourages psychoanalysts to become more precise in their observations. Its uses are many, including the assessment of the inter-rater reliability of psychoanalytic clinical judgements. If psychoanalytic diagnosis is to have any meaning, one would expect experienced clinicians to describe and diagnose the same patient in the same way, just as one would expect experienced radiologists to agree about the interpretation of an X-ray. Shedler and Westen (1998) have shown that, indeed, psychoanalysts using the SWAP produce very high inter-rater reliability coefficients, higher than those typically reported using standard psychiatric diagnostic instruments. This has demonstrated that the hitherto widely held view amongst researchers, that psychoanalytic constructs cannot be assessed reliably, is mistaken.

The SWAP can also be used as a suitably sophisticated instrument to measure change in psychoanalytic outcome research (see p. 114). It can give a uniquely tailored description of a patient (mathematicians should note that the possible number of orderings of the 200 SWAP items is 200 factorial!) and at the same time enable more precise and complex categorisation of personality disorders, which could inform future versions of the standard American psychiatric classification section of the *Diagnostic and Statistical Manual* (*DSM*) (APA, 1994).

The interdisciplinary approach

An intriguing 'fault line' (Whittle, 2001) has traditionally run between on the one hand sciences of the mind like neurobiology, experimental psychology, cognitive neuroscience and developmental psychology, and on the other hand psychoanalysis, which studies subjectivity objectively. Where psychoanalysis is concerned with feelings, ideas and the understanding of mental contents, the approach on the other side of the fault line is concerned with the machinery, so to speak, that gives rise to feelings and ideas. There have tended to be two cultures in the study of mind, which are, as Fonagy (2000) puts it, 'not so much opposed to one another but, rather like neighbours in a large apartment building, quite happy to walk past each other for years without even learning each others' names'.

Perspectives on mother and infant: ethology and developmental psychology

One way of testing aspects of psychoanalytic developmental theory is by placing them alongside the discoveries of experimental parent–infant research. Early psychoanalytic theories saw infants as having rudimentary minds, turned in upon themselves and dedicated mainly to seeking pleasurable sensation. The external world was engaged with gradually, and only through reluctant necessity. The findings of modern developmental psychology show that infants are equipped from the start with remarkably rich perceptual, learning and representational capacities, and that they seek intense and specific relationships to others (see e.g. Stern, 1985; Gergely, 1992). Such findings are much more in tune with modern psychoanalytic **object relations theories**, which were developed independently through psychoanalytic research, and are now in one form or another almost universally accepted by the psychoanalytic community. Parent–infant research is giving us increasing experimental evidence to support psychoanalytic discoveries about the significance of the parent–child relationship and the way disturbance is passed across generations. Some of this comes from the field of **attachment theory**, which owes much to the study of ethology and originates in the work of John Bowlby. In a key experiment, the Strange Situation, designed by Mary Ainsworth, a one-year-old is observed with mother (or sometimes father) over a short period in which the parent and a stranger come in and out of the experimental room in a set pattern. The child's responses to separations from and reunions with the parent, and to the encounter with the stranger, are monitored and found to fall into one of four broad categories of attachment behaviour. These are called 'secure', 'avoidant', 'ambivalent' and 'disorganised'.

This early pattern is found to predict many aspects of later psychological, social and cognitive adaptation. Psychoanalysis would say that this is mediated through the internal representations of significant others, or the internal object relationships. The key issue is whether the child can successfully rely on the mother to help alleviate his distress. Where the child instead has to rely on defensive strategies for dealing with distress, he is likely to appear either superficially undistressed (avoidant) or else inconsolable upon reunion with mother.

The move from measurement of behaviour in the Strange Situation to measurement of the related subjective experience was later pioneered by Mary Main's research group. They devised the Adult Attachment Interview (AAI) in which individuals are asked to describe and evaluate early relationships and experiences. Transcripts are coded by trained raters on the basis not of historical content, but of the manner of discourse as the person remembers and reflects on her past. They fall into four categories of 'states of mind with regard to attachment' (secure/autonomous, dismissing/detached, preoccupied/entangled and unresolved/disorganised).

Fonagy et al. (1993) administered the AAI to a group of parents some months before the birth of their first child, and found that the parent's own attachment category predicted the later attachment pattern of their infant in the Strange Situation. This demonstrates that particular patterns of insecurity and defensive strategy can be transmitted from parent to child. The ability to reflect, on one's own mind or that of another (a capacity for which Fonagy and Target, 1996, coined the term 'reflective self function'), is vital both for self-management when dealing with strong emotion and for raising children. To reflect on an infant's mental state, adapting to and interpreting his perspective, the mother or main carer needs the capacity to have a 'theory of mind' about the child and about herself. Re-examining the transcripts of adult attachment interviews, Fonagy's team found that they could be coded as to the capacity for 'reflective self function'. A good capacity for reflection is strongly associated with secure attachment both in the parent him- or herself and, subsequently, in the child.

This finding from attachment research links with two pieces of psychoanalytic clinical research, showing us the important complementarity of these perspectives. First comes some purely psychoanalytic research from Peter Fonagy, who is unusual in working both as an experimental psychologist and a psychoanalyst. With his psychoanalytic hat on, Fonagy (1991) has studied patients with borderline personality disorder (BPD: see also p. 102 above). Fonagy's patients had been severely neglected or abused by their parents as children. He found that their 'theory of mind' function was impaired, and suggested that they defensively inhibited their knowledge of others' minds in order 'not to know' that the parents had cruel and hostile feelings and impulses towards them.

Britton (1989) has shown a link between this lack of reflective and self-reflective capacity, and a deficient internal concept or working model of collaborating parental couple who can hold the child in mind. Unable to conceive of themselves as part of a benign triangle, these patients seem to lack an internal 'triangular space', which can make analytic work difficult and stormy. The ability to reflect on either self or another from a 'third position' is seriously impaired; there seems to be a fundamental deficit in the thinking process itself. The work of Fonagy, Britton and the attachment theorists can thus be seen to unite internal and external perspectives, and bring together psychoanalytic and experimental psychology research paradigms.

In psychoanalytic terms, such disturbed individuals are often said to have lacked sufficient maternal **containment**; they have been unable as infants and children to convey their distressed states to the mother and have the mother respond by giving both comfort and meaning. It is likely that these patients have often been subject to disturbed projections from the mother. Bion (1967) and Winnicott (1960) among others have intuited from psychoanalytic work that this sort of emotional engagement and response is needed by the parent for a baby to form a properly functioning mind at all, and to be able to give meaning to, and regulate his or her own mental states. These insights have more recently been underpinned experimentally by the findings of Gergely and Watson (1996) who, from the developmental psychology perspective, have considered in detail how the containment process might work, linking their model to what we know about the mechanism of biofeedback.

Perspectives from neurobiology

In recent years some links have been forged between the worlds of developmental psychoanalysis and neurobiology. In 2000 a new journal, *Neuro-Psychoanalysis* was founded by Mark Solms, a leader in this field. Kaplan-Solms and Solms (2000) have made a number of psychoanalytic investigations of patients suffering from emotional disturbances following localised brain damage caused by strokes or tumours. They show how the neurological and psychological domains represent different aspects of reality which complement each other, rather than one being reducible to the other. To try to reduce a mental function to its physiological correlates is like reducing a poem to the letters of the alphabet which constitute it (Solms, 1995).

Allan Schore (1994) has brought together the fields of neurobiology, developmental neurochemistry, evolutionary biology, developmental psychology and developmental psychoanalysis. Schore integrates research findings to show how the emotional responsiveness of an ordinarily good mother through critical periods over the first two years of her child's life actually determines the 'hard wiring' of the brain. As the mother tunes in and responds to the baby's distress, excitement, joy and anger, in repeated, intimate, face to face and bodily encounters, hormones and neurotransmitters are released in the baby's brain which gradually help to mould vital nerve pathways, concerned with the regulation of emotion, and running to and from the right orbitofrontal cortex of the brain. Schore shows how the longstanding psychoanalytic intuition – that the infant first depends on the mother to deal with overwhelming feelings, then internalises this function for him- or herself – actually works, in chemical and anatomical terms.

Schore also shows how problems in the mother–infant relationship, leading to the different sorts of insecure attachment referred to above, are mediated neurochemically and anatomically. Let us take two (simplified and schematic) examples: A depressed mother who does not respond with vitality to her 10-month-old's joyful communications (linking up with Kohut's and Winnicott's psychoanalytic ideas about 'affective mirroring') will inhibit the production of endorphins and dopamine in her infant's brain, and trigger increased production of the stress hormone cortisol. There will be a loss of cells and connections in the arousing pathways into the orbitofrontal cortex, which will thus be out of balance with the reciprocal inhibitory pathways. The mother's depression will in a sense become built in to her infant's brain.

Another example comes from the first half of a baby's second year of life, when in the normal course of events the mother finds that she has moved from frequently reflecting and enhancing her one-year-old baby's excitement and joy, to now just as frequently restricting her active toddler's potentially dangerous and disruptive explorations. The 'shaming' effect of meeting a disapproving, forbidding face, Schore shows, helps to form necessary parasympathetic inhibitory pathways in the right cortex concerned with the damping down of emotional expression. (In psychoanalytic terms we might think that this had a bearing on the formation of the superego.) It is then vital for the mother to repair this shaming effect in a consoling way, reuniting emotionally with her thwarted, angry infant. If this does not happen enough, the child has an unmitigated negative experience from mother, leading again to imbalance in brain chemistry and anatomy. A child in this situation turns away from the mother, and often does not form the capacity to self-regulate anger properly. A psychoanalyst might wonder if this is because the internal representation of the mother becomes a contemptuous, shaming one, that will negatively affect the child's later relationships.

Schore brings together research that shows how the mother–infant relationship determines brain structure, possibly through influencing the way genes are expressed. Although early experiences are importantly formative, human beings retain some plasticity and have the ability to change through intimate relationships in later life. Kandel (1998) has recently argued that psychotherapy may itself be able to achieve neuroanatomical changes in the brain through altering gene expression.

Research on therapeutic outcome

The validity of psychoanalytic **theory of mind** does not stand or fall according to whether psychoanalytic treatment is effective. Research on therapeutic efficacy is thus in a different domain from the research discussed so far. Whereas the impetus for process research arises within the profession, outcome research tends to be stimulated by sources external to psychoanalysis, such as public health funding bodies and private insurance companies, which increasingly demand 'evidence-based medicine' (EBM). Unfortunately demands for EBM may sometimes be motivated as much by the need to ration and cut costs as by the wish to give patients the best treatment.

In 1952 Hans Eysenck reviewed a number of psychotherapy research projects, and concluded that the effectiveness of treatment was no greater than would have been achieved through spontaneous remission. Subsequent research has repeatedly refuted this claim, and re-examination of Eysenck's own data (McNeilly and Howard, 1991) has shown his conclusions to be fundamentally flawed; his own data properly re-analysed reveal statistically and clinically significant efficacy for the brief therapies involved. However, mud sticks and so the Eysenck paper ultimately proved to be a useful spur to systematic psychotherapy research.

The randomised controlled trial (RCT)

There are a number of technical problems for psychoanalytic outcome research, that is research into whether patients are better after treatment. The problems for which help was sought must be clearly identified and ways found for their measurement. Measurement must take place both before and after treatment, preferably with long term follow-up to make sure that changes are not temporary. It also has to be ascertained that it is this specific treatment which has caused the improvement rather than the passage of time, or the non-specific effects of being given attention. For example, we might decide to start by comparing a group of people with psychological problems who have had psychoanalysis, with another group with similar problems who have had no treatment, or have had behaviour therapy or drug treatment. However, since differing people choose differing treatments, how can we be sure meaningful comparisons can be made? Treatment lengths may also be very different, so factors other than the specificity of the treatments are likely to be at work.

These difficulties can be countered by a variety of experimental manoeuvres. To be entirely sure we are comparing like with like, we must randomise patients to **treatment groups** and to control groups. The randomised controlled trial or RCT is currently considered in the scientific community to be the 'gold standard' outcome research tool. This is the typical way that a new drug is tested, in comparison with an old drug or a placebo, an inert substance disguised to look like the drug. In an RCT, half of a consenting group of patients will be allocated entirely at random to treatment A and half to treatment B or to no treatment. All will then be followed up to see how many in each group improve. To discover whether the result is statistically significant, rather than due to chance, a sufficiently large number of patients is needed. The smaller the difference detected between the groups, the more patients are needed to show that the difference is significant.

It is hard to achieve these conditions in psychotherapy research. With such a complex interpersonal treatment, many interpersonal variables may prove important. Is the mix of the two groups similar, for example in terms of variables such as age, sex, type and severity of problem, degree of social support, work status, socioeconomic category? The more variables involved, the larger the number of patients needs to be, to achieve statistically meaningful results. Alternatively, a very narrowly defined group of sufferers has to be selected. For example, middle-aged, working professional men with moderate depression were used in one group of studies of brief psychotherapy (Shapiro and Firth, 1987), but with this degree of selection we would not expect the findings to apply to the community as a whole. And what about taking therapist variables into account? Should one take length of therapist training and experience into account, even perhaps therapist personality factors?

The other major problem with the RCT approach is the necessity of randomisation. With psychoanalysis in particular, we are talking about a penetrating and disturbing treatment requiring collaboration. Some patients welcome this as a relief, others prefer a less intrusive, more educational approach like behaviour therapy. Is it realistic or ethical to allocate people to treatments that are not wanted, or indeed to use no-treatment controls? What conclusions will we really be able to draw for everyday clinical practice?

It is easy to specify drugs to be given, but in psychotherapy research we have to know that therapists in the trial are actually giving the treatments under test. How can one be specific about the exact nature of the treatment that is being given? If a psychotherapy is being tested in a research trial then it must be described in specific detail and the description written down in a manual. It is difficult to manualise a treatment as complex as psychoanalysis without doing violence to it, although some attempts have been made. Further, to ensure that the therapy complies with the manual, audio or video-recordings of sessions are needed. This intrusion into the therapeutic space risks altering what is being measured.

From all these considerations, one can see that it is not too difficult to design an RCT for a very narrow range of patients, with carefully manualised, probably very brief treatments. The trial might show improved efficacy under the conditions of the trial for treatment A as compared with treatment B, but we may be little further forward in assessing the clinical effectiveness of such treatments as they are applied out in the ordinary community. A research design that lends itself well to comparing drug A with drug B may really be stretched beyond its limit when applied to a complex interpersonal process involving such innumerable variables.

Clearly it is going to be very much easier to investigate short term treatments than psychoanalysis itself. In fact a methodologically sound RCT of full psychoanalysis may be impossible in practice. Realistically, we may have to accumulate evidence in ways that have less statistical power, from more naturalistic sorts of research. For example patients suffering from personality disorders which commonly cause long term symptoms and distress, and which are known to respond poorly on the whole to traditional psychiatric care, can be studied before and after a therapeutic intervention, in a sense acting as their 'own controls'. Or a typical inner-city clinic population who receive, say, medium term psychoanalytic psychotherapy can be compared with a broadly similar group elsewhere who are treated with cognitive-behavioural methods simply because the staff are differently trained.

Such studies will involve by definition **comparison groups** rather than strict control groups, and evidence obtained from them has to be regarded as less powerful, more 'circumstantial' if you like, as seen within this research paradigm. However, these, taken together with various sorts of systematised clinical experience and more process-oriented research, will give us strongly suggestive results. We can also gain some useful information about psychoanalytic outcome proper from looking at the results of research trials that are easier to carry out, with short and medium term psychoanalytic psychotherapy.

The outcome of brief psychoanalytic psychotherapy

Very brief psychotherapy, usually around a maximum of 16 sessions, is far easier to study than medium or long term treatments. Control groups and randomisation are easier both ethically and logistically. The problem is that after brief analytic treatment, psychoanalysts would not usually expect more than some symptomatic change. Vital aspects of analytic work are the slow attrition of distorted relationship patterns by repetitive **working through** in the transference relationship with the therapist, and the gradual healing and integrating effect of repeated containment by another mind. Both, like development itself, are time-consuming processes, and are expected to have enduring effects on fundamental structures in the mind.

A treatment such as **cognitive-behaviour therapy (CBT)**, which is compared with analytic therapy in Chapter 8, aims for rapid alleviation of symptoms through the patient identifying faulty thought patterns and learning new ones. Most studies of the effectiveness of CBT measure outcomes in modest ways by symptom scores and simple rating scales. The effectiveness of the two sorts of therapy (CBT and psychoanalytic therapy) are often compared in ways that do not take account of their differing goals and format. Because it is relatively easy to perform, the vast preponderance of published psychotherapy RCT data concerns very brief therapy formats more appropriate for, and typical of, CBT than psychoanalytic therapy. CBT has shown modest though significant efficacy particularly in terms of symptom relief, and on short term follow-up, in both neurotic and psychotic disorder. However, reviewers such as Enright (1999) note that its clinical effectiveness with standard inner-city outpatient populations is yet to be clearly shown. Long term follow-up is rare.

There are now many good published trials of brief psychoanalytic psychotherapy. The relative dearth of them in comparison with RCTs of CBT is sometimes falsely equated with 'evidence against' (Parry and Richardson, 1996) but in fact the research that has been done comes up with strikingly similar results to that of brief cognitive-behavioural work. So-called meta-analytic reviews have been carried out of brief psychoanalytic psychotherapy/CBT comparisons. Meta-analysis is a statistical term which means comparison of results across large numbers of trials. Such comparisons show no significant difference in efficacy between the two brief approaches, in the treatment of a wide range of psychological disturbances. Both approaches are superior to control conditions, with modest but clinically significant effect sizes (Luborsky et al., 1999). It seems that for brief work, the theoretical stance of the therapist is of less importance than the fact that a concerned, skilled professional is listening and helping the patient to make sense of things. This is what many psychoanalysts might have predicted.

The outcome of medium term psychoanalytic psychotherapy

Clinical trials of medium term psychoanalytic psychotherapy, as more typically practised in public sector settings in the UK, with diverse, often severely disturbed patients who have responded poorly to other psychiatric interventions, pose all the methodological problems discussed above. In small NHS departments, run on a shoestring, manpower and funding are in any case rarely available for elaborate research. Naturalistic studies may then have to make up in external validity what they forfeit in statistical power. However, in spite of the methodological difficulties, promising, good-quality RCTs have appeared recently.

To take a few examples, the value of day hospital-based psycho-analytic therapy for severe personality disorder has been shown to compare favourably with routine psychiatric treatment in terms of depression ratings, self-harm and days spent in hospital (Bateman and Fonagy, 1999). In alcohol-dependent patients, abstinence at 15 months is greater in those receiving psychodynamic group therapy compared with CBT (Sandahl et al., 1998). High psychiatric service-utilisers receiving brief psychodynamic psychotherapy improve on measures of symptomatology, social functioning and health utilisa-tion when compared to those who receive the usual outpatient treat-ment (Guthrie et al., 1999).

The London depression intervention study compared three approaches to chronic and complex depression: systemic/dynamic couple therapy, antidepressant medication and cognitive-behaviour therapy. Those receiving couple therapy improved more than the drug treatment group. The CBT arm of the trial was abandoned fol-lowing poor acceptance by patients (Leff et al., 2000).

In children, significantly improved control was obtained in brittle diabetes with a short term intensive psychoanalytic imput (Moran et al., 1991). An advantage was shown for four times weekly as com-pared with once-weekly psychoanalytic psychotherapy for disturbed 11-year-old boys who were failing academically (Heinicke and Ramsey-Klee, 1986). An important 'sleeper effect' has been shown repeatedly after psychotherapeutic treatment of children, their general psychological development post-therapy taking off on a steeper upward curve than before (for example see Kolvin, 1988).

Open, naturalistic trials may be acceptable in circumstances where a predictable chronic relapsing course means patients may provide their own longitudinal controls. Patients diagnosed as hav-ing *DSM III* borderline personality disorder monitored for medical visits, drug-taking, violence, self-harm, hospital admissions and psychiatric symptoms showed significant change in the year follow-ing a year of twice-weekly outpatient psychoanalytic psychotherapy as compared with the year pre-therapy. One third no longer fulfilled the operational definition of BPD (Stevenson and Meares, 1992). Inpatients at the Henderson Hospital therapeutic community, who had severe personality disorder, showed greater improvement than an untreated comparison group. Improvement was related to length of treatment (Dolan et al., 1997).

Outcome measures in psychotherapy research
Good studies use a comprehensive range of outcome measures from different perspectives and different domains of symptomatology and

functioning. Thus a study might measure changes in symptoms (for example 'depression scores' on a standard questionnaire), as well as quality of interpersonal relationships and capacity for work, again as measured on standard questionnaires, or change in use of services (for example GP visits, days in hospital, use of drugs, receipt of welfare payments). Finally, for a treatment which aims to alter aspects of the internal world structure, sophisticated and clinically meaningful ratings which are designed to capture something like this need to be employed. Two examples of these discussed earlier in this chapter were the personal relatedness profile and the SWAP-200.

Research on the effectiveness of psychoanalysis itself
Starting in the 1950s, a number of large studies of psychoanalytic psychotherapy and full psychoanalysis, mostly in the USA (where a much larger number of patients and more funding were available than in the UK) attempted to address many aspects of process and outcome in a global, statistical way. These studies tended to be too ambitious in their attempts to study multiple variables over large numbers of treatments. For example the Columbia Records Project (Bachrach, 1995) made a meticulous study of 1,575 adult analyses, performed mostly by trainees, between 1945 and 1971 in the Columbia University psychoanalytic clinic. The authors comment that paradoxically it is the main strength of the project (i.e. the large number of variables studied among a very large number of diverse cases) which, in retrospect, raises questions about the viability of its methodology. The employment of so-called multivariate statistical methods inevitably results in a statistical averaging of findings, a sacrifice of the individuality specific to cases, and a loss of the kinds of qualitative distinctions that are the essence of psychoanalysis.

Six systematic clinical-quantitative early studies of psychoanalysis, covering the treatment of 550 neurotic and personality-disordered patients in four centres in the USA, have also been critically reviewed by the same author and others (Bachrach et al., 1991). In spite of the huge amount of work that has gone into these studies conclusions seem only to boil down to weak general statements. These include mostly positive outcome, which is linked to treatment length and to treatments that have been completed. The value of supportive as well as interpretive elements of treatment is underlined, as is the difficulty in predicting success from initial assessment.

Looking back with a contemporary eye, we see that such projects implicitly assume a simple linear system with realistically controllable and non-interacting variables (Galatzer-Levy, 1995). The long psychoanalytic process with its myriad patient and analyst variables may resemble more a complex interactive system with feedback better described by a model such as 'deterministic chaos theory' (Moran, 1991; Spruiell, 1993). Such non-linear systems, now known to be ubiquitous in the natural world, show for example extreme sensitivity to small variations in initial conditions, complex interactive effects between multiple variables and oscillations between periodic and near-chaotic behaviour. The weather cannot be accurately predicted beyond a couple of days, although one can be almost certain that it will be warmer on average in July than in January in the UK. In a similar way, one can say now (as was concluded above) that broadly speaking 'psychoanalysis works', and that longer, completed treatments help more, but we are not very good at predicting who will respond best.

In order to say anything more interesting or specific, we have to use research models that are more focused than the blunderbuss techniques referred to above. This is where the wheel tends to come full circle, and less intimidated by scientific fashions of the 1970s and 1980s, we turn again to rigorously conducted clinical research, looking anew for example at formal single-case research methodology (Hillard, 1993; Kazdin, 1992; Moran and Fonagy, 1987). We also realise that we have to focus more modestly on the study of specific outcome and process variables.

In their 1999 review, Fonagy et al. make an extensive and critical review of 55 psychoanalytic outcome research studies, completed or in progress, with useful background epistemological and methodological discussions. These authors, although exposing considerable methodological limitations, adopt a cautiously optimistic attitude to psychoanalytic outcome given the evidence so far available. Key provisional findings include the following: (a) Intensive psychoanalytic treatment is generally more effective than psychoanalytic psychotherapy, the difference sometimes only becoming evident years after treatment has ended, and this applies particularly to the more severe disorders. (b) Longer term treatment has a better outcome, as does completed analysis. (c) There are suggestive findings that psychoanalysis and psychoanalytic psychotherapy are cost beneficial and perhaps even cost effective, and that psychoanalysis can lead to a reduction in other health care use and expenditure. (d) Psychoanalytic treatment appears to improve capacity to work, to reduce the symptoms of borderline personality disorder, and may be an effective treatment for severe psychosomatic disorders.

Three recent studies of psychoanalytic outcome
We will now present three recent good examples of naturalistic psychoanalytic outcome studies. In 1996 Fonagy and Target made

a retrospective study of 763 child analysis and psychotherapy cases treated over a 40-year period at the Anna Freud Centre in London. They made use of detailed diagnostic assessments before treatment, and the weekly reports made during treatment, to work out what factors predicted good outcome. The study showed full analysis (four or five times a week) to be particularly effective for seriously disturbed children under 12 years suffering from a variety of psychiatric disorders, especially those which involved anxiety. These more seriously disturbed children did not do so well in psychotherapy 1–3 times a week although this treatment seemed to suit adolescents better. Children with severe developmental disorders such as autism did not do well, however, even with intensive, prolonged treatment.

In 2000 Rolf Sandell et al. reported on the Stockholm outcome of psychoanalysis and psychotherapy project (STOPP), which is studying over 400 patients treated over four or five years, starting in 1993. Patients, who mostly had long histories of suffering and of psychiatric care, were allocated to intensive or non-intensive treatment, after expert assessment rather than randomisation. The two groups proved broadly comparable on important variables. Outcome was assessed comprehensively, including symptoms, social relations, general health, existential attitudes, health care utilisation and working capacity. Follow-up is not yet complete. So far it appears that both treatments have been of considerable benefit, but that generally psychoanalysis has been more effective than less intensive work in improving mental health. Reduction in health care utilisation has not yet been shown in this study, unlike the one below.

A book by Leuzinger-Bohleber and Target (2001) reports a study which Leuzinger-Bohleber and colleagues conducted. This involved 129 patients who had received psychoanalysis or psychoanalytic psychotherapy from members of the German Psychoanalytic Association. Teams of psychoanalysts assessed the work of colleagues from different regions who were strangers to them. Comprehensive outcome measures included symptoms and diagnosis, functioning in social and work spheres, health care utilisation, and specialised psychoanalytic observations of psychic functioning. The study was striking for its use of psychoanalytic methodology; for example the countertransference of members of the research group was taken into account in understanding the clinical outcome data. Outcome over a range of measures was strikingly positive in this group of patients, who had mostly been significantly psychologically disabled for many years. It was notable that patients themselves tended to rate their improvement higher than did the assessors. This study showed how treatment reduced the expensive use of other health care facilities, an important message to the German insurance companies who have been less willing in recent years to fund long term treatments.

Conclusion

Looking at psychotherapy outcome generally, we can conclude that very brief psychotherapy of any type performed by skilled practitioners is of significant though modest benefit, and that differences between cognitive and psychoanalytic modes tend not to be significant at this brief level. The increase in good quality empirical research in medium term psychoanalytic psychotherapy and psychoanalysis over the last one or two decades is beginning to provide evidence of superior clinical effectiveness in neurotic and some personality-disordered patients. There are also indications that long term complex psychotherapeutic approaches for personality-disordered patients whose condition is refractory to other treatments are effective. This has important implications for future health care planning. Although psychoanalysis itself is labour intensive it might prove cost effective if more widely applied in such groups, and this could be one useful focus for future research.

7

PSYCHOANALYSIS BEYOND THE CONSULTING ROOM

In this chapter we see how psychoanalytic enquiry can be applied to situations outside the consulting room. The chapter is divided into two sections: psychoanalytic consultation and psychoanalysis in the academy. The psychoanalytic understanding of transference and countertransference in relationships has given rise to a research and consultation model which can be applied in a practical way to any setting involving human relationships. Psychoanalysis is also an academic discipline, both in its own right, and in terms of the light it can shed in fields as diverse as sociology, philosophy and literature.

Psychoanalytic consultation

Psychoanalytic consultation is carried out both with organisations, such as business, industry and public sector institutions, and with groups of professionals such as general practitioners, nurses, social workers and teachers. The aim of consultation is to help those involved better understand either the organisation itself or what is going on in the relationship between the professional and a particular patient, client or student. A psychoanalytic consultant does not advise on how to do the work – the practitioners are the experts in their own field – but tries to provide a perspective on unconscious factors operating in the work situation.

In this section, after discussing the background to both organisational and professional consultation, we will consider three specific examples: first, general practitioners, secondly, the nursing profession (an institution) and nurses (as professionals) and finally, child care institutions and professionals who work with nursery-aged children.

Consulting to organisations

The Tavistock Institute of Human Relations (TIHR), an independent neighbour of the Tavistock Clinic, London (see Chapter 8) was founded in 1948, emerging from government concerns about low levels of productivity in post-war Britain. A number of the staff had worked previously in military projects such as officer selection during the war. The projects of the TIHR were concerned with examining unconscious group processes in the workplace, and involved the perspectives of both psychoanalysis and social science, in particular systems theory (see Mosse, 1994; Roberts, 1994). An early action-research project, which continued for eight years, was of work organisation in the newly nationalised coal mining industry (Trist et al., 1963). One important change introduced as a result of this work was 'composite working' in which all members of a team working a coal seam were multi-skilled so that each could engage in a variety of the tasks which made up the whole operation. This allowed teams to be self-regulating and to feel engaged in a common purpose, and led to a marked improvement in productivity, work satisfaction and labour relations.

As government funding became more difficult to secure, the TIHR shifted its focus from grant aided research towards consultation directly commissioned by the client organisation. For example, the Glacier Metal Company in London requested assistance with negotiating a change from piecework payment to an hourly rate (Jaques, 1951). The consultant attended the meetings of various groups – workers, management and both – over a number of months. His function was not to be part of the process in itself but to draw attention to issues in the process of which neither side was fully aware and which were leading to antagonism and stalemate. The outcome of this very successful work was not only that the new wage system was introduced, with satisfaction all round, but also, as a by-product of fully working through the wages problem and all its ramifications, a new 'shop council' was set up which would allow its members fuller involvement in setting policy in future.

In the mid-1960s the London Fire Brigade requested assistance with recruitment. A brief look at this consultation, (Menzies Lyth, 1965) which did not actually lead to change in the organisation concerned, shows something of the way a consultant works and also makes clear the missing element which would have been needed for change to occur. The two consultants spent time in fire stations across London, gaining great respect for the firemen they met. The men had an implicit belief that the authorities did not want too many recruits and, looking at the way things actually were done, the consultants found this plausible. They identified a number of complex issues concerned with working practice: for example the long periods of under-employment on some stations, despite long hours at work, seemed to lead to poor self-esteem in firemen. They came to think that there was an implicit recognition by management that the

Brigade was in fact adequately manned when some of the vacancies were unfilled and that the system then worked better although at the cost of poor morale.

The consultants made a number of recommendations, for example about the organisation of duty rosters and on call time and about selection for promotion, which could have led to much-improved morale and better retention of staff. Sadly the London Fire Brigade did not accept the findings and the authors note that this was probably because the organisation was so big and the local authority committee to whom they reported too distant from the focus of the problem and the people really involved in it. They were not able to discuss the findings with the people directly concerned with decision-making in order to help them start thinking about their meaning and about what could be done.

In 1957 TIHR, in conjunction with Leicester University, set up group relations training conferences and these continue to the present day. Sometimes known as Leicester conferences, these residential events bring together international participants from many different work settings. They are designed to be temporary learning institutions, giving participants the opportunity to learn from their own experience about group and organisation processes and their own part in these. In addition to the almost 50 Leicester conferences which have taken place since their inception, there have been numerous other group relations training events run on a similar model, of varying length, in the UK and many other countries (see Obholzer, 1994).

Consultation expertise continues to be used and developed, not only by the TIHR but also by the Tavistock Clinic and others (see Obholzer and Roberts, 1994; Menzies Lyth, 1989). Consultation has been undertaken with industry, for example a psychoanalyst was involved in the development of safety procedures for Eurotunnel. Work also continues in settings as diverse as child day care centres, hospitals, schools and residential units for troubled adolescents.

Consulting to the helping professions

The first part of a meeting between six student nurses and a psychoanalytic consultant, described below, gives a sense of the rawness and immediacy of the nurses' experience and the way it impacted on the consultant. In the consultant's words (Fabricius, 1991a: 97–108):

As the meeting started there was some lighthearted talk about Alison being tired. Apparently it had been her nineteenth birthday the previous day and she had been out celebrating. This reminded me rather forcibly of the age group of most of these nurses and the contrast between nineteenth-birthday celebrations and their daily work. After a brief pause Bridget said: 'Well I had a really awful week.' This somehow seemed not to get heard. Alison said: 'Did you paint Lisa's ceiling?' and this led to some discussion about painting their rooms in the nurses' hostel. After a while I remarked to Bridget that her comment seemed to have got lost, and everyone laughed slightly in a way that showed they knew they were avoiding the issue.

Bridget then said that yesterday they had had three deaths. One of the deaths, of a patient called Edith, was expected she thought. One patient, Mrs Brown, was very ill but was not expected to die. Bridget had come on duty and seen the curtains round Edith and thought she had probably died but then she was told that Mrs Brown had died at 6 am. The staff nurse Susan was very upset because the doctor had blamed her for bad care. Then the third patient, a lady who was unconscious after a stroke, died. It was Bridget herself who suddenly saw that she was not breathing, and she felt terribly guilty that the patient had died alone like that, and no one had even noticed at first. Bridget helped to lay this third patient out, her first time. She really wished she had not – it was awful putting the sheet over her face and moving her onto the trolley, like a lump of meat. The curtains were pulled round all the beds while each of the bodies was removed, and no one told the other patients what was happening, although they must have known. For the rest of the morning, Bridget said, she neglected her other patients and she felt particularly bad about one who needed two-hourly toileting. She was too occupied with trying to keep a brave face.

After almost no pause, Christine said: 'We had three deaths running too.' At this point I felt 'Oh no, not another three.' There seemed to be more than enough distess already for one group in one hour and I felt that more would be really intolerable. Also I noted that Christine had said this in a slightly throw-away manner, as if to say, 'Three deaths are nothing – one can cope with these things.' So I commented that maybe they were all trying to keep a brave face here and that maybe it felt the only possible course in order not to be overwhelmed. This led to some discussion of Bridget's experience, including how one might manage things better with the other patients.

During the discussion I was strongly aware of my memory of Bridget having told the group previously of her father's death from a heart attack the year before, but no one mentioned this. After a while I commented that people must be remembering her telling us this and wondering what to say. Fiona, who was always quiet, took this up, saying how awkward one felt not knowing whether to mention such things. Bridget then told us that it had made her think about her father and she had telephoned her mother to find out if he had been wrapped up like that. Her mother had said not. We were then able to relate their difficulty of mentioning Bridget's father to the difficulty of talking to the other patients about the patients who had died. They could see how for Bridget it was actually a relief that it was mentioned rather than her being left alone behind a wall of silence about what everyone was thinking and that it might be similarly helpful to give the other patients straightforward information and an opportunity to share their feelings about the deaths.

Doctors, nurses, social workers, teachers and care workers, working with children, chronically sick, old or disabled people, all work within a human relationship. Much of the work is done through the relationship itself. The teacher must control the class and elicit co-operative curiosity for learning to take place, the doctor must establish a relationship of trust for the patient to risk vulnerability and exposure, and the nurse must communicate concerned, yet boundaried, care for the patient to allow complete physical intimacy with a stranger. Psychoanalysts know from their daily study of relationships how many emotional factors, many of them unconscious, come into play and affect relationships, particularly those relationships that tend to bring out a feeling of dependency similar to that of being a child with a parent.

Through consultancy to individual professionals and to work groups of colleagues, psychoanalysts can bring their understanding of the emotions which affect those coming for help and those which affect the giver of that help. Their understanding of the transference and countertransference, as described in Chapter 1, can help illuminate and support professionals engaged in often harrowing or enraging situations with those they aim to help. Psychoanalysts also know about human development and can help professionals think about the major anxieties that the child, adolescent or adult might be facing. A teenager disrupting a class by making sexual comments about an attractive young woman teacher may well be defending himself against confusing sexual feelings of his own. Understanding both the anxiety and the defence against it (see p. 20 on defences), the teacher feels less defensive herself and can think about how to help him to settle in class.

Usually psychoanalytic consultation to helping professionals is offered in small groups. Typically in such a meeting, usually between 1 and 1½ hours, one practitioner will present their work with a client. The consultant facilitates a discussion in which the group members offer observations and hypotheses about the relationship between their colleague and the client. Often a hypothesis will stimulate the presenter to mention some further details, which either add support to the hypothesis or lead to the formulation of an alternative. Sometimes, as in the example above, there is a more general discussion to help a group who are working or learning together to process the emotional impact of the work. In order to work in this way, considerable trust is needed between all the colleagues involved and between the consultant and the other professionals. For this reason such work is done in stable groups which meet regularly over a period of months or years. The consultant works to set up a group culture where it is accepted that the aim is not to judge whether the professional's practice has been right or wrong, or to tell her how to do it better, but to explore and find meaning in the interaction between two human beings, one of whom is in a professional relationship to the other.

Although such work often involves the exploration of a professional's feelings, these are always *feelings in relation to a client*. The consultant and the group need to make a clear distinction between *consultation about work* and *therapy*. Such work aims to assist the professionals in considering their responses *in relation to their work* and *not* to offer personal therapy for the professional. The example above is perhaps somewhat untypical in that a group of very junior student nurses were being helped to process their experience but even there the central focus was on their feelings about the work and not their personal difficulties.

Consultation with general practitioners

Consultation with general practitioners was amongst the earliest work of this type and was pioneered by Michael Balint at the Tavistock Clinic in the 1950s. Balint published an account of this work in 1957 in a book that is still widely read: *The Doctor, his Patient and the Illness*. GPs often have long term relationships with patients, even beyond one generation of the family; they are the first port of call for people with a large variety of complaints.

Working with his GP colleagues, Balint realised that many of the patients they discussed were chronically unhappy, expressing this through the ailments presented to their doctor. Sometimes the GP in these cases had taken the complaints in a literal way, resulting both in a dissatisfied patient who had been fruitlessly referred to a myriad of specialists and a frustrated GP who may have come to hate the patient's continued complaints and even the patient himself. To be told there is 'nothing wrong' is of no help to such patients, since there clearly is *something* wrong, even if this is not the patient's back, head, stomach or other presented organ. Balint encouraged the GPs, using the methods described above, to open up their thinking about these patients and to find new ways to explore their distress. The method could be used not only to think about patients with purely psychological problems, or struggling with the trials of life, but also to consider the psychological responses of those with acute or chronic physical illness.

This way of working with GPs, through what has become known as Balint groups, is still practised. In addition some of the insights gained have been incorporated into general practitioner training so that all GPs these days have better awareness of the effect of psychological factors than perhaps they did in the 1950s. An example of a recent meeting of a Balint group is given below:

As the psychoanalyst consultant came into the room, the seven GP group members had already gathered and were exchanging horror stories about the size of their caseloads. These GPs worked in different practices across a small town, and met every week for an hour and a half in this well-established Balint group. The talk centred around the pressure on them to increase their list sizes; a refugee centre local to two of the GPs, for example, meant long difficult consultations, with problems getting interpreters. Surgeries always overran and lunchtime practice meetings had to be cut short, with home visits still outstanding. Patients complained about long waiting times, but what could they do? The consultant commented that everyone seemed to be feeling particularly burdened. Dr B said that it was his turn to present today, and that the patient he was going to talk about, Mrs A, was a real burden and a worry to him. She was a 68-year-old widow, and he didn't seem to be able to control her blood pressure satisfactorily. The trouble was, every tablet he gave her caused side effects. He'd tried everything, she came every week, and he felt really useless.

Dr B filled in with some more medical and a few basic family details and a prolonged and lively discussion ensued about blood pressure treatment. Everyone had helpful and sensible advice for Dr B about medication, but he still looked despondent. The consultant encouraged him to flesh out a picture for them of what a typical consultation with Mrs A was like. In doing so, he explained that the main trouble was that poor Mrs A was very sensitive to drugs. Literally everything seemed to make her feel sick or give her a horrible taste in her mouth. His colleagues gradually became impatient, and dismissive of these symptoms. Dr B shouldn't be seeing her once or twice a week in surgery like this; he should tell her to stick out the latest drug a bit longer, and not to make such a fuss.

The consultant intervened here to comment that from the reactions of the group, Mrs A seemed to be someone who elicited either lots of worry and medical activity, or an impatient dismissal. That might say something important about Mrs A. Dr B said that people were being a bit unfair. He explained that Mrs A often told him that she was sure she was wasting his time, and that she'd left it ages, feeling really awful, before bothering him. 'So she's a bit of a martyr then,' said Dr S. 'You know, it's guilt,' said Dr B, 'I realise now I'm telling you about her I feel really guilty when I see her name on the day's list. I feel it's my fault that I haven't sorted her blood pressure out yet. I should be able to, and she has a hard enough time, with her sons not bothered about her; they live miles away, and never visit.'

Dr T laughed. 'So you're a substitute son then, are you, Derek?' she said to Dr B. 'And you never know,' said Dr S, 'she's probably like Derek's mother.' There was some more laughter and Dr B smiled and raised his eyebrows, but didn't respond. Dr M suddenly said, 'Can I just check, is this the same patient you were talking about last autumn, Derek, the one you felt you had to keep visiting at home with her leg ulcers?' No, said Derek, that hadn't been her, she'd never had leg ulcers. 'Well it sounds like the same person to me.' 'You know, Derek, I think you're a bit of a soft touch,' said Dr T. 'Anyway, it's not a brilliant idea to keep changing medication for hypertension, is it? I think you should be firm and persuade her to give each one at least a month's trial. By then the initial side effects might have worn off.' Dr B responded more confidently, saying that yes, that made a lot of sense.

The consultant had noticed that Dr P, usually quite an active group member, had said nothing so far, and commented on this. Dr P said with feeling that she really understood what Dr B had been talking about. 'I do that, you know. That feeling of being guilty, and rushing to do something. It stops you thinking when you feel guilty, it stops you doing what you really know is the right thing medically.'

The group returned to Mrs A, this time in a quieter, less jokey way. With the help of the consultant they started to think about what her frequent, anxious presentations might really mean. How was she coping since her husband died three years ago, and what did Dr B remember about the husband and the relationship between them? Would Dr B help by trying to open things up more, encourage her to discuss some other worries besides the blood pressure? Should she be offered a consultation with the practice counsellor?

In this example we can see how the group worked together to make sense of the effect this patient had on this doctor, allowing the sense of filial guilt that was induced in him to be noticed. Becoming aware of this feeling did not diminish the doctor's sympathy for his patient but did allow him to hold this more separately from his judgement of what might be the best way to treat Mrs A herself as well as her blood pressure.

Consultation to nursing and nurses

A psychoanalyst working for the TIHR (see above), Isabel Menzies Lyth, introduced psychoanalytic consultation to nursing. In 1959 she was commissioned by a London teaching hospital which was seeking help in devising new methods of carrying out tasks in nursing organisation. The resulting report (Menzies Lyth, 1959) described nursing practices which were set into the structure of nursing organisation. The practices Menzies Lyth described included the allocation of work in the form of *tasks*, for example taking the temperatures of all the patients in the ward, rather than in terms of *patients*, for example looking after Mrs Smith and Mrs Jones, thus preventing individual nurses from becoming close to individual patients. The terrible phrase, 'Nurse, get a bedpan for the gall bladder in bed 12' illustrates the kind of depersonalisation that can be achieved.

Menzies Lyth noted the ways the organisational culture encouraged detachment and the denial of feelings, and the attempt to eliminate individual decision-making through the use of rules, checks and counter-checks. Menzies Lyth's hypothesis was that these strategies had evolved to protect nurses against the intolerable anxiety which would otherwise be generated as a result of the extreme physical and psychological intimacy inherent in their work. She thought the system was aiding nurses in avoiding awareness of both their patients' intense feelings and their own, to the detriment of their ability to give sensitive nursing care.

Menzies Lyth's report had a mixed reception. In a review in the *Nursing Times* (see Menzies Lyth, 1988) it was described as a 'devastating criticism of the nursing service' and repudiated. Others found the observations interesting and the paper has continued to be cited by nursing authors ever since. Yet usually the acknowledgement has not been accompanied by changes in practice. Since the paper was describing powerful institutionalised unconscious defences this is unsurprising; an article being read by a number of individuals is unlikely to lead to significant change in an institution such as the nursing profession.

However, at the level of professional practice, psychoanalysts (and psychoanalytic psychotherapists) have been involved in consultation with nurses. For example Fabricius has undertaken consultative work both with student nurses (Fabricius, 1991b) and with nurse tutors (Fabricius, 1995) and published several papers commenting on the unconscious factors involved in nursing and its organisation (Fabricius, 1991a, 1996, 1999). In the example of the nurses' group given earlier, the very junior nurses involved were mostly open and sensitive to the emotional issues. They had not yet built up such defences personally although these clearly existed in the staff culture of the ward. This pushed the juniors towards either acquiring the institutional defence or feeling almost intolerable anxiety. It is thus that institutional defences are perpetuated and thus also that many of the more sensitive potential professionals are lost from the caring professions through stress and burnout. It takes special ability, which fortunately does exist, to retain sensitivity while maintaining the capacity to function professionally. The psychoanalytic consultation was an attempt to assist with the development of ways of dealing with the distress that would allow sensitive professional practice to be maintained. Dartington (1994) and Moylan (1994) have also worked and written in this area.

Consultation to professionals who work with nursery-aged children
At the Hampstead Nurseries (see Chapter 3) the everyday work with the children was informed by the understanding of the psychoanalytic leaders (A. Freud, 1944). Subsequently, in the 1950s at the Hampstead Clinic, later known as the Anna Freud Centre, a small nursery school and several parent–toddler groups were started which ran with the assistance of a psychoanalytic consultant (A. Freud, 1975; Zaphiriou Woods, 2000). Although this nursery eventually closed in 1998 (the toddler groups continue, as do a number of nurseries in the United States which were modelled on it), in the UK the principles of offering psychoanalytic consultation to nurseries and other settings for very young children continues. With increasing evidence of the critical effects of optimal or non-optimal care on children during the first years of life (see Chapter 6), it is clear that consultation to workers, which can affect the care of a larger number of children than can individual therapeutic work, is potentially a good use of some of a child psychoanalyst's time.

An example of organisational work which had a major influence on child care practice was that of James Robertson, a social worker at the Hampstead Nurseries who later became a psychoanalyst and worked with John Bowlby. Robertson studied the reactions of children admitted to hospital. At the time, the early 1950s, it was believed that it was unsettling for parents to visit young children in hospital and most hospitals allowed only a few hours of visiting at weekends. Robertson found that children separated for short periods were actively distressed, and as the period of separation grew longer, this gave way to apathy and finally detachment. Finally, mostly to the relief of the hospital staff, the child would make superficial, indiscriminate contact with whatever adult was available. On discharge from hospital a disturbed relationship with the parents persisted for some time.

To try and persuade the hospital authorities to change their practice in relation to children's visiting hours, in 1951 Robertson made a film, *A two year old goes to hospital*. This showed the processes he was describing and still makes harrowing viewing. The film was initially greeted by outrage and rejection of its findings, which Robertson understood as fear of a breakdown of the defences against awareness of the children's emotional pain (See Robertson and Robertson, 1989). However, this piece of psychoanalytically informed research ultimately had a profound effect on the welfare of children through its influence on hospital policy and on the training of nurses and social workers.

A number of authors have written about consultation to child care professionals, in a variety of settings. Often the work of the consultant includes some work with the staff, in the manner described above but with a particular slant to the developmental issues, and also some work with the parents and child. The settings include premature baby units (Fletcher, 1983; Cohn, 1994; Kerbekian, 1995), a baby clinic at a general practice (Daws, 1995), a city toy library (Bowers, 1995) as well as nurseries and nursery schools.

Psychoanalysis in the academy

In the USA, psychoanalysis developed mostly within psychiatry, while in other places, for example France, it started with strong university links. In Britain, however, it developed independently of both the universities and the public health services. There have been both advantages and disadvantages for the British Psychoanalytical Society (BPAS) and Institute remaining an independent body in terms of training, practice and academic research; on the one hand freedom from health service constraints and policies, on the other the danger of intellectual isolation. The BPAS is in frequent dialogue with intellectuals from other fields (for examples see the end of Chapter 9). In 2003, for example a major conference 'The Freudian Century' was held, with psychoanalysts and speakers from diverse academic fields addressing the impact of Freud's ideas on intellectual and cultural life in the twentieth century.

As far as the health professions are concerned, the strong behaviourist and organic traditions of British psychiatry and psychology have for many decades kept clinical psychoanalysis at the margins of these disciplines. Simultaneously, as Michael Rustin (1991) points out, in reaction to this rigidly empiricist tradition, advocates of psychoanalysis in the cultural sphere have turned to a mode of thinking as far away from empiricism as possible, that is, to the ideas of Lacan. This has meant that what Rustin sees as the distinctive strength of British clinical psychoanalysis, its groundedness in the careful observation of emotional experience within relationships, has been relatively neglected in the past both by mainstream psychologists and psychiatrists and by academics.

Rustin discusses major differences between the limited and specific Lacanian reading of the early Freud, and the post-Freudian tradition that has arisen from the whole body of his work. Lacan homes in on what the early Freud showed us about the language of the unconscious through his study of dreams: the mechanisms of symbolisation, condensation and displacement. Lacan uses this work to assert that the psyche is basically structured by the language, and thus also by the culture, in which it is steeped. This converges with structuralist theories of language and literature, giving rise to a whole field of cultural theory with Lacanian underpinning.

Rustin's concern is that those whose psychoanalysis has been learned mainly from Lacan's version of Freud's early classic texts are removed from decades of clinical psychoanalytic advance. The version of psychoanalysis with which they become familiar oddly eschews the body, and is also little concerned with the emotional experience of relationships. However, in recent years the gulf is being bridged, with increasing recognition of British as well as French psychoanalysis in the academy, and also a realisation that since psychoanalytic knowledge is derived from clinical practice, the theory cannot be effectively taught in a way divorced from this.

We will now refer briefly to psychoanalysis as an academic discipline in itself, and then discuss psychoanalysis in relation to some other academic fields. These accounts are inevitably very selective and incomplete, and can only serve as introductions in each case, but we hope to give some idea of the way psychoanalysis can both inform, and be informed by, other disciplines.

Psychoanalytic studies
Psychoanalytic Studies is usually taught at postgraduate level in universities. The unique claim of psychoanalysis to be at once an artistic, scientific and clinical discipline means that it finds itself placed in a variety of faculties, for example health studies (in Kent and Sheffield Universities), social sciences (Brunel and Leeds Metropolitan Universities) and sometimes in departments of its own (UCL: University College London and Essex University).

Different psychoanalytic studies curricula have different emphases. To take some examples from the outlines available in their 2002 postgraduate prospectuses, both the Brunel and the Leeds Metropolitan University MA courses give a grounding in clinical theory, and then foreground a psychoanalytic approach to contemporary cultural phenomena such as literature and film, and to feminist and political theories. In contrast the Universities of Kent and Sheffield have a greater overall emphasis on clinical practice, and besides theoretical courses offer clinically oriented MAs, which can lead to UKCP registration as a psychotherapist (see Chapter 9).

The UCL Psychoanalysis Unit and the Essex University Centre for Psychoanalytic Studies are unique in having senior staff who are all practising psychoanalysts or analytical psychologists (Jungian analysts). Although they offer theoretical rather than clinical teaching, the thorough clinical grounding of the academic staff gives a distinctive flavour to their teaching, and some students have found these degrees to be a staging post along the way to clinical psychoanalytic training.

Finally, another important sign of the *rapprochement* between clinic and academy has been the recent affiliation of certain long-established clinical trainings to universities, enabling integration of academic and clinical qualifications. Examples are the child psychotherapy training at the Tavistock Clinic, London, now linked with the University of East London, and the child analytic training at the Anna Freud Centre, which has academic links with University College London.

Psychoanalysis and philosophy

The philosopher Jonathan Lear points out (1998) that philosophy and psychoanalysis are each in their own way extended conversations. He quotes Socrates' famous dictum, 'The unexamined life is not worth living', and his fundamental question, 'How shall I live?' to illustrate some shared concerns of the two disciplines. In view of this it is surprising that only in the last two decades has psychoanalytic thinking engaged many philosophers other than those involved on either side of the debate about the scientific status of psychoanalysis (see Chapter 5).

Contemporary philosophers such as Richard Wollheim have found the psychoanalytic perspective a useful starting point in considering philosophically what it is to be human and to live a life (for example Wollheim, 1984). Michael Levine (2000), who has edited an important collection of contemporary philosophical papers informed by psychoanalysis, welcomes a recent shift of philosophical energy away from the process of either attacking or defending Freud, towards actually making use of psychoanalytic theory in philosophical thinking.

For example, psychoanalysis can contribute to the debates of moral philosophy through its studies of love, hate, and conscience. Both the psychoanalyst Roger Money-Kyrle (1955) and the philosopher Richard Wollheim (1984) have made use of Melanie Klein's idea of the depressive and paranoid schizoid positions (see Chapter 2). In this theoretical framework, a developmental and love-driven move towards knowing reality, and repairing the damage done to the needed other through thoughtlessness and hate, co-exists with a hateful and/or fearful wish to deny and destroy them. This dynamic gives us the basis of natural morality and moral conflict simply by virtue of our being human and ambivalently needing others.

Psychoanalysis offers a perspective on human life which in some ways is at the opposite pole to that of Descartes, whose central subject is a man alone in a timeless space with a perfectly conscious, rational mind. Even if society is allowed to come into the equation, many earlier thinkers, for example Thomas Hobbes, have explicitly or implicitly based their theories of mind, ethics, society and politics on the model of fully rational adult male citizens in symmetrical relationships to each other. For the purposes of the argument, it was considered quite acceptable for these men to be seen, in Hobbes's (1651) words, 'as if but even now sprung out of the earth, and suddenly like mushrooms come to full maturity, without all kinds of engagement to each other'. Seyla Benhabib (1992), the feminist philosopher and social theorist, quotes this as an example of a denial of our complex interdependence, starting with the universal dependence on the mother. It is as if men can create society without ever themselves having been created and dependent on others.

Emilia Steuerman (2000) discusses how psychoanalysis can help fulfil Benhabib's plea for us to reintroduce the complexity and asymmetry of human relationships. She uses the ideas of Freud and Klein in her analysis of the debate between modernity and post-modernity. For Steuerman the beauty of object relations theory is that it shows us how we come into being through our relationship to the other, beginning with the absolute dependency on the mother. The object of study has to be not simply one person's mind, but an ongoing dialogical process between two subjects.

The social and political theorist Michael Rustin (1999) and the psychoanalyst David Bell (1999) use object relations theory to maintain a modernist and positivist philosophical position. In their view psychic facts are there to be discovered; a person's inner world is simply another part of the natural world, even if the complexity of the transference–countertransference interaction means that its study by another person is complex and specialised. Knowledge of the patient must always be approximate, and is inevitably gained through the analyst's (descriptively) subjective experience. However, this does not mean that it cannot be achieved by means that are objective in the epistemological sense, that of taking a third person position, an observing stance, with respect to one's own subjectivity.

Psychoanalysis, literature and art
The relationship between psychoanalysis and the arts is reciprocal; each can inform the other. Freud's insights about the mind owed much to his knowledge and love of literature; he frequently quoted from Goethe and other great writers. Writers, literary critics and psychoanalysts have in common a deep preoccupation with language, its symbols, resonances and associative links. Freud's original thought was that the content of works of art represented repressed infantile wishes, and he linked artistic production to daydream (Freud, 1908). He initiated the genre of 'psychobiography', for example in his study of Leonardo da Vinci (Freud, 1910). Freud was aware that he had not worked out a psychoanalytic theory of aesthetics, of what makes something truly artistic rather than ephemeral. His early studies have inevitably been considered limited by many artistic and literary critics.

Bell (1999) however, in his edited collection of recent psychoanalytic contributions to the arts, has pointed out that Freud shows he has intuitively grasped something about the relation between the apprehension of beauty and the capacity to mourn, in his paper 'On transience' (1916), where he describes a walking companion of his who turns away from the beauty of their surroundings as it reminds him of the transience of life.

Segal (1952, 1957) extended this early intuition of Freud's to theories of aesthetics and of symbol formation using Klein's ideas about mourning and the depressive position, and the capacity to mourn (see Chapter 2). Art, in Segal's view, has a reparative function, and expresses the creator's struggle to repair internal damage. Artistic talent gives someone, even, or perhaps especially if, they are troubled, a way of expressing and working through dark and painful issues. A work of art which has depth in Segal's view contains both beauty and ugliness; this is shown in the Greek tragedies whose content reflects the horror and ugliness of life, whilst their beauty is expressed in the form. Britton (1998) further explores the phenomenon of depth in artistic creativity, distinguishing the way escapist romance is based on wish-fulfilling daydream or psychic illusion from the way serious fiction is based on psychic reality. The latter process is closer to dreaming than to daydreaming; it is instinctively psychic truth seeking rather than truth evading.

From a different psychoanalytic idiom, the psychoanalyst Marion Milner (1957) addresses a similar area when she stresses the need for reverie, Keats's 'negative capability', and the relaxing of conscious control in the creative act. Her thinking is allied to that of Winnicott (1971), who sees the capacity for play as the essential basis for creativity. The child's early environment must be sufficiently good and trustworthy to allow the development of transitional or potential space, an area between inner and outer worlds which is neither 'me' nor 'not me' but somewhere between, a paradox that Winnicott stresses cannot and must not be resolved. This space is where the child's transitional object first belongs, and where play broadens finally into the cultural world.

Psychoanalysts have both contributed to literary and artistic criticism, and used pieces of literature to illustrate a psychoanalytic theory, sometimes both at once, as Bell's collection illustrates. Academic literary critics have also made extensive use of psychoanalytic theories, and Wright (1984) gives a comprehensive account of the use of different psychoanalytic perspectives over many decades, in studying works of art. Freud's early emphasis on an interpretation of the personality of the artist has given way to analysis of the fictional characters, of the relationship between writer and reader, or a study of the creative process itself.

Influenced by the structural linguistics of Ferdinand de Saussure, Jacques Lacan (whose ideas are also discussed briefly in Chapter 4) extended Freud's discoveries about the hidden and deceptive language of dreams and neurotic symptoms to an idea that the language we are born into structures and limits our very being. Lacan asserts that our sense of identity is an illusion, and that we are constructed in and through language. As Frosh puts it, 'It is not that there is a pre-existent subjectivity which learns to express itself through words, rather that the initially "absent" subject becomes concrete through its positioning in a pre-existing meaning system' (Frosh, 1999: 140). In Lacan's own words: 'It is the world of words that creates the world of things' (Lacan, 1953: 65).

Lacan's ideas were to influence Althusser's theories about the construction of social identity, and transmission of social ideology, through the culture and language of such institutions as family and school. Lacan's work also fed into a new psychoanalytic structural approach in literary theory from the 1970s, which centres on the psychic processes embedded in the text. As a result, the text is no longer taken for granted as a vehicle for transmission of content, but is itself subjected to minute scrutiny, or 'deconstructed'. The reader and writer alike are seen as having transferences to each other and to the text. In its most radical form, this process questions the existence of any meaningful distinction between the reader and writer of a text.

Lacan's idea that gender identity itself is imposed by the language world into which the child is born has been a focal point for developments in feminist literary theory. However, as Frosh (1999) points out, this linguistic determinism creates problems in the way it seems to reduce the individual woman (or man) to a cipher. Lacan's insistence that all culture is patriarchal, the law of the father, also seems to put women in the odd position of being outside culture.

Psychoanalysis and film

Psychoanalysis emerged in 1895 Vienna with the publication of Breuer and Freud's *Studies in Hysteria*, the year the world's first motion pictures were screened by the Lumière brothers in Paris. Diamond and Wrye (1998) introduce a special edition of the journal *Psychoanalytic Enquiry* on psychoanalysis and film. They point out that in over a century of co-existence, both media have been profoundly concerned with psychic reality; understanding it, reflecting it and shaping it. Film often speaks the language of the unconscious. Both psychoanalysis and film have altered our awareness of ourselves, and have influenced each other.

Film-makers have been intrigued and inspired by ideas about the unconscious, and the analytic process, and have popularised psychoanalysis by their representations (sometimes misrepresentations) of it. For their part psychoanalysts continue to be fascinated by film, and the *International Journal of Psychoanalysis* has carried regular film review essays since 1997. Gabbard's (1997) guest editorial introducing this project gives a useful overview of the different psychoanalytic approaches to film, such as the analysis of spectatorship, reflections on the unconscious of the film-maker and the explication of underlying cultural mythology. Psychoanalysts and film scholars have formed creative partnerships, and collaborate for example in an annual psychoanalytic film festival, and in other settings where films are screened and discussed (see Chapter 9).

Psychoanalysis and social issues

We also touch on some sociological and political applications of psychoanalytic theories during the discussion of political and ideological critiques of psychoanalysis in Chapter 5. It is striking that, as we saw in Chapter 4, psychoanalysis is one of the activities that is characteristically proscribed under repressive regimes, bearing witness to its respect for individual freedom and to its expression of unpalatable truths.

Freud's (1930) position on the relationship between individuals and society is that human instincts have to be controlled in order to protect society and mobilise energy for the work of civilisation. The restrictions imposed by society and the internal forces of repression are linked via the inevitability of having to work through the Oedipus complex, relinquish what we cannot have, and develop a superego. For Freud, as for many later thinkers such as Klein, conflict and strife are an inescapable part of being human, and society has to manage this.

Psychoanalytic theorists of a more utopian bent, such as Heinz Kohut, mentioned in Chapter 3 as the founder of the 'self psychology' school of psychoanalysis, are more inclined to view the 'essence' of people as good and potentially even conflict-free. For Kohut, we are deformed by the deficiencies in our parents, our society and, theoretically at least, in an ideal society, we could be perfectible. An extract from one of Kohut's last papers illustrates this:

> Why can we not convince more of those who have espoused the traditional psychoanalytic outlook that intergenerational strife, mutual killing wishes, pathological Oedipus complex (as distinguished from the normal Oedipal stage of development) refers not to the essence of man, but that they are deviations from the normal, however frequently they may occur?…the normal state, however rare in pure form, is a joyfully experienced developmental move forward in childhood…to which the parental generation responds with pride, with self-expanding empathy, with joyful mirroring, to the next generation, thus affirming the younger generation's right to unfold and to be different. (Kohut, 1982: 403)

At the other end of this spectrum, Melanie Klein (1960: 271) stresses the innate conflict between love and hate towards the (m)other.

> The young infant's good relation to the mother and to the food, love and care she provides is the basis for a stable emotional development. However…even under very favourable conditions, the conflict between love and hate (or to put it in Freud's terms, between destructive impulses and libido) plays an important role.…Frustrations, which to some extent are unavoidable, strengthen hate and aggressiveness. By frustration I do not only mean that the infant is not always fed when he wants to be;…there are unconscious desires [for] the continuous presence of the mother and her exclusive love. It is part of the emotional life of the infant that he is greedy and desires more than even the best external situation can fulfil. Together with destructive impulses the infant also experiences

feelings of envy which reinforce his greed and interfere with his being able to enjoy the available satisfactions.

In practice, whichever of these theoretical positions they favour, all psychoanalysts see nature and nurture as interdependent in complex ways, as we have seen throughout this book. In political and sociological terms, however, the pole one favours may have different implications for one's vision of a good society. Both the social psychologist Stephen Frosh (1999) and the sociologist Michael Rustin (1991, 1995) incline towards a view of the inevitability of destructive forces in the personality, whatever their origins, and take this into account in their visions of a more 'containing' society.

If we can better understand the complex internal and external origins of love, hate and envy, say Frosh and Rustin, we are better placed to design institutions, like schools, hospitals, factories and prisons, that will foster human relationships by taking inner states of mind seriously and as matters for reflection rather than for onward projection or punitive reprisal. Here we see a link back to the first half of this chapter, where the psychoanalytic way of thinking is being brought to bear on institutional life.

Psychoanalysis can both learn from, and help to make sense of why certain social experiments do or don't work. A successful example of great relevance and interest to psychoanalysis is the work of the Truth and Reconciliation Commission in South Africa. This was discussed alongside his experiences of other similar projects by Justice Richard Goldstone (2001) in the British Psychoanalytical Society's annual Ernest Jones Lecture.

Finally we may mention the contribution of psychoanalysis to studies of the problem of violence and intolerance in society. Hanna Segal (1987, 1995) has contributed to the study of the nuclear threat. She makes interesting distinctions between a state of mind in which one is waging war in order to save or protect something one values as good, and an omnipotently destructive state of mind linked to the sort of war which nothing can survive. Fahkry Davids (2002) is a current psychoanalytic contributor to the study of racism. In their thinking, both Segal and Davids make use of the idea of 'pathological organisations' of the personality, meaning that cruel and totalitarian structures become embedded in people's character and ways of relating. This field has been well explicated by John Steiner (1993) in his study of 'psychic retreats'. A 2002–3 forum series held by the British Psychoanalytical Society addressed the theme 'Faces of Oppression and Totalitarianism'.

8

PSYCHOANALYSIS AND THE PSYCHOTHERAPIES

The diversity of talking treatments

Since psychoanalysis began, at the start of the twentieth century, a bewildering variety of different psychotherapies has appeared. Close scrutiny however reveals that their different names often represent different 'brands' within quite a limited range of basic types. In this introduction we aim to give the reader a conceptual map, by tracing the influence of five broad traditions within psychotherapy. Then we will focus on the psychoanalytic approach, and see how this can be adapted for less intensive individual psychoanalytic psychotherapy and also used in groups and therapeutic communities, and with couples and families. Finally, we will give a brief account of a small selection of other, non-psychoanalytic psychotherapies, tracing the tradition or traditions from which each arises. In each case we will draw out the differences from psychoanalysis, in particular the different uses made of the therapeutic relationship.

The nineteenth-century idea that mental illness was due to 'degeneracy' was already being challenged before psychoanalysis emerged. Adolf Meyer in the USA, and later Hugh Crichton-Miller in the UK, were early exponents of a more humane approach to psychiatry, in which social and constitutional factors were seen as interacting (Pilgrim, 2002). This model gave rise to an informal, eclectic model of psychotherapy, combining empathy, instruction and persuasion with physical treatments, rather in the way that Freud himself started out. Pilgrim points out that a home-grown pragmatic and eclectic approach has remained on the whole more congenial to British mental health services than the foreign import that the formal psychoanalytic model represented. Although psychoanalytic thinking became established in a few health service institutions such as the Tavistock Clinic in London, it remains on the margins of mainstream psychiatry and psychology in the UK.

Besides the eclectic and psychoanalytic influences on psychotherapy already mentioned, a third major strand has been the behavioural model, based on learning theory and the work of Pavlov, Skinner, Watson and others. The strict behavioural model had its heyday in Britain between 1950 and 1970, and framed psychological disorder in terms of learned patterns of maladaptive behaviour. The idea was that these could potentially be corrected by retraining, following the principles of classical and operant conditioning. Mind as a useful concept was eschewed; what went on in the 'black box' was neither here nor there, if the right set of stimuli could produce an improved set of behavioural responses.

Recent decades have seen the black box reopened, and subjectivity restored in importance, with exploration and attempted retraining of the mis-learned 'cognitions' that are driving distressing feelings and behaviour. This has softened the hard line behavioural approach into a cognitive-behavioural one, which now informs a strong psychotherapeutic tradition that is quite distinct from the psychoanalytic one, as we shall see. This is the model which has always been most influential in British clinical psychology, and which is now strongly taking hold throughout the mental health field, appealing as it does to British rationalism.

A fourth approach to psychotherapy is supplied by the systems model, which has intellectual roots in both anthropology, in the work of Gregory Bateson, and in the study of self-regulating systems in both biology and mechanics. It arose in West Coast America in the 1950s, when clinicians were struggling to help schizophrenic patients and their families. Systems theory proved a useful adjunct to the psychoanalytic ideas that were already available, as it enabled the problems to be studied simultaneously on several levels, in both inner and outer worlds.

The fifth and final strand to be considered is the humanistic movement in psychotherapy. This arose in the anti-authoritarian counter-culture of the 1960s, with influences, amongst others, from the feminist and anti-psychiatry movements, and from existentialist philosophy. The therapies which started to flourish at this time were variously described as existential, humanistic or experiential, and privileged feeling, self-expression and action over thinking, analysing and understanding. Their proponents tended, following the mood of the times, to share an optimistic view of human potential, downplaying negativity and conflict. There was impatience with the slow and measured nature of psychoanalysis, with its repetition and working through, its attention to boundaries, and its asymmetry of roles between analyst and patient. Humanistic styles were either grafted on to psychoanalysis or behaviourism, or operated independently.

Many of these challenges to orthodoxy arose in the USA, in response to the authoritarian medical hegemony that affected psychoanalysis (see Chapter 4). Examples of the new approaches which expanded at this time are the **person-centred psychotherapy** of Carl Rogers (1902–87), the **Gestalt therapy** of Fritz Perls (1893–1970), and the **personal construct therapy** of George Kelly (1905–67). A British example of the 1960s therapeutic counter-culture was the work of R.D. Laing and his experiments with therapeutic regression for schizophrenic patients.

Since the 1970s there has been a huge diversification of labelled therapeutic approaches, and the field has become very confusing for the potential consumer. Small disagreements over theory or technique may still, as we saw historically in Chapter 4, lead a particular individual to break away from their parent organisation and found a new school of therapy, with a different name and a different theoretical language. New schools may also be founded by individuals who integrate different approaches, as with **cognitive-analytic therapy** (CAT) below. Finally, therapies themselves will continue to evolve over time. It has already emerged how psychoanalysis has changed in many ways over the last century, in response to new discoveries in the consulting room. We will see below how, for example, **cognitive-behaviour therapy** (CBT) is also evolving, with a (re)discovery of resistance and transference making treatments longer, and with more attention to the therapeutic relationship.

Psychoanalytic psychotherapies

The relation between psychoanalysis and individual psychoanalytic psychotherapy
Psychoanalysis is the 'parent' discipline of a range of psychoanalytically based approaches, all sharing with psychoanalysis both a base in theory and a particular sort of clinical stance. Psychoanalysis itself continues to provide an important research base, because the fine grain of the mind, and of the therapeutic relationship, is most easily studied in the intensive four or five times weekly individual setting. When sessions can be consecutive, this allows the possibility of deeper involvement than can usually be achieved with longer gaps. The experience in full analysis of continuity through the week, without disruption and loss until the weekend, makes it safer to become immersed in the process, and to take risks. The single day/night gap often means that dream life can be particularly well harnessed into the work.

Neurotic problems tend to become more quickly and thoroughly alive in an intensive therapeutic relationship, often relieving the burden on outside relationships. It might seem paradoxical, but with more sessions the patient is often freer in his or her outside life, less absorbed with neurotic problems and less unhelpfully self-absorbed outside the session. The problems re-emerge rapidly once the patient enters a session, so that the analyst and patient can get on with the work.

Once, twice or three times weekly work is thus in some ways more difficult, although it may often be more practicable and a less unnerving prospect for many patients, especially to start with. It is done both by psychoanalysts and their psychoanalytic psychotherapist colleagues. Chapter 9 mentions some professional links between psychoanalysts and psychoanalytic psychotherapists, including the overarching professional regulating body, the British Confederation of Psychotherapists (BCP). The other psychotherapy regulating body is the United Kingdom Council for Psychotherapy (UKCP), and the history and relationship of BCP and UKCP is also discussed in Chapter 9. The UKCP is a more generic body, representing many different modalities of psychotherapy. Its psychoanalytic section includes a variety of organisations with trainings which do not yet fulfil the stringent requirements of the BCP, although some are actively working towards this.

In psychoanalytic psychotherapy the principles of the setting and of the analytic stance are the same as in psychoanalysis. BCP psychoanalytic psychotherapy trainings are based on the model of three times weekly treatment, using the couch. If the sessions are on consecutive days, the intensity of the experience for the patient, especially in the middle session of the three, can be similar to that of full psychoanalysis, although there is then a long separation to negotiate. Spaced-out sessions will in contrast give a different, more controlled rhythm.

A patient seen once or twice weekly may not always use the couch. This means that the therapist's visible presence can act as a distraction, and may interfere with the range and depth of transference experiences. Indeed at this low intensity it might not be right with some patients to foster too much depth of experience by using the couch, when they then have to wait as much as a week for the next session. This may particularly apply with a psychologically fragile patient who, without the containment provided by intensive work, needs a firm base in external reality to keep his or her inner disturbance within bounds.

Psychodynamic counselling

This book cannot encompass the large field of counselling, which is fully discussed by McLeod (2003). The word 'psychodynamic' refers to the dynamic mental forces, conscious and unconscious, with which psychoanalysis is concerned. There is in practice a somewhat grey area between once-weekly psychoanalytic psychotherapy and the variety of counselling called psychodynamic counselling, the depth of the work depending on the training and experience of the practitioner. (The indistinct boundary between counselling and psychotherapy is reflected in the way the British Association for Counselling was recently renamed the British Association for Counselling and Psychotherapy.) A leading figure in the promotion of psychodynamic counselling has been Michael Jacobs (see Jacobs, 1999).

Psychodynamic counsellors see their clients (the word is usually chosen in preference to patient) face to face, often, but not always, for relatively short term work, and may focus on current external issues and problem-solving, although they will also take account of, and sometimes interpret on the basis of, transference and countertransference. Counselling trainings are shorter and less intensive than BCP psychotherapy trainings, typically lasting two or three years, and not always requiring extensive personal therapy. A good assessment will often show at what intensity and depth a particular person wants and/or needs to work, and whether a referral for counselling or psychotherapy is most appropriate at that point. GP practices often now employ counsellors, and some of these are psychodynamic in orientation. Many counsellors in further and higher education also work psychodynamically. Others will have a different orientation, for example humanistic, cognitive or integrative.

Child and adolescent psychotherapy

Children and adolescents, like adults, can be treated in psychoanalytic psychotherapy once, twice or three times a week, as well as in full four or five times weekly analysis. The basic principles of the work, and the way the therapeutic relationship is used, remain the same as in the adult analytic approach, but there are certain necessary modifications to the setting. In younger children the medium of expression is as much play as speech, so the consulting room has play materials and is appropriately robust. The parents add an important dimension that is missing from adult work, especially in that they have ultimate control over whether or not a younger child attends. Parents are usually offered some form of support and discussion during their child's treatment, often by a colleague of the therapist's so that incursions into the child's private relationship with the therapist are minimised. Child psychotherapy and analysis is thus less straightforward to provide than adult treatment; the setting needed is more complex, and is often best provided in a properly set up clinic rather than a private consulting room. For these and other reasons, a greater proportion of child and adolescent psychotherapy takes place in public settings like health service clinics and charitable sector institutions than is the case for adult psychotherapy. Training for child psychotherapy in the UK is regulated by the Association of Child Psychotherapists. There are five training schools for child psychotherapists in the UK, three in London, one in Birmingham and one in Edinburgh. Child psychotherapists provide individual psychotherapy for children and young people as well as working with parents and with other professionals caring for children. Although much of this training takes place at the practitioner's own expense, in recent years there has been some NHS funding available through the provision of training posts.

Group analytic psychotherapy
The use of groups analytically dates mainly from Second World War experiments in the psychiatric rehabilitation of soldiers. Three key names are those of Wilfred Bion, S.H. Foulkes and Tom Main, each of whom contributed a particular perspective to the analytic study of groups. The principles of individual psychoanalysis are adapted by setting up a neutral, regular, time-boundaried space for a group, which remains largely consistent in its membership. As with individual analytic therapy, unstructured discussion is allowed to arise, rather than a prior agenda being set. The therapist, who may be known as a 'conductor' or a 'group analyst', has a participant observer role as in individual work, helping the group to find out about what is happening in the room, particularly what may be hidden or unspoken.

Bion (1961) writes about the way the group as a whole functions in relation to itself and to its leader. He describes **basic assumptions**, unconscious defences the group as a whole adopts against anxiety, as opposed to a state of creative group functioning, the **work group**. Foulkes (see Foulkes and Anthony, 1973) orientates himself more towards the complex matrix of transferences between members and towards the conductor. The group work styles arising from the work of these two thinkers is rather different, although today's analytic groups often incorporate both perspectives.

The third key figure, Tom Main (see Main, 1989) applied psychoanalytic thinking to **therapeutic community** treatment, where individuals are helped to learn about themselves and their relationships within a residential community. Main worked at the Cassel Hospital in Richmond, Surrey, an NHS therapeutic milieu where a key feature of inpatient work is the attention given to the relationship between the staff. Disagreements and differences in perspective between workers are analysed and worked with for the light they shed on psychic divisions within and between patients. This sort of analysis of the relationship between co-therapists is used in a similar way to gain understanding of the couple or family in **psychoanalytic marital or family therapy**.

Psychoanalytic psychotherapy in the NHS

Psychoanalytic psychotherapy, whether for adults or for children and adolescents, and whether individual or group based, is in very short supply in the NHS. London residents have a greater chance of access to it than many others, but even in London its availability is patchy, limited and usually with very long waiting lists. When it is offered it is usually just once a week for a year or even less, setting a limit on the work which can be done. The Association for Psychoanalytic Psychotherapy in the NHS (APP, for details see p. 172), was formed in 1981 as a special interest and pressure group, concerned to advance the practice of psychoanalytic psychotherapy in the public health sector. The APP now has many sub-sections (for example general psychiatry, general practice, child and family and nursing) and publishes its own journal, *Psychoanalytic Psychotherapy*. The APP also holds lectures and conferences, and administers an educational trust.

The position of psychoanalytic psychotherapy in the National Health Service is complex. Except in the case of child and adolescent psychotherapy, there is no actual *profession* called psychotherapy within the NHS. Rather, psychotherapy is an *activity* which may be carried out by practitioners of a number of professions, provided they have had specialist training. Often in an NHS hospital or health authority the psychotherapy unit is a part of the department of psychiatry and the work of the unit will be under the direction of a consultant psychotherapist, who is a specially trained psychiatrist. These units sometimes offer at least some treatment that is psychoanalytic in orientation. Psychology departments also offer psychotherapy as one of their main functions, but are more likely to offer cognitive, behavioural or eclectic treatment than psychoanalytic psychotherapy.

Other health professionals who may be trained as psychoanalytic psychotherapists include clinical psychologists, social workers and nurses. Often these professionals will have received their specialist training from an organisation outside the NHS and a few will have received psychoanalytic training from the Institute of Psychoanalysis. In the majority of cases this specialist training will have been at the practitioner's own expense. The Tavistock Clinic in north London is a specialist NHS institution which provides psycho-analytically based therapies (as well as systems-based family therapy) for adults and children. It is one of the few institutions which offers in-depth psychoanalytic psychotherapy training in the NHS for psychiatrists, psychologists, social workers and nurses. It also offers many courses for diverse professional groups, enabling them to gain a psychodynamic or systems perspective on their work. A BBC television documentary about the work of the Tavistock, for which there is an accompanying book (Taylor, 1999) was screened in 1999.

There are a few NHS units in the UK where psychoanalytic psychotherapy is part of an intensive programme, either residential or in a day unit. These units include the Cassel Hospital in west London, the Henderson Hospital in Surrey, and the Halliwick Day Hospital at St Ann's Hospital in north London. Such units offer a programme over several months or a year, which usually includes both individual and group therapy within a milieu in which the patients are encouraged to think about their feelings, reactions and impulses rather than merely act on them.

To be offered such a scarce and expensive resource within the NHS the patient has to be suffering severe difficulties, and to be unusually lucky in finding such a setting in their area. Typically the people referred will have problems in many areas of life, such as relationships, work and parenting. There may have been serious self-harm or suicide attempts. There are commonly problems managing impulses and feelings, and often such people have suffered abuse and trauma as children. The suffering of these individuals is severe and long term, and has usually not responded well to standard psychiatric care, so it is encouraging that research is now showing the efficacy of psychoanalytically based treatments (see Chapter 6).

Child and adolescent psychotherapy, unlike psychotherapy for adults, is a well organised NHS profession, although the number of child psychotherapists is small. Child and adolescent psychotherapists usually work as part of the multidisciplinary team in child and adolescent mental health services but also work with children, families and child health care professionals in a number of other settings. The degree of organisation and recognition is helped by their being only one overarching professional body, the Association of Child Psychotherapists (ACP).

Analytical psychology (Jungian analysis)

Although following the split between Freud and Jung in 1913 (see Chapter 3), the psychoanalytic and analytical psychology institutes and trainings evolved separately, over recent years there has been some *rapprochement* both theoretically and clinically. Many Jungian analysts, particularly those trained at the Society of Analytical Psychology (SAP) in London, share with psychoanalytic colleagues a valuing of the importance of intensive work with patients and trainees. The SAP training is similar in depth and intensity to the training at the Institute of Psychoanalysis. Jungian analysts also often make use of the transference and countertransference in a similar way to psychoanalysts, although the theoretical conceptualisation of their findings may differ. This common cause between Freudian and Jungian analysts has led to their collaboration, for example in the formation of the BCP. Jungian analytic perspectives are represented alongside psychoanalytic ones in a number of academic departments, such as the Centre for Psychoanalytic Studies at Essex University, which has both Jungian and Freudian professors. It is of course impossible to do justice to the important field of Jungian analysis here. Interested readers might start by consulting Alister and Hauke (1998) for an account of current post-Jungian perspectives on theory and practice.

Comparing some non-psychoanalytic psychotherapeutic approaches

We have neither the space nor the expertise to do full justice to the theories and methodologies of other psychotherapies. These are dealt with well elsewhere, for example by Bateman, Brown and Pedder (2000) and Dryden (2002). In this section, our main aim is to clarify for the reader the differences between psychoanalytic and a cross-sectional sample of other approaches to psychotherapy. These differences mainly concern the use of the therapeutic relationship, and we will begin by recapping the distinctive features of the analytic stance.

The specificity of the psychoanalytic stance

The analytic stance is hard to maintain partly because it is socially counter-intuitive. As we saw in Chapter 1, the analyst has to hold a certain tension, thinking and observing rather than quickly making things more comfortable. By denying him- or herself automatic social responses, such as sharing personal experiences, becoming authoritative or more openly comforting, the relatively neutral analyst draws the fire of the patient's problematic relationship patterns on to him or herself. Paradoxically, if he or she fitted in with pressures to be more socially ordinary, the analyst would in fact be more likely to go on being experienced as a distorted transference figure.

If the tension can instead be borne and understood, the patient can be given a chance to discover a new and more realistic sort of figure. Many other psychotherapeutic approaches do, in contrast, deliberately make use of a more socially ordinary stance. They can thus be more easily recognised as formalised extensions of familiar relationships, like those of teacher, parent or friend. This can make some non-analytic approaches feel more immediately acceptable to the recipient, and less unnerving. Transference distortions and countertransference pressures will occur with non-analytic therapists as they do with everyone else one meets, and may sometimes get in the way of effective treatment. Non-analytic psychotherapists may sometimes be well aware of transference and countertransference and take these factors into account, but without making direct and central use of them as in psychoanalysis.

The person-centred approach

Carl Rogers (1902–87), an American psychologist, founded what has come to be known as person-centred counselling or psychotherapy. This has roots both in the eclectic approach and in the humanistic movement. Person-centred therapists share a number of features with psychoanalysts: they both view the therapeutic relationship as the main vehicle of change, stress the need for the therapist to be consistent, non-judgemental and empathic, and provide a boundaried but essentially unstructured setting, where the patient brings his own concerns, rather than following any set agenda. Unlike psychoanalysts, however, person-centred therapists do not make use of transference and countertransference as the central source of understanding, neither are they much concerned with unconscious aspects of the mind. They aim for an egalitarian therapeutic relationship, and for this reason usually refer to themselves as counsellors rather than psychotherapists, and to the people they are working with as clients rather than patients (see Thorne, 2002).

The person-centred movement emphasises the existence of the potential in every person for constructive self-fulfilment, which has all too often been constrained by condemnation and conditional love from others, from infancy onwards. Experiences in relationships can both harm and heal, and the therapist aims to provide an honest, unconditionally positive relationship which will allow the client's potential to unfold, like a plant taken from the dark and cold into the warmth and light. Person-centred therapists, as Thorne describes, 'do not hesitate to invest themselves freely and fully in the relationship with their clients...and to reveal themselves, if appropriate, with their own strengths and weaknesses' (2002: 141).

However, as Thorne comments, although person-centred therapy can help clients of many kinds, presenting a wide range of difficulties and concerns, it is probably of greatest help to people who are closest to a reasonable adjustment to life. In Thorne's words: 'Clients who perhaps have most to gain from person-centred therapy are those who are strongly motivated to face painful feelings and who are deeply committed to change. They are prepared to take emotional risks and they want to trust even if they are fearful of intimacy' (ibid.: p. 142).

Gestalt therapy

Gestalt therapy was first developed by Fritz Perls (1893–1970) and Laura Perls (1905–92). They both had some psychoanalytic training in Germany, and were part of the avant-garde movement which flourished there between the wars. In addition to Gestalt psychology, Perls and Perls were involved in existential philosophy and experimental theatre. In the 1930s, as blacklisted left-wing radicals, they were forced to flee the Nazis. Having established themselves in New York, Fritz Perls then moved to the radical Esalen Institute in California. His new approach finally then took off in popularity, as part of the humanistic therapeutic counter-culture of the 1960s. Perls came to encourage his patients, often in groups, to expand their awareness of themselves (to heal their split 'gestalt' or whole) using various exercises and games. In these early days of Gestalt therapy the emphasis was on experimental, confrontational group techniques, sometimes in the form of marathon groups, which released feelings in an intense way. Participants' defences were challenged and penetrated, and the results could be freeing or destabilising. Emphasis was on the here and now of emotional experience rather than on verbal understanding and linking with the past. The early Gestalt therapist was a director/leader, who could become idealised in a charismatic way like a 'guru'.

Over the years Gestalt therapy has matured, and evolved into something much less confrontational and charismatic (see Parlett and Hemming, 2002). It now often takes place on a long term, individual basis, non-intensively and face to face. The therapeutic stance differs in a number of important ways from the analytic one. The therapist often reveals things about herself when this is judged useful, and may still use active techniques at times, which might include occasional physical contact with the patient. Emphasis is on the here and now of experience, as it is in analysis. However, the therapist's transparency and activity means that she does not offer herself as a potential transference figure, but mostly remains aligned with the patient in looking at difficulties in relationships 'out there'.

The systems approach to psychotherapy

Systems theory emerged in the 1950s from an integration of several sources. Firstly these were studies on communication by the anthropologist Gregory Bateson, based in California during the 1950s and 1960s, second, the general systems theory of Von Bertalanffy, and lastly cybernetics, the study of self-regulating systems. Human beings can be seen as existing in a series of open systems, which are distinct but permeable to each other. For example, the individual is part of the mother–child system, itself part of a larger, family system, which is in turn part of further overlapping and concentric systems such as the extended family, the school, the neighbourhood, the country, and so on. Thinking in systems terms, a child with anxiety or tantrums may indicate a problem at some other point in the family system, for example in the parents' relationship. Or at a higher system level, increasing unemployment in a country may lead to more individuals becoming depressed.

Systems theory has given rise to treatment approaches, particularly with families. In child and adolescent mental health services (CAMHS) family therapy is quite commonly offered for a child with an emotional or behavioural difficulty. The family are seen together for a series of meetings, usually one every couple of weeks over a few months. They are often seen by two therapists or by one therapist with a 'reflecting team' behind a one-way screen. The therapists encourage the family members to consider the roles they take in relation to each other and the issues which face them as a family. Sometimes during a family meeting the two therapists may have a conversation with each other, observed by the family, in which they remark on their observations of, and thoughts about, the family. Sometimes the team behind the screen may halt the meeting to make, and reflect on, their observations. By such means the possibility of different viewpoints, and of reflecting on them, can be modelled to the family.

In psychoanalysis and psychoanalytic psychotherapy, family relationships are often discussed but the main interest is in the *internal* relationships of the individual (see Chapter 1) which may affect the way family relationships are experienced and played out. By contrast the central concern of systems family therapy is the operation of the relationships between the people in the family system. The two therapies have in common that the participants are invited to observe themselves and reflect: but in family therapy, unlike psychoanalytic therapy, the relationship between the family and the therapist is usually not the primary focus of attention. However, some family therapists are more interested in the therapeutic relationship (e.g. Scharff and Scharff, 1987) and recently in the family therapy literature there has been some attention to transference and countertransference (e.g. Flaskas, 2002).

Everyone is part of family and social systems but for children in particular an emotional difficulty is likely to be related to both the matrix of the family and the child's own internal state. The contribution of each will vary between individuals and sometimes only trial and error will make the relative contributions clear. As described earlier, even when a child is treated with individual psychoanalytic therapy the parents will also need to be seen, at least from time to time. Sometimes it can lead to quicker relief of a child's immediate distress, and help the family as a whole, to offer family therapy instead of individual therapy for the child. In addition this is usually a less costly option for the NHS. Sometimes, also, a period of family therapy, to work on mutually unhelpful entanglements, may be necessary before either child or parent can allow individual psychoanalytic therapy for a child to take place. Such a possibility is one of the advantages of the multidisciplinary mental health team usually available in CAMHS.

Jack B, aged 14, an only child was referred because of underachievement at school, together with aggressive behaviour at home which his parents were struggling to manage. The B family agreed to attend family meetings and had ten sessions over a nine-month period.

Tension and hostility between the parents was palpable from the outset and the therapist was painfully aware of the extent to which communication passed through Jack. He spoke vividly of being pulled in different directions and of sometimes wanting to run away from home to get away from it all, if only he had the courage. Jack and his mother were very much a couple in the sessions, with Mr B holding a rather authoritarian position whilst clearly feeling rather excluded. Mr and Mrs B were reluctant to address their problems in a marital therapy context but gradually seemed more able to talk directly to each other in family meetings and to protect Jack more from their ongoing disagreements.

After a period of family work Jack was then able to think about having some individual analytic therapy to help him address his own longstanding emotional difficulties, which were impacting considerably on his school life and relationships with peers. For him, one of the most significant aspects of the family meetings seemed to be in signalling that his problems were not just his 'fault', as he put it. The fact that he could articulate this towards the end of the family meetings seemed to help him separate sufficiently from his family to accept the offer of individual therapy for himself.

Systems thinking has also been used to complement the psychoanalytic in the study of group phenomena. A helpful marriage of the two approaches has been used in organisational consultancy, as we saw in Chapter 7.

Cognitive-behaviour therapy (CBT)

CBT was developed by Aaron Beck (b. 1921). Beck trained as a psychoanalyst in 1950s Philadelphia, but became impatient with the long term and, as he saw it, unfocused nature of psychoanalysis (see Milton, 2001). The psychoanalytic root of CBT became an attenuated one, as Beck finally eschewed the idea of unconscious processes altogether, and concentrated on conscious and rational forces within the mind. CBT has another root in the behavioural school, but itself provided an important humanising and deepening influence on the original, strictly behavioural therapeutic model.

CBT is currently favoured in the public sector, as it offers a relatively brief, inexpensive and reassuringly sensible approach to mental distress. The goal is to train the patient to catch hold of, and challenge, the automatic negative thoughts which are maintaining their depressed or otherwise self-defeating moods and behaviour. The CBT therapist takes a collaborative tutor or trainer role. Rather than encouraging expression and exploration of what is in the mind, the CBT therapist aims to help the patient correct it.

CBT sessions are structured and directive, without free association. The therapist helps the patient narrow general complaints down into specific negative cognitions which can then give rise to experimental tasks to be carried out, and the outcome monitored. Thus a patient might be found to have a depressive core belief (or 'schema'), for example that she is uninteresting and unloved. This is found to generate day to day thoughts like 'no one wants to talk to me' and 'other people are luckier than I am in their lives'. Such beliefs can be tested out during sessions through a sort of Socratic discussion, and then experimented with using 'homework exercises' outside the therapy (Beck et al., 1979).

The usual practice is to offer between 10 and 20 sessions of treatment, with follow-up refresher sessions. Training needed for the therapist is relatively brief, not requiring, for example, any personal therapy. Many modern-day CBT therapists working with deeply troubled patients are however coming to rediscover what Freud established about transference. The techniques recommended by Beck et al. (1990) to deal with it sound reminiscent of Freud's early wish (see Chapter 3) to clear transference out of the way by reason and explanation, so that the collaborative work can continue.

Given the intransigence of largely unconscious neurotic structures in the personality (which have been resisting everyday reason all along) psychoanalysts might see this approach as limited. However, CBT is a very useful intervention for patients who cannot tolerate, and/or do not wish for the more disturbing analytic approach. CBT helps people to strengthen their defences (or their rational coping strategies) and gain better control of their emotions. Psychoanalysis in contrast risks just the opposite, encouraging the opening up of the more disturbing and hidden layers of the personality and imagination. Although this potentially provides the opportunity for healing at a more fundamental level, it may prove unacceptable and risky in patients who are deeply troubled or who do not wish to get too stirred up.

Psychoanalysts use reasoning and appeals to logic at times, but if they find themselves doing this too strongly or persistently, for example reasoning with a patient about the logical way to think, or actively encouraging new behaviour, they may stop and wonder what they are enacting with the patient. In such circumstances it is likely that there is something difficult to bear about the patient's intransigence, and that something is getting acted out in the transference and countertransference. An example of this is Mark in Chapter 1, who tantalised his analyst with his plans for getting a job then lapsed into passivity, causing her to become over-active and to proffer ultimately useless suggestions for more 'reasonable' thought and action. The psychoanalyst is not primarily a trainer but a participant observer, trying to make sense of the totality of the interaction; as much concerned with process as content.

Cognitive analytic psychotherapy (CAT)

A number of eclectic and integrated or 'integrative' psychotherapies combine useful approaches and techniques, hoping for even better results. Cognitive analytic therapy (CAT: Ryle, 1990; Dunn, 2002) combines cognitive and psychoanalytic approaches, with an important input from Kelly's (1955) personal construct theory. The therapist works actively with the patient to formulate the central psychic conflicts which are leading to relationship difficulties, then helps the patient to recognise and challenge them. This usually takes place in a brief (16 weeks), focused treatment where transference interpretations are combined eclectically with cognitive or behavioural challenges and 'homework'.

Compared to psychoanalytic therapy, this sort of approach can be initially more acceptable to both patients and therapists, as it involves the therapist being relatively proactive, and taking a stance nearer to that of a trainer. However, as the therapist is taking on this role, rather than striving for neutrality, the full emergence of the transference is compromised. These factors make CAT more immediately accessible, and less risky for therapist and patient (Milton, 2001). CAT has proved popular and useful as a first intervention, especially in settings where therapeutic resources are severely limited (Ryle, 1995).

'Symmetrical' approaches: co-counselling and self-help

Some modes of therapy try deliberately to reduce or abolish inequality between therapist and patient, in an attempt to do away with the idea of a knowledgeable and powerful therapist treating a needy patient. Such enterprises are partly rooted in the anti-authoritarian humanistic movement, but had been anticipated by earlier psychoanalytic work. Freud's talented follower Sandor Ferenczi (1873–1933) experimented as early as the 1920s with disclosing his own thoughts and feelings to his patients, even attempting 'mutual analysis' (see Dupont, 1995). The limitations of this approach became apparent and mainstream psychoanalysis left these experiments behind in the pursuit of greater understanding of therapeutic work in the transference. It is worth noting that although the analytic relationship is highly asymmetrical, its aim is always to restore the patient's autonomy. One advantage of analytic asymmetry and work in the transference is that it enables the patient to work on the unavoidable asymmetries and inequalities of life, not least the relationship to the parents.

In the activity known as co-counselling there is no designated therapist or patient, but two participants come together to help each other in a symmetrical way. Similarly, self-help groups consist only of people who are suffering a common problem, and deliberately have no leader or expert therapist. The most well known and successful example of this is Alcoholics Anonymous. It can be very comforting and inspiring to meet fellow sufferers, particularly people who can offer hope, advice and constructive confrontation through having recovered themselves.

Re-parenting approaches: R.D. Laing

This approach starts with the assumption that patients' problems are essentially the result of poor parenting and that this can concretely be made good in adulthood. In the 1960s Ronald Laing, originally a psychoanalyst, carried out experiments which were representative of the British anti-psychiatry and humanistic movements. The most well known example of these therapeutic experiments is that of Mary Barnes, a patient treated in the therapeutic community, Kingsley Hall, by Joseph Berke (Barnes and Berke, 1973). Mary was encouraged to regress, physically and mentally, to an infantile state, and then to be 're-born' while experiencing total care.

This approach to psychosis mostly proved disappointing, and it is no longer considered advisable or ethical. However, the appeal of the theory of re-parenting or providing a 'corrective emotional experience' persists in some eclectic approaches. The therapist in such situations becomes a very directive and authoritative figure who sets herself up as an ideal parent, and will be the recipient of great idealisation and other primitive infantile feelings.

Psychoanalysts' occasional experiments over the years with providing concrete parenting experiences, over and above the ordinary comfort, safety and security of the analytic setting itself, have mostly led to the same conclusion: that something of the patient's autonomy is sacrificed, and that the patient may even become dangerously regressed and helpless. There is also a certain omnipotence in assuming that one can do an actual parent's job for a person who is no longer a child, especially while also being the therapist. While the analytic situation, like many other therapeutic situations, encourages the uncovering and expression of infantile modes of being, it is important not to let go of the symbolic nature of the parental function. This is particularly difficult at times when the patient herself has lost touch with the symbolic nature of the transference; at such times it is crucial that the analyst or therapist retains a realistic view.

Authoritarian cults

Finally we will mention the authoritarian so-called 'therapies' perhaps better described as cults or quasi-religious sects. Suggestive techniques such as hypnosis are used, with deliberate fostering of highly idealised transferences. The leader sets himself up as a powerful authority, demanding obedience and belief from the followers, who will be healed by giving up their autonomy and following certain sets of rules. The appeal, and the danger, of such cults for fragile, lost people, and the potential for serious abuse and exploitation, hardly need spelling out. Sexual exploitation can arise very easily in such situations, and may even in extreme cases be prescribed as part of the 'cure'.

While the psychoanalytic setting also often involves the exposure and exploration of infantile and childlike modes of relating, in psychoanalysis this is ultimately in the service of developing greater autonomy. The analyst aims to help the patient work through and move beyond infantile modes of dependency, and his or her powerful position carries with it a great responsibility. By contrast, brainwashing aims at keeping the patient's mind fragmented and dispersed (Hinshelwood, 1997).

9

THE PROFESSION

In this chapter we will describe the current organisation of the profession, giving a brief history of its development where relevant.

Main structures

Psychoanalysis in Britain is regulated by the British Psychoanalytical Society (BPAS), itself a member of the International Psychoanalytical Association (IPA), and administered by the Institute of Psychoanalysis.

The British Psychoanalytical Society

This was founded by Ernest Jones and a small group of psychoanalysts working with him in 1919. With the foundation of the BPAS came the establishment of the library and plans to translate the works of Freud and other psychoanalytic writing into English. The key figures in this enterprise were Joan Rivière and James and Alix Strachey who worked closely with Jones.

The BPAS became the seventh psychoanalytic society to be affiliated to the International Psychoanalytical Association, itself founded in 1908. It currently provides the only psychoanalytic training institute in the UK, which from an international perspective is an unusual situation. In Germany and the USA, for example, many major cities contain a society/institute. The UK situation is changing. By 2003 there was an IPA Study Group in Northern Ireland, and one of the London-based psychoanalytic psychotherapy organisations was in discussion with the IPA over whether its standards of training qualified it for membership.

The International Psychoanalytical Association

Freud believed that an international organisation was essential to safeguard and advance his thinking and ideas. The IPA is now the world's primary psychoanalytic accrediting and regulatory body. At the time of writing, it has just over 10,000 members in 30 countries, mostly in Europe, North America and Latin America, with some in Australia. It works with its component societies to establish standards of training, to organise conferences and international congresses, and to develop clinical, educational and research programmes. It fosters the creation of new psychoanalytic groups and acts as a focus for information on international aspects of professional psychoanalytic life.

In recent years the IPA has been supporting the re-emergence of psychoanalysis in Eastern European countries following the lifting of restrictions under communism. There has also been some teaching by IPA analysts in China where interest in psychoanalysis is developing. (We explored the spread of psychoanalysis in Chapter 4.) Membership of the IPA has grown from 240 in 1920, 800 in 1950, 2,450 in 1970 to over 10,000 in 2001 (*IPA*, 2001).

The Institute of Psychoanalysis

With the burgeoning of scientific and commercial activity in the British Psychoanalytical Society of the 1920s, there was a need for a proper administrative structure. The Institute of Psychoanalysis (often referred to as the Institute) was set up in 1924, largely through the initiative of John Rickman, to deal with financial and other matters arising mostly from book publication. The joint structure, a society of members and an institute to administer its affairs, is still in place. Today the Institute runs and administers the clinic, the training, publishing activities, external events and the library. The BPAS provides a forum for members to discuss scientific matters, ethical and other issues arising from the practice of psychoanalysis. Although their areas of responsibility are different, the activities of Institute and society overlap. Thus the major decision-making body is combined as 'Board and Council'; that is the board of the Institute and the council of the Society.

The International Journal of Psychoanalysis

In 1920, the *International Journal of Psychoanalysis* (*IJPA*) was established. It was the first psychoanalytic journal in the English language and remains the only truly *international* psychoanalytic journal. Owned and managed by the Institute of Psychoanalysis in London, under successive editors it has become more and more representative of world psychoanalysis. The Regional Boards (North America, Latin America, European and London) help to encourage the submission of papers from all of the regions. Since 2001 the *IJPA* has been run, on behalf of the Institute of Psychoanalysis, by an international board of guardians and part of the profits of the *Journal* are used to foster the development of psychoanalysis in parts of the world where it is emerging or under-financed. The *IJPA* is read and contributed to widely, not only by clinical psychoanalysts, but also by others who are interested in psychoanalysis and its many applications outside the consulting room, in areas from film studies and literary criticism to politics and philosophy. It is produced six times a year and it runs a website with discussions on psychoanalytic topics (www.ijpa.org).

The London Clinic of Psychoanalysis

Not long after the establishment of the Institute of Psychoanalysis, the London Clinic of Psychoanalysis was founded, in 1926, using a generous donation from an American benefactor, Prynce Hopkins. This made it possible to offer analysis to 'needy patients' unable to afford the usual fees. In the first 50 years, 3,080 patients were psychoanalysed free or for a low fee under the auspices of the London Clinic. The work of the clinic continues and is expanding; anyone may apply for a consultation. In 2003 there were over 100 patients in full psychoanalysis either at the London Clinic (for address, see p. 172) or in the consulting rooms of members of the clinic staff. Fees are agreed on the basis of what the patient can realistically afford.

Psychoanalysis and the medical profession

By 1926 Jones and the core of pioneering British analysts working with him had formed the BPAS and the Institute that continue today. But there was one further battle to be fought to establish psychoanalysis as a profession. It concerned the recognition of psychoanalysis by the medical profession. In those days there was a medical hegemony: the medical profession was charged with the responsibility for treating all illness. Medically qualified analysts were unsure of their position in relation to the General Medical Council when they referred patients to non-medical, or 'lay' analysts, as they were often called (Freud, 1926). In addition there were constant attacks in the press on the profession's ethics and standards. Jones himself encouraged analysts to qualify as doctors as well. However, there were those like James and Alix Strachey who gave up medical training after six weeks and went to Vienna to be analysed by Freud instead, choosing to remain lay analysts. Freud and Jones both favoured a broad base to the profession, rather than restricting entry to doctors. But this did leave Jones and the British Society with the problem of public acceptance.

Jones approached the British Medical Association (BMA) who, in 1927, agreed to set up a committee to investigate psychoanalysis. The BPAS presented evidence, argument, documentation and comment that convinced the committee of 20 eminent physicians. The

BMA finally recommended that '[*The claims of*] *Freud and his followers to use the definition of the term (psychoanalysis) are just and must be respected.*' It defined psychoanalysis as '*the technique devised by Freud, who first used the term, and the theory which he has built upon his work*' (quoted in King and Steiner, 1991).

This was an extremely important report for the new profession. It recognised psychoanalysis as an independent theory and technique, which should be self-regulating and on which the BMA were not competent to pass judgement. It also recognised a distinction between 'psychoanalysts' and 'pseudo' analysts. Psychoanalysts were those trained at the Institute of Psychoanalysis whose training was accredited by the International Psychoanalytical Association. In Chapter 4 we traced the very different way in which relationships between the medical and psychoanalytic professions developed in the USA, where physicians remained in control of psychoanalysis for many decades.

Part of the agreement reached with the BMA at this time was the rule that lay analysts did not practise independently and that for diagnostic purposes a medical colleague took medical responsibility. This requirement held good until the late 1980s. By this stage non-medical analysts were frequently members of other clinical professions that had become autonomous rather than remaining ancillary to medicine. Clinical psychologists in particular made assessments for treatment without necessarily consulting a medical colleague. There was also a recognition that, with their rigorous training, psychoanalysts in their own right could take responsibility for assessments and recommendations for psychoanalytic treatment. The ruling was thus revoked in favour of today's more flexible arrangement, where non-medical analysts seek the opinion of medical colleagues when they judge it necessary or helpful.

Psychiatrists and psychoanalysts both deal with disturbed, distressed and psychologically ill people. Perhaps the best way to describe the relationship of psychoanalysis to medicine today is as an independent specialism, neither split off nor 'alternative', but a discipline, making its own contribution. When the partnership is working well, a GP or psychiatrist will recognise when a psychoanalytic assessment will be useful and will refer suitable patients. Equally, psychoanalysts will recognise when patients need medical help and ensure that they receive it.

Developing the profession

In the development of any profession, there are three crucial steps. The profession starts to regulate entry, the professional body establishes a recognised training and qualification to an approved standard, and it regulates the behaviour of its practitioners through an enforceable code of ethics. Where the client group is potentially vulnerable, some external regulation by the state may also be an important step.

The early membership

In 1925 there were 54 members and associate members of the British Psychoanalytic Society. Many of them had been analysed by Freud in Vienna, by Hans Sachs in Berlin or by Ferenczi in Budapest. It was not uncommon for members to go to more than one analyst, spending time in different cities.

These first British psychoanalysts came from a variety of backgrounds. Eric Rayner (1990) tells us: 'at the start [they] were almost pure English, Welsh or Scots. Their backgrounds were middle class, mercantile and professional, with some from the gentry.' Entry to the profession was open and people brought a range of different experiences. Rayner gives some examples: J.C. Flugel was an academic psychologist; James Glover and his brother Edward were Scottish doctors; James and Alix Strachey were members of the Bloomsbury group, as were Adrian Stephen, brother of Virginia Woolf, and his wife Karin; Ella Sharpe was a teacher of literature and head of a teachers' training college; Susan Isaacs was an educational pioneer; Sylvia Payne, a doctor fresh from running wartime hospitals; William Stoddart was a psychiatrist and John Rickman was a Quaker who had been organising medical services in Russia.

Establishing a training

In 1925 there was a significant IPA Congress in Germany at which the question of international training standards was discussed. The key principles of training were laid down. They were:

1 Institutional responsibility for selection, training and qualification of candidates.
2 A personal training analysis for all candidates.
3 Supervised analysis of patients.
4 Theoretical courses.

Each branch society was to elect a training committee, from which representatives met to form the International Training Board. By 1926 the first Education Committee of the British Psychoanalytic Society had been elected.

The profession today

Training

THE STUDENTS   The students undergoing training in Britain today are a more international group, are more likely to come from related therapeutic fields and span a wider age range than the first analysts described above. Students come from all over the UK and the world. Of a group of 40 student psychoanalysts who responded to a questionnaire in October 2002 (Polmear, 2002 unpublished research), the vast majority, 36 in fact, came from therapeutic professions including medicine (particularly psychiatry), clinical psychology, nursing, social work, music therapy, adult and child psychotherapy and marital psychotherapy. Fifteen were medically trained and 25 were non-medical. Four came from other professional backgrounds: mental health charity management, the law, business management and academe (English literature). These changes in background of the entrants to the profession clearly reflect social changes, the growth of therapy as an occupation (perhaps brought about, to some extent, by the widespread influence of Freud's ideas) and the greater degree of specialism which people tend to have. The Institute continues to encourage applicants from all backgrounds.

Amongst the respondents there were 21 British-born students and 19 non-British born. Three of the latter had dual nationality. Of the 19, there were 3 South Africans, 3 Russians and 3 Irish, 2 Germans, 1 Sri Lankan, 1 French, 1 Italian, 1 Australian, 1 Spanish, 1 Argentinian, 1 Israeli and 1 Canadian. Again changes in society, notably greater geographical mobility, can account for this change in the student body. Where psychoanalysis is in the early stages of being established in a country, or in the case of Russia, re-establishing itself, those wishing to train are prepared to come to the UK to do so, just as in the early days Jones, the Stracheys and other pioneers went to Vienna, Budapest and Berlin.

The age range in the group of students at the time of beginning the training was from 29 to 50. For everyone, it was a second career, which accounted for the relatively late age. Thought is being given to how younger entrants can be encouraged and supported through the training, so that the society replenishes itself and expands.

Applicants are eligible for consideration for training if they have a university degree or its equivalent. They also need to have had some sort of relevant experience working with ill or troubled people. Informal discussions are offered to those wishing to explore their eligibility to apply for training. For those without the necessary relevant experience, help and advice are offered on acquiring or topping up clinical experience. The formal selection process includes two personal interviews to discover whether or not the applicant has an aptitude for this type of work.

COST OF TRAINING The financial commitment largely involves paying for personal psychoanalysis, then later in the training paying for two once-weekly supervisions. In 2003, an analytic session (or supervision) fee was usually within the range of £30–£50, most analysts operating a sliding scale depending on their patients' means. Psychoanalysis, five times a week for around 42 weeks of the year, thus costs £6,000 to £10,000 a year. All the seminar teaching is given free by members of the society, in order to keep the cost of training as low as possible. Some loans and grants are available to help candidates through their training.

Students fund their training in a number of ways. Most continue to work, full or part time, in their original profession while training, and pay for their analysis out of their income with the help of loans when necessary. Clearly the training requires a big commitment, involves long hours, early starts and evening seminars, yet it is manageable and very satisfying.

DESCRIPTION OF THE TRAINING The training is organised by the Education Committee of the Institute, lasts a minimum of four years and has several elements. The personal **training analysis**, that is psychoanalysis with a training analyst appointed by the Education Committee, begins after acceptance and continues throughout the training until qualification. In practice, many qualified analysts continue their analysis until they feel that they have completed it to their own satisfaction, irrespective of when they qualify. Students take a range of **clinical and theoretical seminars**, on two or three evenings a week. These include among other things the study of Freud's writings, various psychoanalytic theories of personality development, different psychoanalytic schools of thought, the theoretical understanding and clinical treatment of various types of disturbance, and ethical issues.

Students take part in a weekly clinical seminar from the second year until qualification. A year-long **infant observation** is carried out during the first year. The student observes a mother with her baby in their home, in the first year of life, for an hour a week, making careful notes afterwards of what went on, including the student's own feelings and reactions. As well as learning about infant development and family relationships, students start to learn the difficult art of observing events and feelings without intruding their own personalities and opinions. This proves valuable in later analytic work. A weekly seminar meets to think about the recorded observations. After the first year of seminars the student may take on the **first training patient**. This patient will be seen in five times a week analysis for at least two years, and probably more, until the analysis is completed. Throughout, the student analyst receives weekly supervision from a training analyst. When this case is well under way, work can begin with the **second training case**. Again this will be a five times a week case, seen under supervision. If the first patient was a male patient, then the second will be a female patient. This case will last a minimum of one year for the purposes of qualification, but like the first case will probably last much longer depending on the needs of the patient in treatment.

Within this framework there is room for individual variation. Students may take 'baby breaks' and extend their training, as may others with heavy commitments. Every student has a progress adviser to help sort out these human variations and make the training possible for them as well as to advise about choices of courses. Students living and working outside London may 'attend' teaching events by telephone link and are given individual assistance to make the training workable.

Following qualification as associate members of the BPAS, and with further clinical work, psychoanalysts can work towards full membership through further advanced study. They may also, or instead, train to work with children and adolescents.

The membership of the BPAS

Listed in the Roster 2002/2003 of the British Psychoanalytical Society are 430 qualified psychoanalysts. Eighty-six of those listed trained in London and now work abroad. There are 42 registered students.

The membership is still heavily London based although strenuous efforts are being made to develop the profession beyond London. As of 2003 there were a few analysts based in the counties around London. Further from London, there were a scattering of analysts in Norfolk, Suffolk, Essex, Avon, Devon, Cheshire, Oxfordshire, Cambridgeshire, Yorkshire, Herefordshire, Lincolnshire, Durham, Tyne and Weir, Greater Manchester, Ireland, Scotland and Wales.

The everyday work of a psychoanalyst

Some psychoanalysts spend their working days seeing patients and supervisees, somewhere between 6 and 10 people a day. These may be all four or five times weekly (patients in full analysis), or may be a mixture of analytic and less intensive psychotherapy patients. Some analysts do some teaching and lecturing in the evenings and at weekends, giving their time free if it is for the Institute training, but being paid if it is for other organisations. Some are involved in psychoanalytic academic writing or research, or in committee work for the BPAS or Institute of Psychoanalysis.

A common pattern is for psychoanalysts to do some psychoanalytic work in their own consulting room, and also to work part time in the public sector, for example in an NHS psychotherapy or psychology department, a child guidance clinic or a university student health service. In the public sector a psychoanalyst is often employed as a member of their original profession, for example as a consultant psychiatrist or clinical psychologist specialising in psychotherapy. Some of the complexities of psychoanalytic psychotherapy in the NHS are discussed in Chapter 8. Psychoanalysts may also become involved in sessional consultation work of various kinds, as described in Chapter 7.

We described in Chapter 1 how important the setting is as part of the psychoanalytic process. When establishing a practice, care is given to making sure that there is very little of the analyst's personal life on display. Analysts set up their consulting rooms either away from their home or in such a way that family members and patients don't meet. There is usually a waiting area and toilet facilities. Psychoanalysts take care to minimise the intrusion of their personal life into their analytic work and endeavour to avoid interruptions to the sessions. All these issues involved in providing a safe and boundaried analytic setting need to be thought about when the analyst is considering setting up a private practice.

Clinical governance

Clinical governance is an umbrella term describing the structures needed for good professional practice. These include, for example, structures for **continuing professional development (CPD)**. Clinical governance structures also include open and straightforward ethical and complaints procedures, formalised standards for record-keeping and for confidentiality, and ways of ensuring that patients have been properly assessed and have given informed consent to treatment.

In the BPAS, regular detailed discussion of clinical work (care being taken to protect the patient's identity) with a small group of colleagues is the central CPD requirement. Groups enable colleagues to take pastoral responsibility for each other, and be alert to difficulties caused by illness or ageing in a colleague, but one to one supervision may sometimes be more suitable. Members also take part in a yearly minimum of 30 hours of mixed CPD activity. This can include attendance at the BPAS scientific meetings where clinical and theoretical papers are presented and discussed, attending postgraduate lectures and seminars, taking part in conferences or getting involved in various teaching, writing and research activities. CPD helps guard against the complacency that can lead to bad practice. Each new patient will present the analyst with different technical and emotional problems, which may need further research and study.

Ethics
Because of the uniquely intimate and emotional nature of the relationship with a patient in analysis, psychoanalysts must conduct themselves in a strictly professional way; disregard of this can be seriously damaging for the patient. During the profession's development accusations of misconduct by psychoanalysts have occurred, some unfortunately true. This was at no time more so than in the early pioneering days when knowledge of the transference and countertransference was limited and regulation of the profession in its infancy.

Today, it would not be acceptable for an analyst to analyse his own daughter as Freud did. Equally it would not be right to analyse family friends, or for the analyst to talk about the patient to the patient's spouse. Again Freud did this. Freud was clear, however, about the need for strict sexual boundaries between patient and analyst, while some other early analysts were not. In subtler ways ethical boundaries were broken too. Analysts deeply involved with their patients and failing to consult with colleagues could become engrossed in a relationship in which they became gratified by aspects of their patients' transference to them.

Although we understand more about all this now and have in place rigorous structures for investigating complaints, our problems are by no means confined to the past. Regrettably, violations by the analyst of the professional relationship do sometimes still occur. Challenges to an analyst's boundaries are inevitable, with the nature of the work pushing analysts towards fulfilling patients' wishes and fantasies (Gabbard and Lester, 1995). As well as the need for a rigorous training including particular attention to such issues, it is essential for a psychoanalytic institution to have a good clinical governance structure, one central part of which is an ethics committee administering a well worked out code of practice.

The ethical code and guidelines

The code sets out the principles and main tenets by which psychoanalysts must conduct themselves. In the event of a serious breach of the code being confirmed, it lies finally with the council of the BPAS, advised by the ethics committee, to decide what sanction is appropriate. The ultimate sanction is to have membership of the society withdrawn and thereby lose the title Psychoanalyst. The guidelines set out in more detail specific applications of the code that may occur in common practice. Both code and guidelines are available to the public on request. In brief, the areas covered by the code and guidelines are as follows:

1 that psychoanalysts must act at all times in the best interests of their patients.
2 that psychoanalysts must exercise restraint towards patients physically, verbally and socially.
3 that psychoanalysts must respect patients' confidentiality. Patients' anonymity must be preserved.
4 that psychoanalysts must conduct themselves in a manner which will not bring psychoanalysis into disrepute.
5 that psychoanalysts must be considerate to colleagues, other professionals and members of other organisations and institutions.

The Ethics Committee

This committee of the British Psychoanalytic Society is elected annually at the AGM of the society. It consists of five elected senior and experienced analysts and a panel of invited, non-analyst experts who are called upon for specialist advice from time to time.
Their brief is:

1 To offer discussion and advice about matters of ethics and professional conduct to any member or candidate in training and any member of staff employed by the Institute.
2 To receive and adjudicate upon complaints concerning the professional conduct of any member, candidate in training or member of staff of the Institute. Professional conduct includes conduct that may affect patients, colleagues, the society or the Institute, other professionals, members of the public, or the good name of psychoanalysis as a discipline.
3 To bring general ethical issues to the membership for consideration.

Equal opportunities

The Institute of Psychoanalysis has an equal opportunities policy which governs all psychoanalysts, support staff working at the Institute, and the selection of applicants to join both the staff and the training. The Institute's equal opportunities statement says:

The training of students and the provision of treatment at the clinic, whilst both necessarily involving selection, are provided without discrimination on grounds of ethnicity, religion, gender or sexual orientation and the Institute is committed to maintaining the highest professional standards through on-going student evaluation, supervision, clinical debate and self-monitoring.

THE ISSUE OF HOMOSEXUALITY Concerns are sometimes expressed by patients and those wishing to train as analysts that homosexuality might not be acceptable or that they might be expected to change their sexual orientation. Although homosexuality was never an exclusion criterion for psychoanalytic training in the UK, it seems likely that there was prejudice in the past, causing pain and disappointment to some who may have wished to train. The statement above clearly spells out that, in the UK today, no discrimination on grounds of ethnicity, religion, gender or sexual orientation is tolerated in any aspect of the Institute's work.

It appears that Freud did not consider homosexuality to be a negative indicator for becoming an analyst. Bisexuality is at the very heart of Freud's theory of psychosexual development. Freud believed that we all begin with bisexual potential and that gradually through the resolution of the Oedipus complex our sexual and gender identities coalesce around a more male, or more female pole. This identity becomes fixed at the end of adolescence. For example, it is known (Holroyd, 1973, 1994) that James Strachey had a consummated affair in 1906 with the economic theorist Maynard Keynes and that he was passionately and hopelessly in love with Rupert Brooke over a long period of time. When James and his wife to be, Alix, returned from being analysed by Freud in Vienna they were reported to be very much in love.

As we learn more about sexuality, we find that there are likely to be as many different forms of homosexuality as there are different forms of heterosexuality. Homosexuality itself is not a negative indicator for acceptance on the training, just as heterosexuality is not a positive one. The key factor is whether the applicant is able to know him- or herself sufficiently to be able to understand the complexity and multi-determined nature of each patient's developmental background and personality, and to respond to patients in an unbiased, concerned and thoughtful way. In relation to any concern prospective patients might have that their analyst will hold a desire to change them from one orientation to another, we cannot state too strongly that the work of analysis is to help people to become more fully themselves and that attempts to change or manipulate patients are not a part of the process. Many homosexual patients feel that it is in analysis that they have felt fully and deeply understood for the first time and have been able to become more accepting of themselves.

External regulation of the psychotherapeutic professions

Since the British Psychoanalytical Society was founded in 1919 there has been a proliferation of psychotherapy and counselling organisations, some whose theory and practice derive directly from psychoanalysis, some based on other modalities as diverse as systems theory, learning theory, hypnosis, yoga, and astrology. Each runs its own training and they differ greatly in standards of training and professional regulation. As yet there is no statutory regulation of the overall profession, although work is in progress towards this. However, individual professional organisations have been well aware of the need to regulate themselves for the protection of their patients, and many have worked together on this for decades.

Concern about the need for regulation first surfaced in 1971 when the Foster Report, responding to alarm about scientology, called for a register of specialist psychotherapists and recognised trainings. The Professions Joint Working Party was formed to take this forward and this led, in 1978, to the Seighart Report, then to a series of annual conferences known as the Rugby conferences, and finally to the inauguration of the United Kingdom Standing Conference on Psychotherapy (UKSCP) in 1989. The United Kingdom Council for Psychotherapy, one of the two current voluntary registers for psychotherapists, developed out of the UKSCP.

The UKCP has come to encompass a very broad range of different types of psychotherapy and counselling. Besides psychodynamic therapies, its eight sections include some very different types of therapy such as 'Hypno-Psychotherapy', 'Experiential and Constructivist Therapies' and 'Behavioural and Cognitive Psychotherapies'. Forms and standards of training are inevitably very different across the member organisations.

BRITISH CONFEDERATION OF PSYCHOTHERAPISTS   In 1993 the British Confederation of Psychotherapists was formed by a group of organisations, the members of which were all engaged in working in a psychoanalytic way. This new body arose out of a desire to ensure thorough and intensive personal training analysis/therapy and supervision for their trainees. These organisations also needed rigorous standards of professional practice and accountability for their members. They were concerned that an umbrella body like the UKCP, which provided for such an inclusive and diverse range of treatments, was not fully appropriate for their specialised field.

The move away from the UKCP proved difficult and painful at first, but dialogue has been resumed between the two bodies, and both are involved in ongoing discussions with government about eventual statutory regulation for all psychotherapies. The UKCP continues to be a large, inclusive, regulatory body for a diverse range of psychotherapeutic approaches, while the BCP has become the organisation specifically regulating those groups who share psychoanalysis and analytical psychology as their theoretical underpinning. These are organisations that, for example, require that their trainees receive at least three times weekly training psychotherapy/analysis over a number of years, with carefully selected training therapists or analysts.

Within the BCP each professional organisation controls its own training, ethical code and CPD programme. However, aspiring member organisations are thoroughly scrutinised in order to confirm that standards are acceptable, and that ongoing checks are in place. The BCP also lobbies government on issues affecting the profession, brings to practitioners' attention relevant issues and developments and provides a forum for discussion. For example, conferences have been held to explore the vital and complex issue of confidentiality in publishing and reporting case material. Consensus is being forged on ways in which patients will be protected from breaches in confidentiality at the same time as allowing scientific debate and developments in theory and practice to take place.

The BCP publishes an annual register of qualified psychoanalysts, analytical psychologists (Jungians) and psychoanalytic therapists. All bona fide psychoanalysts are listed either as a Psychoanalyst of the British Psychoanalytical Society, in the alphabetical section, or in the section that lists members of the British Psychoanalytical Society. The BCP register is to be found in libraries or can be purchased from the British Confederation of Psychotherapists (address on p. 172). For information about the

BCP and its member organisations visit their website at: www.
bcp.org.uk

Psychoanalysis and the wider world

*The relationship between psychoanalysis and the psychoanalytic
psychotherapy organisations*
Psychoanalysts were closely involved in the origin of the profession
of psychoanalytic psychotherapy, and continue to collaborate with
their colleagues in psychoanalytic psychotherapy organisations, particularly those which are also in the BCP or are working towards
BCP membership. Psychoanalysts work alongside psychotherapist
colleagues as training analysts, teachers and supervisors within
many psychoanalytic psychotherapy trainings, with the co-operative
and collegial relationship. With the same theoretical base, research
and scientific interests are shared, and members of different BCP
organisations participate in each other's conferences and other
events.

Psychoanalysis and other disciplines
Despite its detractors, psychoanalysis has had far-reaching influence
on many other fields of learning. In particular there has been fruit-
ful interchange between psychoanalysts and academics, writers and
artists of various kinds, and some of this is explored in Chapter 7.
The first International Psychoanalytic Film Festival in 2001 proved
so successful that it has become an annual event. Conferences on
psychoanalysis and history, psychoanalysis and philosophy and
psychoanalysis and religion bring analysts and academic thinkers
together to explore and debate the interrelations of their subjects.
    The relationship between psychoanalysis and the neurosciences
was first explored in Freud's 1895 book, *Project for a Scientific
Psychology*, which he abandoned as too ambitious a task at that stage
of development of both the disciplines. Now we are seeing the
beginnings of a new *rapprochement*, and the International Neuro-
Psychoanalysis Society was founded in 1999. This society brings
together an international interest group of psychoanalysts, psychoanalytic psychotherapists and neuroscientists. Some links between
psychoanalysis and the neurosciences are mentioned in Chapter 6.

Teaching and discussion events open to members of the public
The Institute offers a range of courses, lectures and discussion
events open to members of the public. In 2003 these included those

that are listed below. For those seeking current information, details of the BPAS website, telephone number and postal address are given at the end of the chapter.

THE INTRODUCTORY LECTURES This two-term course is open to members of the general public who are curious about psychoanalysis. It consists of a series of weekly lectures held on Wednesdays during the autumn and spring terms. Each lecture covers a central topic in psychoanalysis and is given by a member of the BPAS. The lectures are followed by discussions in smaller groups. The feedback on this course has been consistently good and participants have sometimes gone on to apply to train as a psychoanalyst.

CENTRE FOR THE ADVANCEMENT OF PSYCHOANALYTIC STUDIES Courses of seminars are offered by senior analysts for psychoanalysts and psychoanalytic psychotherapists. Some of the topics studied have included: psychoanalytic views on psychosomatic phenomena, the treatment of borderline mental states, and interpretations and their relation to psychic change.

THE PSYCHOANALYTIC FORUM The Psychoanalytic Forum offers members of the public a chance to hear and participate in interdisciplinary discussions on topics of current interest. Papers are presented by psychoanalysts and eminent speakers from other fields in exploration of important topics. For example in 2003 there was a meeting on 'The faces of totalitarianism'.

THE ERNEST JONES LECTURE This biennial lecture is organised by the Scientific Committee of the BPAS and is open to members of the public as well as members of the society. Different subjects are chosen for their topical interest. The lecture is given by someone with outstanding expertise in their field, whether psychoanalysis or another profession, in the UK or abroad. The first Ernest Jones Lecture was given in 1946 when Lord Adrian spoke on 'The mental and physical origins of behaviour'. In 2000 Richard Holmes's lecture was entitled: 'The biographer's footsteps', in 2001 Justice Richard Goldstone spoke about 'Crimes against humanity' and in 2003 Lady Onora O'Neill spoke on 'Trust and professionalism'.

THE ANNUAL RESEARCH LECTURE Organised by the Research Committee, a sub-committee of the Scientific Committee, this important annual event focuses on an aspect of research relevant to the profession. It is well attended by psychoanalysts and those in related fields. At the time of writing there have been 11 such lectures. The first, given in

1987 by Professor Robert Wallerstein, was called 'Psychoanalytic therapy, one paradigm or many?' In 2001 Professor Mark Solms spoke on 'An example of neuro-psychoanalytic research: Korsakoff's Syndrome'. In 2002, Professor Marianne Leuzinger-Bohleber, from Frankfurt, asked: 'Can we study psychoanalytic outcome in truly psychoanalytic ways?' In 2003 Professor Rolf Sandell described 'An outcome study of 434 cases in psychoanalysis and long-term therapy'.

'ON THE WAY HOME' This is a series of conversations, usually held on Friday evenings at the Institute of Psychoanalysis, in which writers, thinkers and artists are in conversation with a psychoanalyst and with the audience. They are informal and quite social events covering a very wide range of topics. In the autumn term 2002 three evenings saw choreographer Shoban Jeyasingh, writer Lawrence Norfolk and playwright Shelagh Stephenson in a conversation, led by psychoanalyst Dr Sheilagh Davies, about the book, *Art Not Chance: Nine Artists' Diaries*; Professor Susan Greenfield CBE in conversation with psychoanalyst Professor Mark Solms; and Professor Stuart Hall discussing 'The interface between personal and cultural identity' with psychoanalyst Fakhry Davids. Well known writers such as A.S. Byatt, Colm Toibin, Rose Tremain and Philip Pullman have discussed their work.

FILMS AND DISCUSSIONS ON 'THE LIFE CYCLE' The common ground between psychoanalysis and film is vast. Linked with the International Psychoanalytic Film Festival (see p. 169 above), the BPAS, in co-operation with the Institute of Contemporary Arts, runs a series of films and discussions each term capturing aspects of a particular phase of the life cycle. In the current series (2003), after viewing the film, the audience joins psychoanalyst Andrea Sabbadini and film historian Peter Evans in a discussion.

Beyond the couch is an information leaflet published three times a year by the Institute of Psychoanalysis listing all the external events in the coming term. Anyone wishing to receive a copy should contact the Institute of Psychoanalysis.

Useful addresses

The Institute of Psychoanalysis and the British Psychoanalytical Society, 112A Shirland Road, Maida Vale, London W9 2EQ. Telephone number: 020 7563 5000 Website: www.psychoanalysis.org.uk

The London Clinic of Psychoanalysis, at the above address.
Telephone number: 020 7563 5002
E mail: catherine.avoh@iopa.org.uk Also see page on Institute website.

The International Journal of Psychoanalysis, at the above address.
Telephone number: 020 7563 5012
E mail: maned@ijpa.org

The Library of the BPAS, at the above address.
Telephone number: 020 7563 5008
E mail: library@iopa.org.uk

The British Confederation of Psychotherapists
West Hill House, 6 Swains Lane, London N6 6QS
Telephone number: 020 7267 3626
E mail: mail@bcp.org.uk
Website: www.bcp.org.uk

The Association for Psychoanalytic Psychotherapy in the NHS
Administrative Secretary: Joyce Piper
5 Windsor Road, London, N3 3SN
Telephone number: 020 8349 9873

REFERENCES

Abraham, K. (1924) A short study of the development of the libido, viewed in the light of mental disorders. In *Selected Papers on Psychoanalysis*. London: Hogarth Press, 1927.

Abrams, S. (1974) Book review of Ellenberger's *The Discovery of the Unconscious*. *Psychoanalytic Quarterly*, 43: 303–306.

Alister, I. and Hauke, C. (eds) (1998) *Contemporary Jungian Analysis*. London: Routledge.

American Psychiatric Association (1994) *Diagnostic and Statistical Manual of Mental Disorders*, 4th edition. Washington DC: American Psychiatric Association.

Anderson, R. (ed.) (1992) *Clinical Lectures on Klein and Bion*. London: Routledge.

Bachrach, H. (1995) The Columbia Records Project. In Shapiro, T. and Emde, R. (eds) *Research in Psychoanalysis: Process, Development, Outcome*. Madison, CT: International Universities Press.

Bachrach, H., Galatzer-Levy, R., Skolnikoff, A. and Waldron, S. (1991) On the efficacy of psychoanalysis. *Journal of the American Psychoanalytic Association*, 39: 871–916.

Balint, M. (1957) *The Doctor, His Patient, and the Illness*. London: Pitman.

Balint, M. (1968) *The Basic Fault: Therapeutic Aspects of Regression*. London: Tavistock.

Barnes, M. and Berke, J. (1973) *Mary Barnes: Two Accounts of a Journey through Madness*. Harmondsworth: Penguin.

Bateman, A. and Fonagy, P. (1999) The effectiveness of partial hospitalisation in the treatment of borderline personality disorder – a randomised controlled trial. *American Journal of Psychiatry*, 156: 1563–1569.

Bateman, A. and Holmes, J. (1995) *Introduction to Psychoanalysis*. London: Routledge.

Bateman, A., Brown, D. and Pedder, J. (2000) *Introduction to Psychotherapy. An Outline of Psychodynamic Principles and Practice*. London: Routledge.

Beck, A., Rush, A., Shaw, B. and Emery, G. (1979) *Cognitive Therapy of Depression*. New York: Wiley.

Beck, A., Freeman, A. and associates (1990) *Cognitive Therapy of Personality Disorders*. New York: Guilford Press.

Bell, D. (1999) Psychoanalysis, a body of knowledge of mind and human culture. In Bell (ed.) *Psychoanalysis and Culture*. London: Duckworth.

Benhabib, S. (1992) *Situating the Self: Gender, Community and Postmodernism in Contemporary Ethics*. Cambridge: Polity Press.

Benvenuto, B. and Kennedy, R. (1986) *The Works of Jacques Lacan: An Introduction*. London: Free Association Books.

Bion, W. (1961) *Experiences in Groups*. London: Tavistock.

Bion, W. (1967) *Second Thoughts*. London: Heinemann.

Bowers, M. (1995) White City Toy Library: a therapeutic group for mothers and under-5s. In Trowell, J. and Bower, M. (eds) *The Emotional Needs of Young Children and Their Families: Using Psychoanalytic Ideas in the Community*. London: Routledge.

Bowlby, J. (1969) *Attachment and Loss. Vol. 1. Attachment*. New York: Basic Books.

Bowlby, J. (1973) *Attachment and Loss. Vol. 2. Separation: Anxiety and Anger.* New York: Basic Books.

Bowlby, J. (1980) *Attachment and Loss. Vol. 3. Loss: Sadness and Depression.* New York: Basic Books.

Brecht, K., Friedrich, V., Hermanns, L., Karuner, I., Juelich, D. (eds) (1985) *Here Life Goes On in a Most Peculiar Way...*, English editions. Goethe Institute, London: Kellner.

Breuer, J. and Freud, S. (1895) *Studies on Hysteria. Standard Edition 2.* London: Hogarth.

Britton, R. (1989) The missing link. In Steiner, J. (ed.) *The Oedipus Complex Today: Clinical Implications.* London: Karnac.

Britton, R. (1998) Daydream, phantasy and fiction. In *Belief and Imagination.* London: Routledge.

Cardinal, M. (1975) *The Words to Say It.* London: The Women's Press.

Chasseguet-Smirgel, J. (1985) *Creativity and Perversion.* London: Free Association Books.

Chasseguet-Smirgel, J. (1988) *Female Sexuality.* London: Karnac.

Chodorow, N. (1978) *The Reproduction of Mothering.* Berkeley, CA: University of California Press.

Chrzanowski, G. (1975) Psychoanalysis: ideology and practitioners. *Contemporary Psychoanalysis*, 11: 492–499.

Cioffi, F. (1970) Freud and the idea of a pseudo-science. In Berger and Cioffi (eds) *Explanation in the Behavioural Sciences.* Cambridge: Cambridge University Press.

Cohn, N. (1994) Attending to emotional issues on a special care baby unit. In Obholzer, A. and Roberts, V.Z. (eds) *The Unconscious at Work.* London: Routledge.

Cosin, B.R., Freeman, C.F. and Freeman, N.H. (1982) Critical empiricism criticized: the case of Freud. In Wollheim, R. and Hopkins, J. (eds) *Philosophical Essays on Freud.* Cambridge: Cambridge University Press.

Crews, F. (1997) *The Memory Wars: Freud's Legacy in Dispute.* London: Granta Books.

Crews, F. (ed.) (1998) *Unauthorised Freud.* Harmondsworth: Penguin.

Crockatt, P. (1997) Book review of *Why Freud Was Wrong* by R. Webster, *Psychoanalytic Psychotherapy*, 11: 87–90.

Dartington, A. (1994) Where angels fear to tread: idealism, despondency and inhibition of thought in hospital nursing. In Obholzer, A. and Roberts, V.Z. (eds) *The Unconscious at Work.* London: Routledge.

Davids, F. (2002) September 11th 2001: some thoughts on racism and religious prejudice as an obstacle. *British Journal of Psychotherapy*, 18: 361–366.

Daws, D. (1995) Consultation in general practice. In Trowell, J. and Bower, M. (eds) *The Emotional Needs of Young Children and Their Families: Using Psychoanalytic Ideas in the Community.* London: Routledge.

Diamond, D. and Wrye, H. (1998) Prologue to 'Projections of Psychic Reality: A Centennial of Film and Psychoanalysis'. *Psychoanalytic Inquiry*, 18: 139–146.

Dolan, B., Warren, F. and Norton, K. (1997) Change in borderline symptoms one year after therapeutic community treatment for severe personality disorder. *British Journal of Psychiatry*, 171: 274–279.

Dryden, W. (2002) (ed.) *Handbook of Individual Therapy*, 4th edition. London: Sage.

Dunn, M. (2002) Cognitive analytic therapy. In Dryden, W. (ed.) *Handbook of Individual Therapy*, 4th edition. London: Sage.

Dupont, J. (ed.) (1995) *The Clinical Diary of Sandor Ferenzci.* Cambridge, MA: Harvard University Press.

Edgcumbe, R. (2000) *Anna Freud: A View of Development, Disturbance and Therapeutic Technique.* London: Routledge.

Ehlers, H. and Crick, J. (1994) *The Trauma of the Past: Remembering and Working Through.* London: Goethe-Institut.

Eickhoff, F-W. (1995) The formation of the German psychoanalytical association (DPV): regaining the psychoanalytical orientation lost in the Third Reich. *International Journal of Psychoanalysis*, 76: 945–956.

Eissler, K. (1971) *Talent and Genius: The Fictitious Case of Tausk Contra Freud.* New York: Quadrangle.

Ellenberger, H. (1970) *The Discovery of the Unconscious.* London: Penguin Books.

Enright, S. (1999) Cognitive-behavioural therapy – An overview. *CPD Bulletin Psychiatry*, 1(3): 78–83.

Eysenck, H. (1952) The effects of psychotherapy: an evaluation. *Journal of Consulting Psychology*, 16: 319–324.

Fabricius, J. (1991a) Running on the spot or can nursing really change? *Psychoanalytic Psychotherapy*, 5(2): 97–108.

Fabricius, J. (1991b) Learning to work with feelings: psychodynamic understanding and small group work with junior student nurses. *Nurse Education Today*, 11: 134–142.

Fabricius, J. (1995) Psychoanalytic understanding and nursing: a supervisory workshop with nurse tutors. *Psychoanalytic Psychotherapy*, 9(1): 17–29.

Fabricius, J. (1996) Has nursing sold its soul? A response to Professor Banks. *Nurse Education Today*, 16: 75–76.

Fabricius, J. (1999) The crisis in nursing. *Psychoanalytic Psychotherapy*, 13(3): 203–206.

Fairbairn, W. (1952) *Psychoanalytic Studies of the Personality.* London: Tavistock.

Feltham C. (1999) Facing, understanding and learning from critiques of psychotherapy and counselling. *British Journal of Guidance and Counselling*, 27: 301–311.

Fenichel, O. (1945) *The Psychoanalytic Study of Neurosis.* London: Routledge & Kegan Paul.

Flaskas, C. (2002) *Family Therapy Beyond the Postmodern: Practice Challenges Theory.* Hove, Sussex: Brunner-Routledge.

Fletcher, A. (1983) Working in a neonatal intensive care unit. *Journal of Child Psychotherapy*, 9(1): 47–55.

Fonagy, P. (1991) Thinking about thinking: some clinical and theoretical considerations in the treatment of a borderline patient. *International Journal of Psychoanalysis*, 72: 1–18.

Fonagy, P. (2000) British Psychoanalytical Society Annual Research Lecture. Unpublished.

Fonagy, P. and Target, M. (1996) Outcome and predictors in child analysis: a retrospective study of 763 cases at the Anna Freud Centre. *Journal of the American Psychoanalytic Association*, 44: 27–77.

Fonagy, P., Steele, M., Moran, G., Steele, H. and Higgitt A. (1993) Measuring the ghost in the nursery: an empirical study of the relation between parents' mental representations of childhood experiences and their infants' security of attachment. *Journal of the American Psychoanalytic Association*, 41: 957–986.

Fonagy, P., Kachele, R., Krause, R., Jones, E., Perron, R. and Lopez, L. (1999) *An Open-Door Review of Outcome Studies in Psychoanalysis.* London: International Psychoanalytical Association. Also available at http://www.ipa.org.uk/R-outcome.htm

Forrester, J. (1997) *Dispatches from the Freud Wars.* Cambridge, MA: Harvard University Press.

Foulkes, S. and Anthony, E. (1973) *Group Psychotherapy: The Psychoanalytic Approach.* Harmondsworth: Penguin.

Freud, A. (1926) *Four Lectures on Child Analysis.* Reprinted in *The Writings of Anna Freud.* New York: International Universities Press, 1974.

Freud, A. (1936) *The Ego and the Mechanisms of Defence.* London: Hogarth, 1987.

Freud, A. (1944) *The Writings of Anna Freud Vol. III: Infants without Families (1939–45).* London: Hogarth, 1974.

Freud, A. (1965) *Normality and Pathology in Childhood.* London: Hogarth.

Freud, A. (1975) The nursery school of the Hampstead Child Therapy Clinic. *Psychoanalytic Study of the Child Monograph Series,* 5: 127–132.

Freud, S. (1895) *Project for a Scientific Psychology. Standard Edition 1.* London: Hogarth.

Freud, S. (1900) *The Interpretation of Dreams. Standard Edition 4 and 5.* London: Hogarth.

Freud, S. (1901) *The Psychopathology of Everyday Life. Standard Edition 6.* London: Hogarth.

Freud, S. (1905a) *Three essays on the theory of sexuality. Standard Edition 7.* London: Hogarth.

Freud, S. (1905b) *Fragment of an Analysis of a Case of Hysteria. Standard Edition 7.* London: Hogarth.

Freud, S. (1905c), *Jokes and their Relation to the Unconscious. Standard Edition 8.* London: Hogarth.

Freud, S. (1908) *Creative writers and daydreaming. Standard Edition 9.* London: Hogarth.

Freud, S. (1909a) *Notes upon a case of obsessional neurosis. Standard Edition 10.* London: Hogarth.

Freud, S. (1909b) *Analysis of a phobia in a five year old boy. Standard Edition 10.* London: Hogarth.

Freud, S. (1910) *Leonardo da Vinci and a memory of his childhood. Standard Edition 11.* London: Hogarth.

Freud, S. (1911) *Formulation of the two principles of mental functioning. Standard Edition 12.* London: Hogarth.

Freud, S. (1916) *On transience. Standard Edition 14.* London: Hogarth.

Freud, S. (1917a) *Introductory Lectures on Psychoanalysis. Standard Edition 16.* London: Hogarth.

Freud, S. (1917b) *Mourning and melancholia. Standard Edition 14.* London: Hogarth.

Freud, S. (1918) *From the History of an Infantile Neurosis. Standard Edition 17.* London: Hogarth.

Freud, S. (1923) *The ego and the id. Standard Edition 19.* London: Hogarth.

Freud, S. (1925a) *Negation. Standard Edition 19.* London: Hogarth.

Freud, S. (1925b) *An autobiographical study. Standard Edition 20.* London: Hogarth.

Freud, S. (1926) *The question of lay analysis. Standard Edition 20.* London: Hogarth.

Freud, S. (1930) *Civilisation and its discontents. Standard Edition 21.* London: Hogarth.

Frosh, S. (1999) *The Politics of Psychoanalysis,* 2nd edition. London: Macmillan.

Gabbard, G. (1997) The psychoanalyst at the movies. *International Journal of Psychoanalysis,* 78: 429–434.

Gabbard, G. and Lester, E. (1995) *Boundaries and Boundary Violations in Psychoanalysis.* New York: Basic Books.

Galatzer-Levy, R. (1995) Discussion: the rewards of research. In Shapiro T. and Emde, R. (eds) *Research in Psychoanalysis: Process, Development, Outcome.* Madison, CT: International Universities Press.

Gardner, S. (1995) Psychoanalysis, science and common sense. *Philosophy, Psychiatry and Psychology*, 2: 93–113.

Gay, P. (1988) *Freud: A Life For Our Time*. New York: Norton.

Gedo, J. (1976) Book review of Roazen's *Freud and his Followers. Psychoanalytic Quarterly*, 45: 639–642.

Gergely, G. (1992) Developmental reconstructions: infancy from the point of view of psychoanalysis and developmental psychology. *Psychoanalysis and Contemporary Thought*, 14: 3–55.

Gergely, G. and Watson, J. (1996) The social biofeedback model of parental affect mirroring. *International Journal of Psychoanalysis*, 77: 1181–1212.

Godley, W. (2001) Saving Masud Khan. *London Review of Books*, 22 February.

Goldstone, R. (2001) Crimes against humanity – forgetting the victims. British Psychoanalytical Society Ernest Jones Lecture. Published on the BPAS website: www.psychoanalysis.org.uk

Green, A. (1980) The dead mother. First appeared in *Narcissism de vie, Narcissism de mort*. Paris: Editions de Minuit; English edn, *Life Narcissism Death Narcissism*, Trans. Andrew Weller. London: Free Association Books, 2001.

Green, A. (2000) Response to Robert S. Wallerstein. In Sandler, J., Sandler, A-M. and Davies, R. (eds) *Clinical and Observational Psychoanalytic Research: Roots of a Controversy*. Madison, CT: International Universities Press.

Greer, G. (1971) *The Female Eunuch*. London: Paladin.

Grünbaum, A. (1984) *The Foundations of Psychoanalysis*. Berkeley, CA: University of California Press.

Guthrie, E., Moorey, J. and Margison, F. (1999) Cost-effectiveness of brief psychodynamic-interpersonal therapy in high utilizers of psychiatric services. *Archives of General Psychiatry*, 56: 519–526.

Hale, N. (1995) *The Rise and Crisis of Psychoanalysis in the US*. New York: Oxford University Press.

Heinicke, C.M. and Ramsey-Klee, D.M. (1986) Outcome of child psychotherapy as a function of frequency of session. *Journal of the American Academy of Child Psychiatry*, 25: 247–253.

Hillard, R. (1993) Single-case methodology in psychotherapy process and outcome research. *Journal of Clinical and Consulting Psychology*, 61: 373–380.

Hinshelwood, R. (1994) *Clinical Klein*. London: Free Association Books.

Hinshelwood, R. (1997) *Therapy or Coercion? Does Psychoanalysis Differ from Brainwashing?* London: Karnac.

Hobbes, T. (1651) Philosophical rudiments concerning government and society. In: W. Molesworth (ed.) *The English Works of Thomas Hobbes*. Darmstadt: Wissenschaftliche Buchgesellschaft, 1966.

Hobson, P., Patrick, M. and Valentine, J. (1998) Objectivity in psychoanalytic judgements. *British Journal of Psychiatry*, 173: 172–177.

Holmes, J. and Lindley, R. (1989) *The Values of Psychotherapy*. Oxford: Oxford University Press.

Holroyd, M. (1973) *Lytton Strachey: A Biography*. London: Heinemann.

Holroyd, M. (1994) *Lytton Strachey: The New Biography*. London: Chatto & Windus.

Hopkins, J. (1988) Epistemology and depth psychology: critical notes on *The Foundations of Psychoanalysis*. In Clark, P. and Wright, C. (eds) *Mind, Psychoanalysis and Science*. Oxford: Blackwell.

IPA Membership Handbook and Roster 2001. London: International Psychoanalytic Association.

Jacobs, M. (1999) *Psychodynamic Counselling in Action*, 2nd edition. London: Sage.

Jaques, E. (1951) Working through industrial conflict: the service department at the Glacier metal company. In Trist, E. and Murray, H. (eds) *The Social Engagement of Social Science*, Vol 1. Philadelphia: University of Pennsylvania Press, 1990.

Jones, E. (1953–57) *Sigmund Freud: Life and Work Vols I–III*. London: Hogarth Press.

Jones, E. (1964) *The Life and Work of Sigmund Freud*. London: Penguin.

Joseph, B. (1989) *Psychic Equilibrium and Psychic Change*. London: Routledge.

Kandel, E. (1998) A new intellectual framework for psychiatry. *American Journal of Psychiatry*, 155: 457–469.

Kaplan-Solms, K. and Solms, M. (2000) *Clinical Studies in Neuro-Psychoanalysis*. London: Karnac.

Kazdin, A. (1992) *Methodological Issues and Strategies in Clinical Research*. Washington, DC: American Psychological Association Press.

Kelly, G. (1955) *The Psychology of Personal Constructs*. New York: Norton.

Kerbekian, R. (1995) Consulting to premature baby units. In Trowell, J. and Bower, M. (eds) *The Emotional Needs of Young Children and Their Families: Using Psychoanalytic Ideas in the Community*. London: Routledge.

King, P. and Steiner, R. (1991) *The Freud–Klein Controversies 1941–45*. London: Routledge.

Klein, M. (1940) Mourning and its relation to manic depressive states. In *Love, Guilt and Reparation and Other Works. Vol. I of The Writings of Melanie Klein*. London: Hogarth, 1985.

Klein, M. (1946) Notes on some schizoid mechanisms. In *Envy and Gratitude and Other Works. Vol. III of The Writings of Melanie Klein*. London: Hogarth, 1984.

Klein, M. (1960) On mental health. In *Envy and Gratitude and Other Works. Vol. III of The Writings of Melanie Klein*. London: Hogarth, 1984.

Kohon, G. (ed.) (1999) *The Dead Mother: The Work of André Green*. London: Routledge.

Kohut, H. (1977) *The Restoration of the Self*. Madison, CT: International Universities Press.

Kohut, H. (1982) Introspection, empathy and the semi-circle of mental health. *International Journal of Psychoanalysis*, 63: 395–407.

Kolvin, I. (1988) Psychotherapy is effective. *Journal of the Royal Society of Medicine*, 81: 261–266.

Kuhn, T. (1970) *The Structure of Scientific Revolutions*. Chicago, IL: Chicago University Press.

Lacan, J. (1953) The function and field of speech and language in psychoanalysis. In *Écrits: A Selection*. London: Tavistock, 1977.

Lear, J. (1998) *Open Minded: Working Out the Logic of the Soul*. Cambridge, MA: Harvard University Press.

Leff, J., Vearnals, S., Brewin, C., Wolff, B., Alexander, E., Asen, E., Dayson, D., Jones, E., Chisholm, D. and Everitt, B. (2000) The London intervention trial: an RCT of antidepressants versus couple therapy in the treatment and maintenance of depressed people with a partner. Clinical outcome and cost. *British Journal of Psychiatry*, 177: 95–100.

Leuzinger-Bohleber, M. and Target, M. (2001) *Psychic Change in Psychoanalyses and Psychoanalytic Long-Term Psychotherapies. Clinical and Research Perspectives*. London: Whurr.

Levine, M. (ed.) (2000) *The Analytic Freud. Philosophy and Psychoanalysis*. London: Routledge.

Luborsky, L., Diguier, L., Luborsky, E. and Schmidt, B.A. (1999) The efficacy of dynamic versus other psychotherapies: Is it true that 'everyone has won and all must have prizes'? – An update. In Janovsky, D.S. (ed.) *Psychotherapy: Indications and Outcomes*. Washington: American Psychiatric Press.

Mahoney, P. (1974) Book review of Ellenberger's *The Discovery of the Unconscious*. *Contemporary Psychoanalysis*, 10: 143–153.

Main, T. (1989) *The Ailment and Other Psychoanalytic Essays*. London: Free Association Books.

Marty, P. and M'Uzan, M. (1963) La Pensée operatoire. *Revue Français de Psychoanalyse*, 27 (no. spécial): 345–356.

Masson, J. (1984) *The Assault on Truth*. London: Faber & Faber.

Masson, J. (1985) *The Complete Letters of Sigmund Freud to Wilhelm Fliess 1887–1904*. London: Karnac.

Masson, J. (1989) *Against Therapy*. London: Collins.

McDougall, J. (1986) *Theatres of the Mind*. London: Free Association Books.

McLeod, J. (2003) *Introduction to Counselling*, 2nd edition. Buckingham: Open University Press.

McNeilly, C. and Howard, K. (1991) The effects of psychotherapy: a re-evaluation based on dosage. *Psychotherapy Research*, 1: 74–78.

Meisel, P. and Kendrick, W. (eds) (1986) *Bloomsbury/Freud: The Letters of James and Alix Strachey 1924–1925*. London: Chatto & Windus.

Menzies Lyth, I. (1959) The functioning of social systems as a defence against anxiety: a report on the study of a nursing service of a general hospital. *Human Relations*, 13: 95–121.

Menzies Lyth, I. (1965) Recruitment into the London Fire Brigade. In *The Dynamics of the Social: Selected Essays*. London: Free Association Books, 1989.

Menzies Lyth, I. (1988) *Containing Anxiety in Institutions: Selected Essays*. London: Free Association Books.

Menzies Lyth, I. (1989) *The Dynamics of the Social: Selected Essays*. London: Free Association Books.

Millett, K. (1970) *Sexual Politics*. New York: Doubleday.

Milner, M. (1934) *A Life of One's Own*. London: Chatto & Windus. [Published under the name 'Joanna Field'.]

Milner, M. (1957) *On Not Being Able to Paint*. London: Heinemann. [Published under the name 'Joanna Field.]

Milner, M. (1987) *The Suppressed Madness of Sane Men*. London: Routledge.

Milton, J. (2001) Psychoanalysis and cognitive behaviour therapy – rival paradigms or common ground? *International Journal of Psychoanalysis*, 82: 431–447.

Mitchell, J. (1974) *Psychoanalysis and Feminism*. Harmondsworth: Penguin.

Mitchell, S. and Black, M. (1995) *Freud and Beyond. A History of Psychoanalytic Thought*. New York: Basic Books.

Mollon, P. (1998) *Memory and Illusion*. Chichester: Wiley.

Money-Kyrle, R. (1955) Psychoanalysis and Ethics. In *The Collected Papers of Roger Money-Kyrle*. Strathtay, Perthshire: Clunie Press, 1978.

Money-Kyrle, R. (1971) The aim of psychoanalysis. *International Journal of Psychoanalysis*, 52: 103–106. Reprinted in *The Collected Papers of Roger Money-Kyrle*. Strathtay, Perthshire: Clunie Press, 1978.

Moran, G. and Fonagy, P. (1987) Psychoanalysis and diabetic control: a single case study. *British Journal of Medical Psychology*, 60: 357–372.

Moran, M.G. (1991) Chaos theory and psychoanalysis. *International Review of Psychoanalysis*, 18: 211–221.

Moran, G., Fonagy, P., Kurtz, A., Bolton, A. and Brook, C. (1991) A controlled study of the psychoanalytic treatment of brittle diabetes. *Journal of the American Academy of Child and Adolescent Psychiatry*, 30: 926–935.

Mosse, J. (1994) The institutional roots of consulting to institutions. In Obholzer, A. and Roberts, V.Z. (eds) (1994) *The Unconscious at Work*. London: Routledge.

Moylan, D. (1994) the dangers of contagion: projective identification processes in institutions. In Obholzer, A. and Roberts, V.Z. (eds) *The Unconscious at Work*. London: Routledge.

Obholzer, A. (1994) Authority, power and leadership. In Obholzer, A. and Roberts, V.Z. (eds) *The Unconscious at Work*. London: Routledge.

Obholzer, A. and Roberts, V.Z. (1994) *The Unconscious at Work*. London: Routledge.

Oliner, M. (1988) *Cultivating Freud's Garden in France*. Northvale, NJ: Jason Aronson.

Parlett, M. and Hemming, J. (2002) Gestalt therapy. In Dryden, W. (ed.) *Handbook of Individual Therapy*, 4th edition. London: Sage.

Parry, G. and Richardson, A. (1996) *NHS Psychotherapy Services in England: A Review of Strategic Policy*. London: Department of Health.

Pascal, Blaise (1623–62) *Pensées* iv 277, trans. A.J. Krailsheimer. Harmondsworth: Penguin, 1995.

Pilgrim, D. (2002) The cultural context of British psychotherapy. In Dryden, W. (ed.) *Handbook of Individual Therapy*, 4th edition. London: Sage.

Popper, K. (1969) *Conjectures and Refutations*, 3rd edition. London: Routledge & Kegan Paul.

Psychoanalytic Electronic Publishing (2001) Archive 1 version 3 1920–98.

Puget, J. (1992) Belonging and ethics. *Psychoanalytic Inquiry*. 12: 551–569.

Rayner, E. (1990) *The Independent Mind in British Psychoanalysis*. London: Free Association Books.

Roazen, P. (1969) *Brother Animal: The Story of Freud and Tausk*. New York: Knopf.

Roazen, P. (1971) *Freud and his Followers*. Harmondsworth: Penguin.

Roazen, P. (1977) Orthodoxy on Freud: the case of Tausk. *Contemporary Psychoanalysis*, 13: 102–114.

Robert, M. (1966) *The Psychoanalytic Revolution*. London: Allen & Unwin.

Roberts, V.Z. (1994) The organisation of work: contributions from open systems theory. In Obholzer, A. and Roberts, V.Z. (eds) *The Unconscious at Work*. London: Routledge.

Robertson, J. and Robertson, J. (1989) *Separation and the Very Young*. London: Free Association Books.

Robinson, P. (1993) *Freud and his Critics*. Berkeley and Los Angeles: University of California Press

Rosenfeld, H. (1965) *Psychotic States*. London: Hogarth.

Rosenfeld, H. (1987) *Impasse and Interpretation*. London: Routledge.

Roustang, F. (1982) *Dire Mastery: Discipleship from Freud to Lacan*. Baltimore, MD and London: Johns Hopkins University Press.

Rustin, M. (1991) *The Good Society and the Inner World*. London: Verso.

Rustin, M. (1995) Lacan, Klein and politics: the positive and negative in psychoanalytic thought. In Elliott, A. and Frosh, S. (eds) *Psychoanalysis in Contexts*. London: Routledge.

Rustin, M. (1999) Psychoanalysis: the last modernism. In *Psychoanalysis and Culture*. London: Duckworth.

Rycroft, C. (1985) *Psychoanalysis and Beyond*. London: Hogarth.

Ryle, A. (1990) *Cognitive Analytical Therapy*. Chichester: Wiley.

Ryle, A. (1995) Psychoanalysis, cognitive-analytic therapy, mind and self. *British Journal of Psychotherapy*, 11: 568–574.

Sandahl, C., Herlittz, K., Ahlin, G. and Ronnberg, S. (1998) Time-limited group therapy for moderately alcohol dependent patients: a randomised controlled trial. *Psychotherapy Research*, 8: 361–378.

Sandell, R., Blomberg, J., Lazar, A., Carlsson, J., Broberg, J., and Schubert, J. (2000) Varieties of long-term outcome among patients in psychoanalysis and long-term psychotherapy: a review of findings in the Stockholm outcome of psycho-analysis and psychotherapy project (STOPP). *International Journal of Psychoanalysis*, 81: 921–942.

Sandler, J. (1983) Reflections on some relations between psychoanalytic concepts and psychoanalytic practice. *International Journal of Psychoanalysis*, 64: 35–46.

Sandler, J. (1987) *From Safety to Superego*. London: Karnac.

Sandler, J. (ed.) (1988) *Projection, Identification and Projective Identification*. London: Karnac.

Sandler, J. and Sandler, A-M. (1998) *Internal Objects Revisited*. London: Karnac.

Sandler, J., Dreher, A.U. and Drews, S. (1991) An approach to conceptual research in psychoanalysis illustrated by a consideration of psychic trauma. *International Review of Psychoanalysis*, 18: 133–141.

Sandler, J., Dare, C., Holder, A. and Dreher, A. (1992) *The Patient and the Analyst*. London: Karnac.

Sands, A. (2000) *Falling for Therapy*. London: Macmillan.

Scharff, D.E. and Scharff, J.S. (1987) *Object Relations Family Therapy*. Northvale, NJ: Aronson.

Schore, A. (1994) *Affect Regulation and the Origin of the Self*. Hillsdale, NJ: Lawrence Erlbaum.

Sebek, M. Presidential address 2001: Gates we try to open. EPF website www.epf-eu.org

Segal (1952) A psychoanalytic approach to aesthetics. *International Journal of Psychoanalysis* 33: 196–207. Reprinted in *The Work of Hanna Segal*. London: Free Association Books, 1988.

Segal, H. (1957) Notes on symbol formation. *International Journal of Psychoanalysis*, 38: 391–397. Reprinted in: Bott Spillius (ed.) *Melanie Klein Today Vol. 1: Mainly Theory*. London: Routledge, 1988.

Segal, H. (1973) *Introduction to the Work of Melanie Klein*. London: Karnac, 1988.

Segal, H. (1981) *The Work of Hanna Segal*. Northvale, NJ: Jason Aronson.

Segal, H. (1987) Silence is the real crime. *International Review of Psychoanalysis*, 14: 3–12.

Segal, H. (1995) From Hiroshima to the Gulf War and after: a psychoanalytic perspective. In Elliot, A. and Frosh, S. (eds) *Psychoanalysis in Contexts*. London: Routledge.

Segal, H. (1997a) *Psychoanalysis, Literature and War*. London: Routledge.

Segal, H. (1997b) On the clinical usefulness of the concept of the death instinct. In *Psychoanalysis, Literature and War*. London: Routledge.

Shapiro, D. and Firth, J. (1987) Prescriptive versus exploratory psychotherapy. *British Journal of Psychiatry*, 151: 790–799.

Shedler, J. (2002) A new language for psychoanalytic diagnosis. *Journal of the American Psychoanalytical Association*, 50: 429–456.

Shedler, J. and Westen, D. (1998) Refining the measurement of Axis 11: a Q-sort procedure for assessing personality pathology. *Assessment*, 5: 335–355.

Solms, M. (1995) Is the brain more real than the mind? *Psychoanalytic Psychotherapy*, 9: 107–120

Spruiell, V. (1993) Deterministic chaos and the sciences of complexity: psycho-analysis in the midst of a general scientific revolution. *Journal of the American Psychoanalytical Association*, 41: 3–44.

Steiner, J. (1993) *Psychic Retreats*. London: Routledge.

Steiner, R. (2000) *'It Is a New Kind of Diaspora'*. London: Karnac.

Stern, D. (1985) *The Interpersonal World of the Infant*. New York: Basic Books.

Steuerman, E. (2000) *The Bounds of Reason.* London: Routledge.

Stevenson, J. and Meares, R. (1992) An outcome study of psychotherapy for patients with borderline personality disorder. *American Journal of Psychiatry,* 149: 358–362.

Stewart, H. (1992) *Psychic Experience and Problems of Technique.* London: Routledge.

Strachey, J. (1934) The nature of the therapeutic action of psychoanalysis. *International Journal of Psychoanalysis,* 15: 127–159.

Strachey, J. (1953–74) *Standard Edition of the Complete Psychological works of Sigmund Freud* (24 vols). London: Hogarth Press.

Stubley, J. (2000) Review article: *Memory wars* by F. Crews and others. *Remembering Trauma* by P. Mollon. *Memory in Dispute* by V. Sinason. *Psychoanalytic Psychotherapy,* 14, 83–92.

Sulloway, F. (1979) *Freud, Biologist of the Mind.* New York: Basic Books.

Sutherland, S. (1976) *Breakdown.* London: Weidenfeld & Nicolson.

Szasz, T. (1969) *The Ethics of Psychoanalysis.* London: Routledge & Kegan Paul.

Taylor, D. (ed.) (1999) *Talking Cure: Mind and Method of the Tavistock Clinic.* London: Duckworth.

Thorne, B. (2002) Person-centred therapy. In Dryden, W. (ed.) *Handbook of Individual Therapy,* 4th edition. London: Sage.

Timpanaro, S. (1974) *The Freudian Slip.* English edition London: NLB, 1976.

Trist, E., Higgin, G., Murray, H. and Pollock, A. (1963) The assumption of ordinariness as a denial mechanism: innovation and conflict in a coal mine. In Trist, E. and Murray, H. (eds) *The Social Engagement of Social Science, Vol. 1: The Social-Psychological Perspective.* London: Free Association Books, 1990.

Tylim, I. (1996) Psychoanalysis in Argentina: a couch with a view. *Psychoanalytic Dialogues,* 6: 713–727.

Wallerstein, R. (ed.) (1992) *The Common Ground of Psychoanalysis.* Northvale, NJ: Jason Aronson.

Webster, R. (1995) *Why Freud Was Wrong.* London: HarperCollins.

Whittle, P. (2001) Experimental psychology and psychoanalysis: what we can learn from a century of misunderstanding. *Neuro-psychoanalysis,* 2: 233–245.

Will, D. (1986) Psychoanalysis and the new philosophy of science. *International Review of Psychoanalysis,* 13, 163–173.

Winnicott, D.W. (1958) *Through Paediatrics to Psychoanalysis.* London: Hogarth, 1987.

Winnicott, D.W. (1960) The theory of the parent–infant relationship. *International Journal of Psychoanalysis,* 41: 585–595.

Winnicott, D.W. (1964) Further thoughts on babies as persons. In *The Child, the Family and the Outside World.* Harmondsworth: Penguin.

Winnicott, D.W. (1965) *The Maturational Process and the Facilitating Environment.* London: Hogarth.

Winnicott, D.W. (1971) *Playing and Reality.* London: Tavistock.

Wolf, E. (1976) Book review of Roazen's *Freud and his Followers. Journal of the American Psychoanalytic Association,* 24: 243–244.

Wollheim, R. (1984) *The Thread of Life.* Cambridge: Cambridge University Press.

Wollheim, R. (1993) *The Mind and its Depths.* Cambridge, MA: Harvard University Press.

Wright, E. (1984) *Psychoanalytic Criticism.* London: Methuen.

Zaphiriou Woods, M. (2000) Preventive work in a toddler group and nursery. *Journal of Child Psychotherapy,* 26(2): 209–233.

INDEX